READable.

A Comprehensive Guide to Teaching Your Child to Read

Janelle Curry

from Educatable

Cover Image: Busybird Publishing

Cover design: Busybird Publishing

Layout and typesetting: Busybird Publishing

Busybird Publishing
2/118 Para Road
Montmorency, Victoria
Australia 3094
www.busybird.com.au

Contents

This book is dedicated to my husband Paul and children Avalee, Hudson and Campbell. Without you guys, this book would have been finished a year ago! I love you all more than words can say.

This book is also dedicated to every one of the families I have worked alongside over the years. You are my inspiration!

About the Author

Janelle Curry, Certified Practising Speech Pathologist.

I've always loved children, so when deciding on which allied health stream to follow, it made sense to become a paediatric speech therapist.

I have been working with struggling readers and their families for over 20 years in both private practice and in the education systems of Australia, New Zealand and the UK. I have had additional literacy training including countless webinars and workshops, and professional development days.

Whilst I can talk excitedly all day about what I do professionally, I also have other things in my life that keep me busy! I have three awesome children of my own who do everything from basketball to singing and dancing, and I'm a keen netballer who throws the odd ball around in a local mum's team. It's no surprise that I read fiction voraciously, and I also love a glass or two of wine around the campfire with friends. The beach is my happy place and I'm blessed to live just five minutes away from it.

How to Use This Book

This book is intended to be used by parents of toddlers to children in their first three years of school (and higher grades if you have a struggling reader). In this book you will learn about all of the components needed to become a great reader and speller, why they are necessary, as well as activities and scripts to help teach your child these skills.

If your child is not yet at school, then please read chapter 1: Foundational Skills and chapter 2: Oral Language. To be able to give your child a solid foundation in oral language, vocabulary, phonological awareness as well as fine and gross motor skills is the best gift you can give them before they start to learn to read and write.

Once your child is of school age, I suggest you read the book in its entirety first, so that you are familiar with the language used and the progression your child will make in their reading and spelling journey. Afterwards, you can go back to each chapter and work out where your child is at so that you know what activities are suitable for them.

The chapter on phonics contains a suggested "timetable" so you have some guidance on what to teach your child and when. This should help reduce any overwhelm you may feel! It will become clear how the many different aspects of learning to read can fit together in one teaching session.

Please feel free to photocopy the activity pages in the book or download and print them from the website (details are in the back of this book). The website also has videos demonstrating how to do the activities with a real child rather than just read about it. Also included are printable boardgames which you can use to practise different sound-letter links or words.

The book has further suggested readings if you would like to deepen your knowledge, as well as other resources if your child requires additional activities. I have not cited references throughout the book as it can make reading disjointed. All references can be found in the bibliography.

You may wonder why this book is necessary if your school is teaching a structured literacy approach. Firstly, not all schools are teaching a structured literacy approach, so many children are missing out on the best chance to learn to read well and parents are none the wiser. Secondly, if you are lucky enough to have children attend a school with a great literacy program, then offering support at home to reinforce the school learnings, plus placing extra focus on fluency, vocabulary, comprehension and word origins, will only enhance your child's ability to become a successful reader and speller.

Glossary

There are many terms used in the teaching of reading and spelling that you'll need to be familiar with to support your child. Here are some definitions used in this book as well as other sources.

Blending – This is the process of hearing or reading individual sounds and placing them together to form a word. For example, h – o – t blend together to form hot.

Consonants – A letter that is used to represent speech sounds which are formed by closing off (partially or completely) the vocal tract. For example, /p/ – lips closed, /t/ – tongue partially obstructs airway, /f/ and /s/ – air is forced through narrow gap. Consonants are all the letters of the alphabet that are not vowels.

Decodable books/texts – These are books that are carefully sequenced to progressively incorporate words that are consistent with the letter-sound relationships that have been taught to the new reader. They are great to practise sound-letter links and blending at the early stages of reading.

Decoding – Sounding out written words by using knowledge of sound-letter relationships to correctly pronounce them.

Encoding – Segmenting a word into its sounds and writing down a letter for each sound to spell the word.

Grapheme – A grapheme is a way of writing down a phoneme (speech sound). It is a letter, or a combination of letters. Graphemes can be made up of one letter (*p, b, t, s*), two letters representing one sound (digraphs such as *sh, ch, th, ey, ai*), three letters representing one sound (trigraphs such as *tch, igh, oor, air*), and four letters representing one sound (quadgraphs such as *ough, eigh*). In some countries, graphemes are called **phonograms**.

Manipulating – This is the last and most challenging of the phonemic awareness tasks. It is the ability to change individual sounds in spoken words. For example, say the word *tram*. Now say it again and change the /t/ to a /k/ – *cram*. Children who can think about and manipulate phonemes become better readers and spellers.

Onset and Rime – These are parts of a word. Onset is the first consonant sound or blend, and rime is the rest of the word. For example, *fr-esh, m-at, ch-air*.

Orthographic mapping – A mental process used to store words so that we can read them automatically. This process allows us to develop a memory for the specific order of the letters in words. An example is when we see the word *hair* we think of the hair on our head, but if we see the word *hare* we think of a rabbit. These two words are pronounced the same but due to orthographic mapping and orthographic memory we think of the correct meaning.

Phoneme – This is a speech sound and is the smallest unit in spoken language. Phonemes combine to form syllables and words. For example, the word *mat* has three phonemes: /m/ /a/ /t/. There are 44 phonemes in the English language, including sounds represented by letter combinations such as /th/.

Phoneme-grapheme correspondence – For reading and spelling, children need to know which phonemes or sounds correspond with each grapheme or letter. For ease of reading in this book I am going to refer to this as "sound-letter link" or "sound-letter relationship".

Phonemic awareness – This comes under the broader phonological awareness umbrella and refers to the specific ability to hear and to manipulate individual speech sounds (phonemes) in spoken words. Phonemic awareness is one of the best predictors of how well children will learn to read during the first two years of school instruction. For great decoding (reading), encoding (spelling) as well as understanding spoken language, children need to be able to blend, segment and tell the difference between phonemes. Changes in a single phoneme changes the meaning of a word, even if it is just the change of voice. For example, *pat* versus *bat* where /p/ is unvoiced and /b/ is voiced.

Phonics – This is the teaching of reading by learning the relationships between speech sounds and the spelling patterns that symbolise them.

Phonological (sound) awareness – This is the umbrella term for the knowledge of spoken language. Children need to know that sentences break down into words, words break down into syllables and syllables break down into onset and rime (defined above). It is the awareness that some words sound similar (rhyme) and some sound different, and the awareness that some words have the same sound at the start (alliteration).

Predictable texts – A text where merely one or two words may change on the page and the reader can guess the word from the picture.

Schwa – This is the most common vowel sound. A schwa sounds like "uh" and is tricky for children to read and to spell since any vowel letter can stand for the schwa sound. You may hear it being called the "lazy" vowel as you hardly open your mouth. Words with two or more syllables can have a schwa and it is found in an unstressed syllable. Examples: *woman, bottom, bacon, camel, complicated.*

Segmenting – This is the opposite of blending. Children are given a word and they learn to break it into its parts. For example, *slid* is segmented to *s-l-i-d*. This process is necessary for spelling.

Structured Literacy approach – Explicit, systematic teaching that focuses on phonological awareness, phonemic awareness, sound-letter relationships (phonics), morphemes, and vocabulary at the sentence, paragraph and text levels. Structured literacy is sequential and follows a scope and sequence (what is going to be taught and the order in which it is taught). A structured literacy approach uses decodable books and passages to practise what has been taught.

Syllable – A sound or word chunk that contains one vowel sound and at least one consonant sound. Example: *bug* is a one-syllable word, *snowball* is a two-syllable word, and *computer* is a three-syllable word.

Systematic synthetic phonics – The way that the phonics portion of a structured literacy program should be taught. It follows a scope and sequence, so that all sound-letter relationships are explicitly taught, and children learn to blend them together to form words.

Unvoiced speech sounds – Sounds that are made without vibrating the vocal cords. They can be compared with voiced speech sounds. Unvoiced sounds include: /p/ as in *pet*, /t/ as in *top*, /k/ as in *cat*.

Voiced speech sounds – All vowels are voiced as well as the speech sounds in the column below. Voiced sounds have the voice box turned on and you can feel the vibration in your throat.

Unvoiced (quiet sounds)	Voiced (noisy sounds)
	All vowel sounds
p	b
t	d
k	g
s	z
f	v
sh	zh (measure)
ch	j
th (thumb)	th (that)
h	l
	n
	m
	r
	w
	y
	qu (kw)

Vowels – A letter that represents speech sounds made by keeping the mouth open and without using the tongue to touch your teeth, lips or roof of the mouth. These are *a, e, i, o, u* and the letter *y* is sometimes counted as a vowel too. A vowel may be considered long or short depending on where the vowel is in the word and the way the word is said.

Long vowels – When the vowel says the name of its letter. For example, the name of *a* is /ai/ so in the following words you can hear long vowel sounds: *cake, tape, rain, way*. The name of *e* is /ee/: *dream, tree*. The name of *i* is /ie/: *try, my, sight, bike*. The name of *o* is /oa/: *no, grow, home, boat*. The name of *u* is the "long u" is /ue/ – *unicorn, use, shoe, boot*.

Short vowels – These are pronounced in their "short" form (although the length of time to say a long vowel sound and a short vowel sound only differs slightly): *a* as in *pat*, *e* as in *red*, *i* as in *ship*, *o* as in *hot*, *u* as in *nut*.

The age when children start school and what each grade is called differs between countries and even states within Australia and the US.

Australia – The first year of school is called Preparatory, Foundation, Pre-primary or Kindergarten depending on what state you are in (age 5–6 years). Children then go on to Year 1, Year 2, etc.

US – The first year of school is called Kindergarten (age 5–6 years); however, this is not compulsory in many states (but a child must be enrolled in kindergarten or first grade in the calendar year in which they turn 6 years old). They then move into first grade, second grade, etc.

UK – The first year of school is called Reception (age 4–5 years) and then they move into Key Stage 1 (two years of schooling known as Year 1 and Year 2) when they are aged between 5 and 7 years.

New Zealand – The first year of compulsory school is called Year 1 (age 5–6 years). NZ have different times of the year that children can start school once they turn 5. Children who start in the first half of the year are Year 1, children that start in the second half are Year 0 (who would then do Year 1 the following year).

In this book I will use the phrases "first year of schooling", "second year of schooling" and so on in order to avoid confusion.

Sounds and Letters Chart

This chart has the phonemes on the left, and the different graphemes used to spell the sound. The ones highlighted are taught in this book.

Phonemes (speech sounds)	Graphemes (different ways the speech sounds can be spelt)								
/s/	sat	hiss	city	house	voice	scene	listen		
/a/	ant								
/t/	ten	litter	jumped						
/i/	in	gym							
/p/	pet	happy							
/n/	not	dinner	knee	gnome	gone				
/k/	cat	kid	duck	school					
/e/	egg	bread	said						
/h/	hen	whole							

/r/	run	ca__rr__ot	__wr__ong						
/m/	__m__at	ha__mm__er	cli__mb__	autu__mn__	so__me__				
/d/	__d__ot	la__dd__er	rain__ed__						
/g/	__g__ate	e__gg__	__gh__ost	__gu__ess					
/o/	__o__dd	w__a__s[1]							
/u/	b__u__t	M__o__nday	c__ou__sin						
/l/	__l__amp	we__ll__	turt__le__						
/f/	__f__ish	stu__ff__	__ph__one	enou__gh__					
/b/	__b__at	bu__bb__le							
/ai/	__ai__m	l__a__ke	s__ay__	__a__pron	th__ey__	st__ea__k	w__ei__ght	r__ei__n	
/j/	__j__og	__g__erm	lar__ge__	fri__dge__					
/oa/	b__oa__t	h__o__me	sn__ow__	g__o__	t__oe__	d__ough__			
/ie/	t__ie__	b__i__ke	m__y__	r__igh__t	k__i__nd				
/ee/	b__ee__	bunn__y__	th__e__me	__ea__t	m__e__	ch__ie__f	hon__ey__		
/or/	f__or__	s__au__ce	p__aw__	t__al__k	f__our__	m__ore__	d__oor__	b__oar__	
/z/	__z__oo	Bu__zz__	ha__s__	chee__se__	snee__ze__				
/w/	__w__et	__wh__en							
/ng/	so__ng__	pi__n__k							
/v/	__v__an	lo__ve__							
/oo/	b__oo__k	sh__oul__d	p__u__t						
/oo/	sp__oo__n	gl__ue__	fl__u__te	ch__ew__	d__o__	s__ou__p	fl__u__	fr__ui__t	thr__ough__
/y/	__y__es								
/x/ (ks)	bo__x__								
/sh/	__sh__ip	__ch__ef	__s__ugar	na__ti__on	spe__ci__al	ti__ss__ue	man__si__on		
/ch/	__ch__eap	wa__tch__	na__t__ure						
/th/ (voiceless)	__th__ink								
/th/ (voiced)	__th__at								
/qu/ (kw)	__qu__een								
/ou/	__ou__t	h__ow__	pl__ough__						
/oi/	b__oi__l	t__oy__							
/ue/ (yoo)	resc__ue__	c__u__te	n__ew__	__u__nicorn					
/er/	h__er__	b__ir__d	b__ur__n	__ear__th	w__or__m[2]				
/ar/	sh__ar__k	f__a__st	h__a__lf	h__ear__t	__au__nt				
/air/	h__air__	c__are__	b__ear__	wh__ere__					
/eer/	p__eer__	d__ear__	h__ere__	w__eir__d					
/zh/	vi__si__on	trea__s__ure							

---

1 Only following *w*.
2 Only following *w*.

Pronunciation guide

Pronunciation between countries, and even within countries, differs. It is important that when teaching your child, you say the sounds without a schwa added (say the phoneme without adding "uh").

Australian phonemes, Alison Clarke, Spelfabet

youtu.be/KlMDwolcfzU and for each phoneme separately www.spelfabet.com.au/2018/05/phonemes-are-sounds-and-articulatory-gestures/

American phonemes, Rollins Center for language and literacy

youtu.be/wBuA589kfMg

British phonemes, Oxford Owl

youtu.be/UCI2mu7URBc

New Zealand phonemes, Emma Nahna, Sound Foundations for Literacy

youtu.be/SePU-T4S-js

Introduction

I love reading and always have. Reading allows me to travel to other countries, learn new words, research things that I am passionate about and escape from the humdrum of life for a while. Reading is not a struggle for me, except for one time when I picked up a book and many of the words were not easy or automatic for me to read. There was a lot of technical jargon and the sentence structure was unusual. I struggled through the first chapter but lost interest because it was such an effort, so I didn't finish it. I felt defeated, and a bit stupid to be honest.

So how do we think children feel when they struggle to read? And how do the parents of struggling children feel when they do not know how to help? This is the reason I am writing this book.

I have been working with struggling readers and their families for over 20 years. I have witnessed the frustration, pain, self-doubt and the impact this has on their wellbeing. Reading is used in all areas of the curriculum at school. Children cannot escape it. My heart aches for the children who, day in and day out, have to turn up to a place where they feel out of place and awkward. Which is why I do what I do. When I help these children to become great readers, my heart sings. I love witnessing their little faces glow when they can confidently read as their self-esteem skyrockets. But as much as I love helping each individual child, I want to make a bigger impact. How can I help these children *before* they start to struggle? How can I help *more* families?

There are many amazing professionals out there bringing the literacy plight to the fore through amazing research, books, and blogs. What's the literacy plight you might ask? The alarming fact is that literacy levels in Australia are declining. One million Australian children are at risk of not learning to read adequately, and 500,000 students went to secondary school in 2018 with weak literacy skills. This worrying trend has to be arrested.

Let me introduce some of the remarkable professionals from around the world who are making it their business to help.

In Australia:

- Professor Pamela Snow – Psychologist and Speech Pathologist, Head of the La Trobe Rural Health School. Professor Snow's blog, *The Snow Report* (pamelasnow.blogspot.com), is one to follow.

- Alison Clarke from *Spelfabet* – Speech Pathologist, Masters in Applied Linguistics, ESL teaching certificate. Alison's *Spelfabet* website (spelfabet.com.au) is a treasure trove of information and resources.

- Lyn Stone from Lifelong Literacy – Linguist, author of three books (*Spelling for Life, Language for Life* and *Reading for Life*), many wonderful webinars and programs. She is a literacy consultant to schools as well as a private clinician.

- Dr Jennifer Buckingham – Director of Strategy and Senior Research Fellow, MultiLit, founder of *Five from Five* project. This is another amazing website (fivefromfive.org. au) full of information and resources.

- Dr Lorraine Hammond – Researcher and lecturer at Edith Cowan University, Perth. Dr Hammond has a particular interest in preventing literacy-based learning difficulties.

In the US:

- Dr David Kilpatrick – Professor of Psychology, State University of New York. Dr Kilpatrick is a reading researcher, and the author of *Essentials of Assessing, Preventing, and Overcoming Reading Difficulties* (2015), and *Equipped for Reading Success* (2016).

- Natalie L. Wexler – Education journalist. She is the author of *The Writing Revolution* (2017), *The Knowledge Gap: The Hidden Cause of America's Broken Education System and How to Fix It* (2019) as well as numerous articles.

- Emily Hanford –Public media journalist. She has put together some insightful and hard-hitting documentaries.

In the UK:

- Professor Kate Nation – Experimental psychologist and expert on language and literacy development in school-age children. Professor Nation directs the *ReadOxford* project and the Language and Cognitive Development Research Group.

- John Walker – Managing Director of Sounds-Write (a quality first phonics program) and author of *The Literacy Blog*.

In New Zealand:

- Carla McNeil – Former principal, mathematics advisor, classroom teacher and parent of a dyslexic child. Carla runs *Learning Matters* (learningmatters.co.nz) who provide specialist learning support for students and families and consult with schools and education centres.

- Professor James Chapman and Distinguished Professor Bill Tunmer –one of the most successful research teams on the aspects of reading. They have published over 150 journal articles, book chapters and books.

With all of these amazing brains on the job, how I am going to add value to this conversation? Let me state right up front: I am *not* a researcher. (In fact, I nearly failed statistics at university! Ha!) What *I am* is a highly practical "people person" who has years of first-hand experience working with families on this particular problem. I see my role in spreading the literacy message about how best to teach children to read, and as an educator of parents. In addition to workshops, this book will become my primary vehicle to upskill parents and carers of struggling readers.

In the pages that follow I bring all the research of these incredible leaders in the field of literacy together and combine it with activities and real-world examples to create an easy to use, hands-on book to help your child.

What you need to know as a parent or primary carer

- Reading is not a natural process. Unlike learning to speak, where most children learn by being spoken to and being surrounded by oral language, our brains are not hardwired for reading. Written history seems to date back to about 6,000 years ago, so that was probably when writing and reading systems were invented.

- Reading is best taught with a Structured Literacy approach. This is explicit, systematic teaching that focuses on phonological and phoneme awareness, word recognition, phonics and decoding, spelling, and syntax at the sentence and paragraph levels. We will discuss what this means and how to do it in more detail in Structured Phonics. It is the most effective and evidence-based way of teaching children to read and spell.

- Unfortunately, some teachers or schools are not equipped to teach reading in the abovementioned way, which means you will need the skills to help your child learn to read at home.

- Even if your child's teacher *is* doing all the right things at school, you should understand how to support your child and continue their learning at home.

- You need to know the difference between a decodable book and a non-decodable one and their importance for beginner readers.

- Just because you read to them every day since birth doesn't guarantee they will be good readers.

- You need (and have the right to know) how to help your struggling reader as early as possible in their reading journey.

If all children were taught from a young age how to read with a structured synthetic phonics approach, then we would eliminate a large number of reading difficulties that present later. The number of children we see for literacy difficulties at my speech pathology practice would decrease – which would be a wonderful outcome! As much as I *love* working with children on reading and spelling, I shouldn't need to.

Current research on teaching children to read

You may have heard of the "Reading Wars'. It is a "fight" between two opposing views on how to best teach reading – Whole Language versus Structured Literacy. It sounds very dramatic and, in a sense, it is. Learning to read is a human right. Being able to read well impacts on success at school and is closely aligned to a person's self-esteem.

How best to teach children to read has been researched to death and there are two main schools of thought around learning to read which have been hotly debated for decades. This gave rise to the term "reading wars". One is **Whole Language** and the other is **Structured Literacy** (also called structured synthetic phonics).

The philosophy behind **Whole Language** is that children will just learn to read naturally, as they learn oral language, without the need to explicitly teach them sound-letter links or how to sound out words. The theory is that you merely need to immerse them in books – teaching is incidental. This method emphasises learning whole words and phrases in the context of making meaning from what the children are reading.

The philosophy behind **Structured Literacy** explicitly teaches children that there are 26 letters of the English alphabet which are used to represent the 44 speech sounds that make up our spoken language. It also teaches phonemic awareness (the ability to focus on and manipulate individual sounds – phonemes – in spoken words), which is one of the main skills required for reading and spelling.

But phonics alone is not enough. Children also need instruction in all of the areas as noted in the US National Reading Panel in 2005 – phonemic awareness, phonics, vocabulary, comprehension and fluency. Oral language is now also being added to the "Big Five". Using a structured synthetic phonics approach has the soundest evidence base.

In 2005, the Australian Government conducted a National Inquiry into the Teaching of Literacy. It is a lengthy read, so I have quoted some of the main points below for your interest. I'm sad to report that 15 years later these recommendations are still not standard practice in schools.

1. The Committee recommends that teachers be equipped with teaching strategies based on findings from rigorous, evidence-based research that are shown to be effective in enhancing the literacy development of all children.

2. The Committee recommends that teachers provide systematic, direct and explicit phonics instruction so that children master the essential alphabetic code-breaking skills required for foundational reading proficiency. Equally, that teachers provide an integrated approach to reading that supports the development of oral language, vocabulary, grammar, reading fluency, comprehension and the literacies of new technologies.

3. The Committee recommends that programs, guides and workshops be provided for parents and carers to support their children's literacy development. These should acknowledge and build on the language and literacy that children learn in their homes and communities.

The last point is where this book comes in. My intention is to provide practical, easy-to-follow guidance for parents to confidently assist their children to become successful readers, whether they are at the start of their reading journey or are struggling to keep up.

Why structured literacy isn't being used in all schools

Unfortunately, the research is not filtering down to teachers during their teacher training. A friend of mine who trained as a teacher was told during her studies that *phonics is the way to go, but realistically, just do whatever the school you are working in is doing.* Many schools think that they are using the most effective methods, so any new teacher who joins the staff is typically going to follow suit.

My friend, like most teachers, was not taught how to implement a phonics-based program nor was she taught about phonemic awareness. Whilst it is unbelievable that teachers are not all teaching our children to read in the correct way, it's not their fault. Teachers are one of the most dedicated, hardworking and caring group of professionals, yet they are being let down by outdated curriculum at universities. They are not equipped with a solid understanding of the evidence-based approaches to the teaching of reading.

Further complicating the situation is that where schools *are* using some sort of phonics approach, many of the teachers lack the structure, systematic teaching and phonemic awareness needed to successfully implement the program in their classrooms. A number of flawed strategies are unfortunately also being used in the classroom, and reinforced at home, which compounds the issue. I bet you have all used or at least heard of these:

- Eagle eye – "Look at the picture." "Use the first letter."
- Skippy frog – "Skip the tricky word."
- Trying Lion – "Try to re-read the sentence. Think about what would make sense; guess the word based on context."

The above are prompts that are part of the "three-cueing system" often used by teachers. In this system they encourage children to look away from the word and to use other information, not decoding, to guess the word.

The first part is based on semantic clues – that is, the meanings around the word. For example, one of my clients was reading a story about horses. When she came to the word colt and didn't know it, she used the context of the sentence and said, "Pony". ("The mother horse came over to her colt.") So, we discussed not to guess words but read from the start to the finish of the word.

The second cueing system is syntactic. This is when the reader is able to guess what part of speech is required next, for example, a noun or a verb. For instance: "Jesse was _____ at the beach." Clearly, the unknown word has to be a verb, which rules out all the naming words like *towel*, *sand* and *water*. It could be *digging*, *jumping* or *swimming*.

Lastly, the readers may use the initial sound to narrow down the choices. So, in the example above, if s is given, then that rules out the other options and the reader would guess *swimming*. Everyone thinks the child has read beautifully when this happens, but the truth is they simply guessed beautifully.

Decodable books versus predictable texts

Reading is not a guessing game. Teaching children early on to guess words is a terrible habit to fall into, and it becomes hard to break when they are older.

Some schools have spent a lot of money buying sets of predictable texts for early readers. These are the books where one word may change on the page and the children can guess that word from the picture. Here is an example:

"I went to the farm."

"I went to the shops."

"I went to the beach."

"I went to the circus."

The above "book" contains the following digraphs – *ar*, *sh*, *ch*, *ir*. (We'll talk more about digraphs in chapter 5: Phonics.)

The young reader has barely learnt any sound-letter relationships, yet they are being sent home with books that contain words with sounds they haven't been taught. How are they supposed to decode it? They can't, so they guess. They guess from the repeated sentences and they guess from the pictures. Reading seems easy! Until they get to books that are more difficult (and not repetitive) and require words to be sounded out. Now all of a sudden, the child struggles.

This struggle can lead to a lack of confidence, lack of motivation and frustration, as well as pressure from parents. You could be forgiven for thinking that if a book has been sent home with your child then he/she must be able to read it! Unfortunately, this is not always the case. What ensues is a whole lot of frustration and bad habits that can last for years.

An example of how predictable texts lead to guessing was evident when I did weekly parent reading at school whilst my oldest child was in Prep. My middle child, who was three years old at the time, would come along with me, and as the preps were reading out loud, he would fill in the gaps with the right word if they paused. Of course, they were all amazed that he could "read" but the truth was he was just guessing from the sentence structure.

A gorgeous client of mine was reading her reader every night with her mum. Her mum was proud as punch as she was reading them wonderfully. Then one day Lila said, "Look mummy, I can read this without looking at the words." And she did. The whole book. This made her mum wonder what she was actually reading and what she was memorising or guessing.

Often children read a book earlier in the day with a parent helper, then do a re-read for their parents in the evening. I assessed Lila and it turns out she had poor phonemic awareness and little knowledge of phonics. Had there not been some intervention, she would have ended up struggling as a reader. Fortunately, with some guidance and dedication from her mum, she is now reading decodable books brilliantly and is all set to become a great reader.

Decodable books are just what their name suggests – books that are able to be decoded (or read). In the early stages of reading, children should only be given a book that has the sound-letter relationships that they have been taught. For example, once the sound-letter links for *s*, *a*, *t*, *p*, *i*, and *n* have been taught, the child should be given lots of practice blending these sounds into words, and then provided with readers that only contain these sounds as well as direct teaching of words such as *the*. For example:

"The ant."

"The ant sat."

"The pin."

"The pins in."

"The pins in the ant."

As you can see, the only word they have to be told is *the*, the rest they can sound out for themselves.

Learning to read "effortlessly"

Some children do learn to read effortlessly no matter which way they are taught. You may have been one of them! Your first child may have been one of those lucky ones, but now you have a struggling reader and you don't know why. Children that learn to read without a structured phonics approach actually teach themselves the code.

We don't know which children are going to learn to read "effortlessly" and which ones will require a structured literacy approach. So why take the chance when there is strong evidence to show that a structured literacy approach works for all? It is not easy for struggling readers to catch up to their peers once they have slipped behind, so it is best to start all children off on the right track.

Learning to read

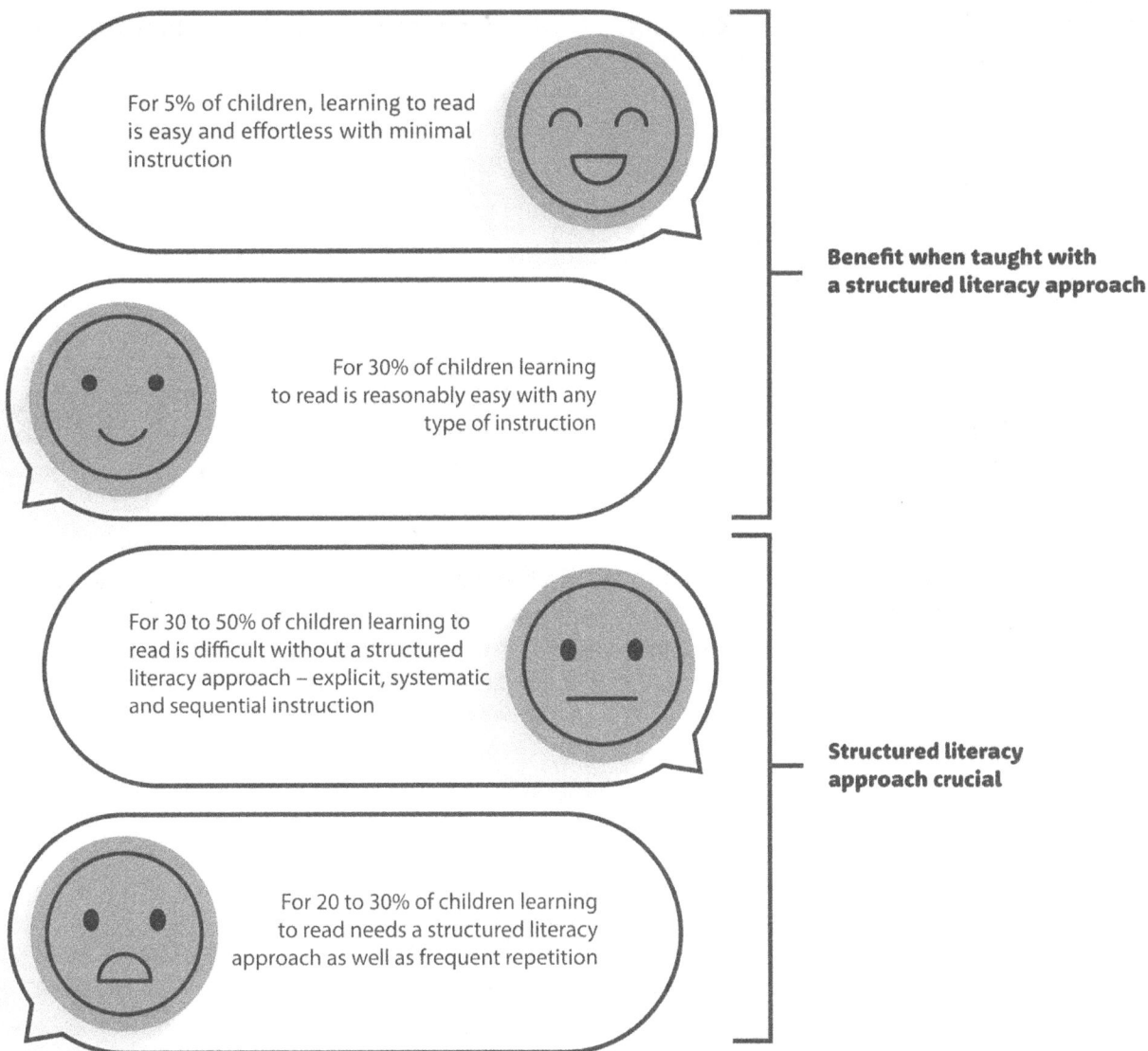

For 5% of children, learning to read is easy and effortless with minimal instruction

For 30% of children learning to read is reasonably easy with any type of instruction

Benefit when taught with a structured literacy approach

For 30 to 50% of children learning to read is difficult without a structured literacy approach – explicit, systematic and sequential instruction

For 20 to 30% of children learning to read needs a structured literacy approach as well as frequent repetition

Structured literacy approach crucial

Parents often feel guilty when their child is struggling to read. Questions such as "Did I not read to them enough as a baby or toddler?" is a common one I hear. I can assure you, it's not your fault. Reading to children is wonderful for many reasons. It teaches them new vocabulary and the structure of sentences. (Chapter 2: Oral Language will go into this in more detail.) It is also a lovely time for parents and children to snuggle up and spend quality time together at the end of the day. *But* reading to your child does not guarantee that they will become a good reader.

This book discusses the skills and knowledge children need in order to become great readers and spellers. Each chapter has information about why the particular skill is important, assessments to see where your child is currently at, and specific activities for you to do at home.

How children learn to read and spell

The end goal of reading, and therefore reading instruction, is comprehension. It is to get the meaning from what we have read. To do this, children have to be able to read, or decode, the words as well as having the vocabulary and background knowledge in order to understand them. The starting point is to explicitly teach them sound-letter relationships and then show them how to blend them together to read a word, not guess a word.

I ran a workshop recently for parents of Prep children (first year of schooling) on how children best learn to read and how to support them at home. It still amazes me how much parents are left in the dark about one of the most important things we can teach our children. The parents at the workshop were from different schools and they had all been given varying advice on how children learn to read and how to help them at home.

Most schools have a parent information night before children start school for the first time, where they cover lots of information rather quickly. There is rarely enough time to go into detail about how children are taught to read and how they can be supported at home, and yet it is the most critical skill to learn.

Well-meaning parents put their faith in the system and assume their children will be taught in the best manner possible. I was disappointed to see that one parent at my workshop had been given a single-page that contained the three-cueing system which she'd been following and assumed was perfectly fine. As discussed earlier, this method doesn't work and can actually be detrimental to a child's progress. Hard news for me to hand out to an enthusiastic parent!

The good thing is that there is always time to make a change and get children back on track with their learning. It was beautiful to see these parents walk away from the workshop feeling enlightened about why their child was struggling and empowered and confident that they can actually help.

As mentioned before, there have been umpteen studies on how to teach reading and spelling in the most effective way for children. Most studies report five core areas that children need to master in order to be successful readers. More recent studies (Konza, 2011, 2014) have added oral language to these fundamental areas.

1. Phonemic Awareness – The ability to hear and manipulate individual speech sounds in spoken words.

2. Phonics – The relationships between speech sounds and the spelling patterns that symbolize them.

3. Vocabulary – Words that children know the meaning of so that they can understand what they hear or read and communicate through speaking or writing.

4. Fluency – When children can read effortlessly, at a good rate and with expression.

5. Comprehension – Being able to understand what has been read.

6. Oral Language – Understanding what is said to us and using language to express ourselves.

The Simple View of Reading

"The Simple View of Reading" (Gough and Turner, 1986) provides a useful way to think about reading development and how we need both the ability to decode the words and the language to understand them. The diagram illustrates how the six core areas work together.

Simple View of Reading

Reading comprehension requires proficient skills in both **decoding** (reading written words) and **language comprehension** (understanding the words read)

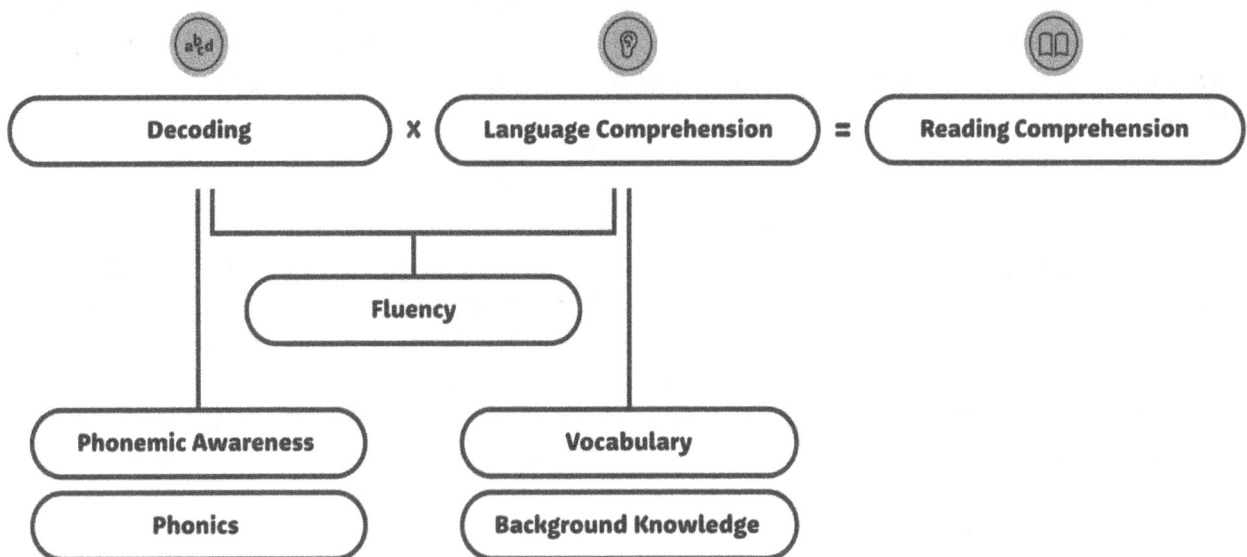

| Decoding | X | Language Comprehension | = | Reading Comprehension |

Fluency

Phonemic Awareness

Phonics

Vocabulary

Background Knowledge

Based on Gough and Tunmer, 1986

In the first two to three years of schooling, most of the child's brainpower is focused on working out what the words say – "Decoding" on the diagram on page 19. They should be explicitly taught all of the sound-letter links (phonics) and the most common spelling choice for the sound.

There are 44 phonemes (speech sounds) in spoken English and only 26 letters from which to spell them. There is not a one-to-one correspondence. As there are only 26 letters, we need to put two or three or four together to spell the other sounds. We can do this in over 150 ways. Yes, you heard right. Don't panic! If you introduce the sound-letter relationships in a structured and systematic way, give the child lots of practice and teach them phonemic awareness at the same time, then most children can "crack the code". In chapter 4: Structured Phonics, I will give you activities for teaching the sound-letter links needed in the first three years of schooling.

Once children know several thousand words, it doesn't take as much effort. Lots and lots of practice, plus explicit teaching of all of the remaining spelling choices for each sound, and the children are well on their way to being proficient readers and spellers.

If a child's decoding skills are adequate and they read daily, their fluency dramatically increases. As you can see from the Simple View of Reading diagram, fluency is needed to help children understand what they have read. If a child is struggling with their word-level decoding (or printed word recognition), then they will not develop their reading skills and fluency, and will need more support at this foundational level until the skills are automatic.

As children are developing their decoding ability, they should also be developing their language comprehension, vocabulary and background knowledge, so that when they read, they can understand and remember what they have read.

In Grade 3 (age 9 years) children are reading to learn, not learning to read. Now the child's language skills and background knowledge come even more into play. Knowledge of vocabulary and morphemes become more important and children benefit from them being explicitly taught as well. For example, if your child knows that the root word *hydro* is a Greek word meaning "water", then they can work out the meanings of other words, such as *hydroplane* and *hydro-electric*.

Sight words

Your child may have been sent home "sight" words, or "magic" words, to memorise. Children are encouraged to remember the whole word and to memorise it as a word shape, instead of learning how to decode and sound it out from left to right. There are very few words that are unable to be sounded out. Have a look at the Magic 100 list – *from, went, had, and, in, it, but, not, they, with* … the list goes on. They can all be sounded out. Some of them are trickier than others, for example, *they* and *her*. However, once a child has been taught that *e* and *r* together make the sound at the end of *her*, they can then read *fern, sister, germ* and *herd*.

It can be confusing to a child when asked to visually remember some words but sound out others. Sounding out should always be the first strategy children choose, not looking at the whole word.

Years ago, I was working with a darling little boy who would read a whole page out loud to his mother and I. His mother said, "Great reading, I only had to tell you five words." Unfortunately, mum thought her son was doing well, but in reality, most of the words read by her son were the "Magic 100" words that were taught at school. The remaining five words that he could not work out needed to be decoded, but her son didn't know where to start or what to do. These words are the words that give the story meaning, so it's imperative that a child has a strategy to tackle them.

All words eventually become "sight words" or words known without having to decode them. It is not often as adult readers that we need to work out a word. This is the goal: for children to have a large "sight" vocabulary that in turn improves reading fluency and comprehension.

So how do children turn unknown words into words known by sight? By having a solid basis of sound-letter links and phonemic awareness.

Recently, some very clever scientists have worked out how we store words so that we can recall and read them effortlessly. For children, storing new words quickly is going to make them a good reader. Contrary to what most people think though, we don't recall words through visual memory. It is through a process called orthographic mapping. Simply put, this is when a word we have read many times is stored as a unique letter string and can be read instantly. Please refer to the definition in the glossary.

I feel like I'm repeating myself but I want to stress the importance of this point: children need explicit teaching to learn to read. This means that teachers and parents must clearly explain and model the sound-letter links, phonemic awareness and how to apply those skills to segment and blend words. Children need to be taught each new sound-letter link or phonemic task until it becomes automatic.

If a child is taught only to memorise whole words they cannot teach themselves new words. When children have a good grasp of sound-letter links and segmenting and blending, then they can apply this knowledge to work out how to say new words. With varying amounts of repetition of the new word, they add it to their orthographic memory. And voila! Another word is known by sight. In the following chapters I will explain each of the six core areas and offer activities that you can do with your child at home.

Further information

"Simple View of Reading." *The Center for Development & Learn.*
cdl.org/the-simple-view-of-reading/
    Explanation of Simple View of Reading.

Stone, L. (22 September 2019) "Orthographic Mapping."
youtu.be/KIuwKnZqJEQ/
    This is a good explanatory video on the topic.

Hanford, E. (22 August 2019) "At a Loss for Words: How a flawed idea is teaching millions of kids to be poor readers." APM Reports.

apmreports.org/episode/2019/08/22/whats-wrong-how-schools-teach-reading/

> This article discusses the ineffective three-cueing system.

Ginsberg, M. (18 September 2019) "How Children Learn to Read – the Science of Reading by Sound." Phonics Hero.

phonicshero.com/how-children-learn-to-read/

> This article provides an explanation of how children learn to read.

If you are interested in learning more about each of the clever reading experts mentioned earlier, here are some references:

- Alison Clarke, *Spelfabet* – spelfabet.com.au

- Pamela Snow – pamelasnow.blogspot.com/p/about-me.html

- Lyn Stone, *Lifelong Literacy* – lifelongliteracy.com

- Jennifer Buckingham, *ResearchED* – researched.org.uk/the-fight-for-phonics-in-early-years-reading/

- Natalie Wexler – nataliewexler.com

- Emily Hanford, *APM Reports* – apmreports.org/profile/emily-hanford/

- John Walker, *The Literacy Blog* – theliteracyblog.com

- Carla McNeil, *Learning Matters* – learningmatters.co.nz

1

Foundational Skills

Before children start primary school, there are foundational skills that will benefit them enormously if they get really good at them! These include oral language, speech sounds, phonological awareness, fine and gross motor skills and print knowledge. Let's take a look at each of these areas.

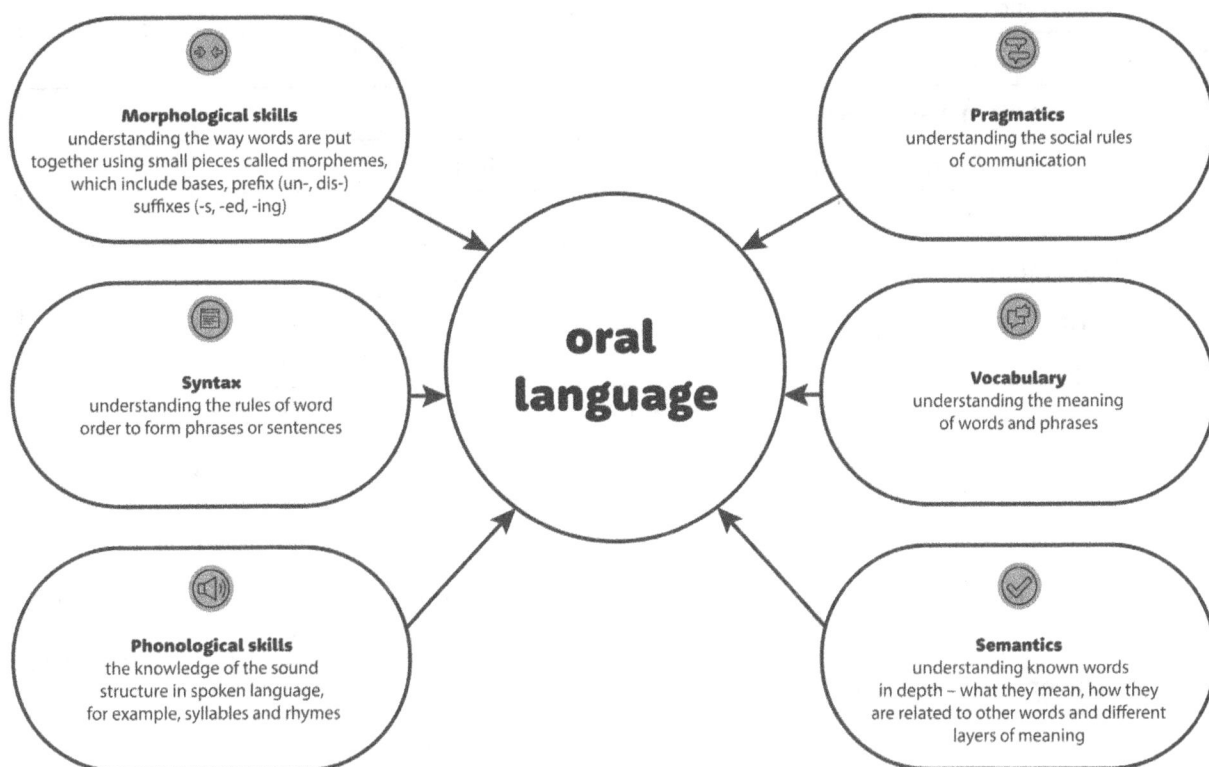

Morphological skills
understanding the way words are put together using small pieces called morphemes, which include bases, prefix (un-, dis-) suffixes (-s, -ed, -ing)

Pragmatics
understanding the social rules of communication

Syntax
understanding the rules of word order to form phrases or sentences

oral language

Vocabulary
understanding the meaning of words and phrases

Phonological skills
the knowledge of the sound structure in spoken language, for example, syllables and rhymes

Semantics
understanding known words in depth – what they mean, how they are related to other words and different layers of meaning

Why oral language is important for reading

We read for meaning. If children have poor language skills, then it doesn't matter if they can read every word put in front of them. There is literally no point if they cannot attach meaning to it. Having a good vocabulary also helps with decoding the words. If a child sounds out a word incorrectly and it doesn't match a word they have stored in their vocabulary, then they will know to sound it out a different way.

What your child should be able to understand and say at what age

Below are some basic guidelines from Speech Pathology Australia's Communication Milestones (freely available on their website) for what your child should be able to do before they start school.

If your child is 5 years old, then they should have mastered all of the areas in the 3- and 4-year-old norms. Place a tick or cross or comment next to each skill. If you are concerned that your child is not where they should be, then seek professional help for an assessment; the earlier you do so, the better the outcomes.

At 3 years old, children can usually:

Understand …	
Two-part instructions (e.g. give me the teddy and throw the ball).	
Simple "wh"-questions, such as *what*, *where* and *who*	
The concepts of "same" and "different"	
How to sort items into groups when asked (e.g. toys vs food).	
Name some basic colours.	
Say …	
Four or five words in a sentence.	
A variety of words for names, actions, locations and descriptions.	
Questions using *what*, *where* and *who*.	
Something about the past, but may use *-ed* a lot (e.g. "he goed there").	
A number of sentences during a conversation with you, but may not necessarily take turns or stay on topic.	

At 4 years old, children can usually:

Understand …	
How to answer most questions about daily tasks.	
Most "wh"-questions, including those about a story they have recently heard.	
Some numbers.	
That some words start or finish with the same sounds.	
Say …	
Conjunctions such as *and*, *but* and *because* to make longer sentences.	
Descriptions of recent events, such as morning routines.	
Lots of questions.	
Sentences using personal pronouns (e.g. *he/she*, *me/you*) and negations (e.g. *don't*, *can't*).	
Numbers up to five in order and name a few colours.	

At 5 years old, children can usually:

Understand …	
Three-part instructions (e.g. put on your shoes, get your backpack and line up outside).	
Time-related words (e.g. *before*, *after*, *now* and *later*).	
The meaning of words when learning.	
Instructions without stopping to listen.	
How to recognise some letters, sounds and numbers.	
Say …	
Well-formed sentences that are understood by most people.	
Sentences in turn with another, making increasingly longer conversations.	
Simple short stories with a beginning, middle and end.	
Verbs in past and future tenses correctly (e.g. *went*, *will go*).	

Speech sounds

Speech sounds (also called phonemes) are the individual sounds we produce that are put together to make words. There are 44 different speech sounds.

Why is having good speech sounds important for reading?

If a child cannot say the /k/ sound and they are sounding out a word, such as *cat* or *cold*, then when they blend it back together it will make *tat* and *told* which are totally different words with different meanings. A point I like to stress here is the importance of getting your child's hearing tested! Yes, I know that they can hear a chip packet opening from a mile away, but speech sounds have different frequencies and even a mild hearing loss makes it hard to distinguish particular sounds.

Regardless of whether your child passed the hearing screen at birth, they should be tested again before school as they can develop "glue ear" where sticky mucus in the eustachian tubes muffles speech sounds. Your GP can refer you to an audiologist.

What speech sounds should my child be able to say?

The following tables outline the average age children learn to pronounce English consonants correctly.[3]

---

3   McLeod, S.& Crowe, K. (2018), Children's consonant acquisition in 27 languages: A cross-linguistic review. *American Journal of Speech-Language Pathology.* doi: 10.1044/2018_AJSLP-17-0100, ajslp.pubs.asha.org/article.aspx?articleid=2701897

At 3 years old, children can usually use the following:

Speech sound	Word example	
p	pie	
b	bee	
m	me	
d	do	
n	no	
h	he	
t	to	
k	car	
g	go	
w	we	
ng	sing	
f	foot	
y	yes	

At 4 years old, children can usually use the following:

Speech sound	Word example	
l	leaf	
j	jaw	
ch	chew	
s	sock	
v	van	
sh	she	
z	zoo	

At 5 years old, children can usually use the following:

Speech sound	Word example	
r	red	
zh	measure	
th (voiced)	this	

At 6 years old, children can usually use the following:

Speech sound	Word example	
th (voiceless)	thing	

Preschool children's (age 3 and 4 years) speech should be understood by unfamiliar people (outside of the family) about 75% of the time. By 5 years of age, anyone (including unfamiliar listeners) should be able to understand the child's speech in conversation 95–100% of the time.

If your child makes an error with a sound, do not repeat the error (even though it may be cute). Repeat back the word several times using the correct sound for them to hear. Your child does not have to repeat the word.
For example,

Child: I am **pour**!

Adult: Yes, you are **four**. What a big **four**-year-old you are. I'm not **four**. I'm forty-**four**.

If you are concerned about the way your child is making his/her speech sounds, then please contact a speech pathologist for an assessment and advice.

Phonological awareness

Phonological awareness may sound complicated but, simply put, it is the awareness that "sentences" are made up of "words" and these "words" are made up of "sounds". It is the awareness that some words sound similar and some sound different, that words can be broken up into syllables, and words can be broken up into sounds. (Onset and rime are parts of a word – onset is the first consonant sound or blend, and rime is the rest of the word.)

Why Phonological awareness is important for reading

Research shows that children are at risk of having a reading difficulty if they have poor phonological and phonemic awareness. Step-by-step practice of these skills can improve reading and spelling, so it is important to encourage this before children start school. Phonological awareness develops in stages which build upon each other.

What should my child be able to do before school?

Phonological awareness skill	Example	Should be mastered by:
Breaking words into syllables.	car (1 syllable) ta-ble (2 syllables) all-i-ga-tor (4 syllables)	5 years
Alliteration: Children need to hear the sounds (phonemes) within words, rather than see the letter patterns (graphemes).	**Peter Piper picked a peck of pickled peppers.** **Six swans swam slowly.**	5 years

Rhyming: Being able to identify which words sound the same.	chair, stair, hare cat, fat, bat, that	5 years
Being able to make up their own rhyme or tell you a word that rhymes.	"Can you tell me a word that rhymes with *bat*?" Or "Can you tell me a word that sounds the same as *back*?"	5 ½ years
Blending the start of a word and then the end together (onset and rime). Onset — any consonant sounds that come before the vowel. Rime — includes the vowel sound and any consonants that follow.	"What word do these sounds make if you push them back together?" s – ock m – an h – at spl – ash	5 ½ years

Activities to develop phonological awareness

Remember that this is an oral awareness activity, so you don't need resources or materials. You are simply playing with the oral language. You may have to do a lot of teaching and modelling first before your child can do it themselves.

Breaking words into syllables

Your child does not have to count the syllables said, as long as they pause long enough for you to know that they have broken the word into its syllables.

- Ask your child to put their hand under their chin and say the following words: *table, alligator, mummy, daddy, car, basketball*. Notice how your jaw drops when a vowel is said? This is a syllable.

- Practise saying compound words which are words that combine two separate words to create a new word. For example: *football, doghouse, footpath, rainbow, pancakes*. These are great introductions to awareness of syllables in words.

- You can also clap or tap beats in words. Try these ones: *paper – pa-per, basket – bas-ket, computer – com-pu-ter, phone – phone, Saturday – Sat-ur-day*.

- How many beats in your child's name; for example, *Timothy – Tim-o-thy*.

- Practise identifying verbally things/toys around the house. Break the word into its syllables; for example, *lion – li-on, ball – ball, octopus – oct-o-pus, table – ta-ble, refrigerator – re-frig-er-a-tor*.

- Say the syllables in every family member's name.

Now that your child knows what a syllable is and has practised separating them in words, it's time to take it up a notch. You may need to model this several times with different compound words.

The parent is to say a compound word for the child to repeat. After that, the parent instructs the child to omit one of the words. For example:

Parent: Say *cupcake*.

Child: Cupcake.

Parent: Now say it again but don't say *cup*.

Child: Cake.

Try these compound words, using the instructions above, and then think of some of your own.

- football – foot = ball
- sunlight – sun = light
- milkshake – milk = shake
- bathtub – bath = tub
- rainbow – rain = bow

Now let's try deleting the end part of the compound word.

- popcorn – corn = pop
- snowball – ball = snow
- toothbrush – brush = tooth
- campfire – fire = camp
- cowboy – boy = cow

Alliteration

Alliteration is using the same consonant sound at the beginning of words in a sentence.

- Alliteration – "Peter Piper picked a peck of pickled peppers."
- Make up your own – "Seven silly sausages were sizzling sideways." "Jack jumps giant jelly." "Many mummy's make muffins."
- Alliteration with yours and your children's names – "Happy Hudson's on holidays." "Jumping Jenny." "Busy Belinda." See if they can think of ones for their own name.
- Find books that have alliteration throughout. Bring it to the attention of your child. "Can you hear how all of the sounds at the start **sound** the same? They are all the /m/ sound."

Identifying words that rhyme

- Sing nursery rhymes!

- Read books that contain rhyming words. Consider reading books by authors such as Dr Seuss or Pamela Allen.

- Model rhyming words to help your child hear the rhyming component of the words. "Billy … silly … they sound a bit the same … they rhyme."

- Ask your child to listen as you say two words. Then ask, "Do they rhyme?" "Do they sound the same at the end? If they rhyme give me a thumbs up, if they are different give me a thumbs down."

Producing words that rhyme

- When reading a rhyming book, ask your child to tell you a word that would rhyme; for example, "The dog sat on a … ?" or "The mouse went into the … ?"

- Have fun with rhymes. Try the game "Hospital Rhyme". Ask your child to complete the rhyme: "Mrs Peck hurt her (neck). Mr Beg hurt his (leg).

- Tell your child two words that rhyme and ask them to think of another. For example, "Cat and mat. What's another word that sounds the same? Cat … mat …" If they can't think of one, then give them another example. "Try to add another word to this rhyme: cat … mat … sat …"

Blending onset and rime

This is a much trickier skill and children may not master this before they enter school. It is the first time that children have to blend syllables together.

Tell your child that you are going to speak in a "slow, funny" way and they have to work out what word you are saying by "pushing" the sounds back together. Say the first part of the word, pause for one second and then say the rest of the word. Try these:

- f – ish
- d – oor
- b – ook
- ch – air
- sh – op
- c – at

In the next chapter on Oral Language, there are additional activities for phonological awareness that can be done when engaged in an activity with your child.

Fine motor skills

Fine motor skills are the ability to use the small muscles in your hands and wrists to complete actions such as cutting with scissors, using pencils, doing up buttons, shoelaces and zips, opening lunch boxes and containers, using cutlery, brushing teeth, dressing toys and creating things with Lego.

Why are they important for reading?

Fine motor skills are the building blocks for handwriting. Pencil control is needed to write letters, which are formed by connecting different lines together. Being able to write the letter as you learn the associated sound helps consolidate letter-sound links.

What should my child be able to do?

At 3–4 years old, children can usually:

Draw a cross while watching you draw one.	
Copy a circle.	
Snip paper with scissors and hold paper independently.	
Start to cut out a circle.	
Build a tower with 9–10 blocks.	
Draw a person with a head and one other part.	
Write several capital letters.	
Occasionally go outside of the lines when colouring.	
Hold a pencil in a tripod grasp; however, they may not be able to move their fingers independently of their wrist.	

At 4–5 years old, children can usually:

Draw diagonal lines, squares and triangle shapes while watching you draw them.	
Cut along a straight line for 10 cm.	
Fold paper three times.	
Draw a person with 4–6 elements.	
Copy simple words in uppercase letters.	
Colour within the lines.	
Use dynamic tripod grasp – movement of the pencil is now from the fingers but this may take until 6 years old to fully develop.	

Typical Development of Pencil Grasp

10 months
Pincer Grasp

12-15 months
Palmar Supinate Grasp

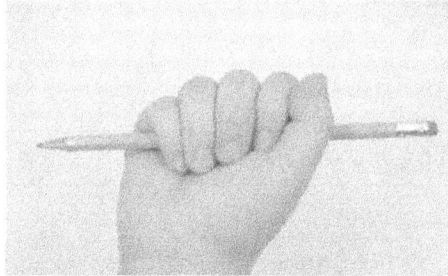

2-3 years
Digital Pronate Grasp

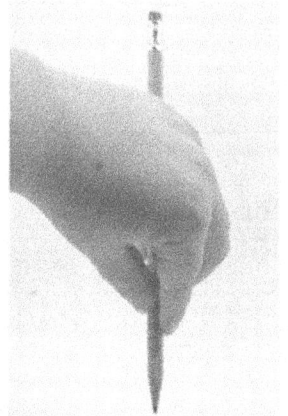

3-4 years
Quadrupod Grasp and/or Static Tripod Grasp

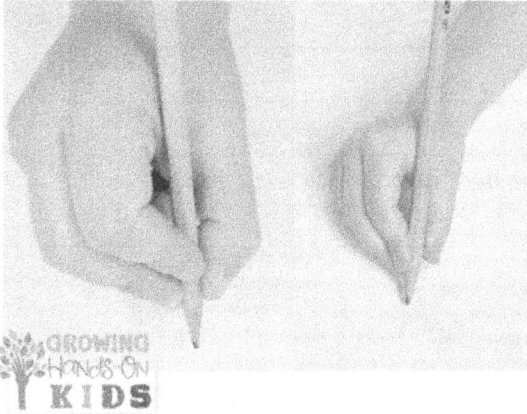

4-6 years
Dynamic Tripod Grasp

GROWING
Hands·On
KIDS

Activities to develop fine motor skills

- Play with playdough or clay.
- Paint.
- Thread beads.
- Play with Lego or other building blocks.
- Draw and colour with chalk, pencils and crayons or on a whiteboard.
- Learn to hold and use scissors correctly. Once you think they will not cut off a finger, then let them cut on their own!

Gross motor skills

Gross motor skills are the use of whole-body movements, such as standing, walking, sitting upright, climbing, catching, kicking and throwing and running.

Why are gross motor skills important for reading?

If a child does not have good core strength, then their posture is affected; this makes them "slumpy" when they are writing, cutting, drawing and sitting up to listen which can affect their concentration and form.

What should my child be able to do?

At 3–4 years old, children can usually:

Hop forward on one foot.	
Run around objects and turn corners.	
Jump forward with feet together, at least 50 cm.	
Jump over low objects.	
Walk down steps, alternating feet.	
Walk on tiptoes.	

At 4–5 years old, children can usually:

Balance on one foot.	
Maintain own momentum when swinging on a swing.	
Bounce and catch a tennis ball.	
Jump sideways with feet together.	

Activities for gross motor development

- Outdoor play – running, climbing, jumping, hopping, swinging themselves on swing, rope ladders, wobble bridges, popping bubbles, throwing or kicking a ball back and forth.

- Riding a scooter or bike.

- During winter, indoor activities work just as well, such as balloon play (keeping the balloon off the ground by hitting and kicking it), dancing (throw on your favourite 90s music or nursery rhymes), or obstacle courses made from pillows, chairs, hula hoops that require jumping over or crawling under.

Print knowledge

Before your child starts school, they need to know that a printed word means something. They need to understand the idea that the "squiggly" lines on a page represent what we say and that when an adult reads to them, the story is from the words on the page and not the picture.

Your child should also know where the front of the book is, how to hold a book the right way up, that in English you read a book from left to right and from top to bottom. They should know that there is an author, a person that writes the book and an illustrator, a person who draws the pictures.

Many children recognise some letters, such as the ones in their name.

Activities to develop print knowledge

- When reading a book, point out: "This is the front of the book, we hold it up this way. When we read, we start at the top of the page."

- As you read track the words across the page: "We read from left to right." Also talk about the author, the illustrator, the title.

- When at a restaurant or café, point to the words as you read the menu to them.

- When out and about, point to a variety of signs, such as "No Parking" and highlight that those words let you know what you may and may not do.

- Write a shopping list in front of your child and say the words as you write them.

All of the above skills are foundational and should be developing nicely in the year before children start school, allowing for more complex skills to be added when they start school.

Further information

Oral Language

The Hanen Centre – hanen.org
  This is a not-for-profit organisation that provides handouts for parents and educators.

Raising Children – raisingchildren.net.au
  This website has lots of information about promoting language and literacy skills.

Hungry Little Minds – hungrylittleminds.campaign.gov.uk
  This website has suggestions based on the age of children with links to other resources.

Phonological awareness

Five from Five – fivefromfive.org.au/parent-resources/parent-resources-phonological-phonemic-awareness/
  More activities can be found on this amazing website.

Prof. Gillon G., University of Canterbury, NZ – www.canterbury.ac.nz/education-and-health/research/phonological-awareness-resources/
  Professor Gillon provides free resources.

Fine and gross motor skills

"Kids health information", Royal Children's Hospital Melbourne – rch.org.au/ot/information_sheets/Kids_health_information/
  The Royal Children's Hospital website has a range of fact sheets with activities.

Growing Hands-on Kids – growinghandsonkids.com
  Another treasure trove of activities can be found on this website.

"Child Development Charts", Kid Sense – childdevelopment.com.au/resources/child-development-charts/
  This website provides more detailed checklists for both speech pathology and occupational therapy milestones (from 0–8 years).

If you think that your child is struggling with their speech sounds, their understanding or use of language or phonological awareness, then please book an assessment with your local speech pathologist. Contact your community health service or not-for-profit organisation for a public speech pathologist.

Private speech pathologists

- Speech Pathology Australia – speechpathologyaustralia.org.au

- New Zealand Speech-language Therapists' Association – speechtherapy.org.nz/employing-a-speech-language-therapist/

- American Speech-Language-Hearing Association – asha.org/profind/

- Speech-Language & Audiology Canada – sac-oac.ca/find-speech-language-pathologist-or-audiologist-service

- Association of Speech and Language Therapists in Independent Practice (UK) – asltip.com/therapy-for-children/

If your child is struggling with their motor skills, please book an assessment with an occupational therapist. Contact your community health service or not-for-profit organisation for a public occupational therapist.

Private occupational therapists

- Occupational Therapy Australia – otaus.com.au

- Occupational Therapy New Zealand – otnz.co.nz/find-an-occupational-therapist/

- Find an Occupational Therapist (US) – findanoccupationaltherapist.com

- Canadian Association of Occupational Therapists – caot.ca/site/findot

- Royal College of Occupational Therapists (UK) – rcot.co.uk/about-occupational-therapy/find-occupational-therapist/

Remember to always check the child's hearing!

2

Oral Language

Oral language is made up of many different components, and it is the ability to understand what is said to you (receptive language) and to communicate your message (expressive language).

Why is it important?

Good oral language skills are necessary to recognise instructions, understand and respond to questions, ask questions, re-tell an event that happened, follow conversations, follow the story lines in books, solve problems, express thoughts and ideas, wants and needs, engage in social interactions, *and* to be a great reader and writer. Being able to comprehend oral language comes before reading comprehension.

Remember, written words are our spoken language in print. If your child cannot understand the words orally, then they will not understand them in writing. Similarly, if your child cannot tell you a wonderful sentence, then they will not be able to write a wonderful sentence. Oral language is not something you only put effort into before school, it has to continue to be developed throughout primary and secondary school.

Strategies to develop oral language skills

Learning to understand and to use language is biologically natural. However, children still need frequent exposure to language-rich activities and conversations. Children may hear many words from the TV, iPad, computers, but they do not learn these as readily. Children learn through live interaction – that is, they say something, you say something, they say something and so on. This is called "serve and return".

Talk out loud about what you are seeing, hearing, doing or feeling at any point in time. Describe what your child is doing, seeing or hearing. This provides great language exposure for your child. They do not need to repeat or imitate what you say.

Model language while playing with your child. Talk about the toys, discuss how to play with them, narrate what you and your child are doing with the toys. Pretend-play is a wonderful way to expose your child to lots of language and to develop their imagination. Also sing lots of songs and nursery rhymes.

Expand on their message by adding extra words or phrases to what your child has said when you respond to them. This allows you to add new words and information to their thoughts by making your sentences slightly more complex than your child's. For example, if your child uses a two-word sentence, you can respond to them and add more words:

Child: Mummy kick.

Adult: You want Mummy to kick the ball. – Okay, I will kick the ball. – I did a big kick. (Remember to pause between each sentence.)

When interacting with older children, model sentences that use the following:

- Cause and effect – "The train crashed into the tunnel **because** it was too low." "Many rainforests are being destroyed, and **as a result** some species have nowhere to live."
- Comparatives such as *longer, faster, bigger, taller* – "My sandcastle is bigg**er.**"
- Superlatives such as *longest, fastest, biggest, tallest* – "She was the fast**est** runner."
- Conjunctions to join ideas and sentences together such as *but, whereas, because, although* – "I am very hungry, **but** the fridge is empty."
- A sequence of events, whether real events that have already occurred or those that may occur during imaginative play. Model to your child to re-tell an event with a start, middle and an end. "First, we did [x], then we felt [y], and finally we discovered [z]."
- Questions and answers – "I wonder why the beach ball went flat? Oh look, here is a tiny hole where the air is escaping."

Modelling correct language structures

Your child is going to have errors in their word order and grammar. The key to helping your child is to give them a model immediately after their sentence. Don't change the meaning, merely correct it by modelling back the way it should be said. Your child does not need to repeat the sentence or be told that they are wrong.

This modelling should occur naturally as part of your conversation with your child, without interrupting the flow of communication and without getting in the way of listening to their message. Try to model the correct word or sentence at least 2–3 times, as well as add new language where possible.

Example 1

Child: We **is** going to have lunch now.

Adult: Yes, we **are** going to have lunch now. We **are** going to clear the tables **first.** Then we **are** going to wash our hands. Then we **are** ready for lunch! So, what are we doing **first**?

Child: Wash our hands?

Adult: We are going to clear the tables **first,** then wash our hands.

Child moans, of course, about clearing the table!

Adult: Let's sing a nursery rhyme while we do it. (Some phonological awareness!)

Example 2

Child: I **runned** all the way to car.

Adult: Wow, you **ran** all the way to **the** car. I don't think I could have **run** all the way to **the** car. You must be tired.

Child: I am very tired.

Adult: Yes, I can see you are tired. You look exhausted.

Child: What's that?

Adult: It means really, really tired. You look exhausted. Are you exhausted?

Child: Yes, I need a rest. I'm so exhausted. (They may not pronounce the word correctly the first time they try the new word.)

Example 3

Child: When daddy get here?

Adult: When **will** daddy get here? Mmm … I don't know when daddy **will** get here. Shall we call him and ask him, "When **will** you get here, Daddy?"

Child: Yes, let's call him.

Adult: Ok, remember to ask, "Daddy, when **will** you get here?"

Child: Daddy, when **will** you get here?

Example 4

Child: I seen a big car.

Adult: You **saw** a big car! What colour was the car you **saw**?

Child: Blue.

Adult: You **saw** a big, blue car. How big was it?

Child: This big. (The child gestures with arms out wide.)

Adult: Wow. That seems like a **huge** car. You saw a **huge**, blue car.

Once your child has a good grasp of lots of different sentence structures, then the need for modelling and expanding their language reduces. To keep the conversation and the learning going, use good questions and comments.

Keep the conversation going

The quality of the conversations that you have with your child really counts. Aim for at least five conversation turns to encourage positive, engaging experiences with language. You can see from the above examples that I have used comments and questions to keep the conversation going.

Everyday experiences

Rich language experiences happen in everyday activities. Sometimes, we just need a reminder to be more intentional with our language. The examples below can be done with children of varying ages and language levels by simply adapting the complexity of the vocabulary (words and concepts). For example, with your 4-year-old, use other words to describe "big" such as *huge* and *large*. For your Grade-2 child, you could say it's *colossal* or *gigantic*.

If your child does not know what a word means, take the time to explain it. Try to use it in another context as well to help your child understand the new word. For example, you are reading a book and the character was walking too close to the **edge** of the pool. Ask, "Do you know what edge means?" If they don't know, then you can explain it, and show them with pictures or real objects. "It's the outside of something, the edge of a piece of paper, the edge of the table. "Arrrgggghhh, I'm falling off the edge of the couch!"

When engaged in an activity with your child, please do not feel as if you have to model every one of the parts of language listed below and in the Real Life scenario examples. You may lose the naturalness of your special time together.

Parts of language

Parts of language	What it means	Examples
Nouns	Naming words for people or things.	table, dog, mummy
Pronouns	Words that take the place of nouns so that we don't have to continue repeating them.	she, he, his, hers, him, we, us, them, I, me, mine, our, you, herself, himself
Adjectives	Words that describe nouns.	pretty, cold, yellow, small, humungous, vast, tiny
Verbs	Doing or action words.	jump, run, sleep, gallop, hop, appear, imitate
Adverbs	Words that describe a verb or adjective.	carefully, slowly, sing loudly, ate greedily
Prepositions	Words that join pronouns, nouns and phrases to other words in a sentence. They describe the position of something, the manner in which something is completed or the time when something occurs.	in, on, under, next to, between, through, over, during, since, ago

Morphemes	These can change the meaning of the word and include:	
	• plurals	dogs, cats
	• irregular past tense	fell, came, broke
	• regular past tense (-ed)	jumped, walked
	• continuous tense (-ing)	jumping, walking
	• possessives	Michael's
	• comparatives	later, slower
	• superlatives	busiest, easiest
	• prefixes and suffixes.	dis – disappear
		un – unhappy
Conjunctions	A word that connects phrases or sentences together.	and, because, if, but, unless, after, in order

Real-life scenario 1: Cooking

Nouns	Name the utensils needed; for example, spatula, wooden spoon, whisk, measuring cup.
Pronouns	"It's **her** turn first." "**I** will do this one." "Can **you** give the egg to **me** please?" "**They** are going to love this cake." "Wow, you did that by **yourself**."
Adjectives	Discuss the ingredients: **What they look like** – colour, shape, how they look similar and different. **What they feel like (texture)** – slimy, smooth, hard, bumpy, sticky. **What their weight is** – heavy, light, "Which one is the heaviest, which is the lightest?" **How many or much of each ingredient you need** –some, all, the rest, half, etc. **How they taste** – spicy, sweet, delicious, yummy, bland, salty.
Verbs	Stir, pour, measure, roll, break, spread, melt, grate, boil.

Prepositions	**in** the bowl
	on the table
	it is **between** the milk and flour
	pour the water **over** the mixture
Morphology	two egg**s**
	"Stir slow**er**."
	"Let's do some roll**ing** together."
	"**Is it** ready?"
Conjunctions	"Let's stir some more **because** it is not all mixed together."
	"Should we put in more milk **or** do you think it's enough?"
Following instructions	"Can I have two eggs please?"
	"Can I please have the milk **and** the butter?"
	"Can you please stir the batter faster?"
Phonological awareness	**Syllables** – break names of utensils or ingredients into syllables like *spa-tu-la, fork, mea-su-ring, cup, sif-ter, a-pple, egg, flo-ur*.
	Alliteration – say words with the same sound at the start like "**M**mmmmm, I'd like to **m**unch **m**ore **m**arshmallows."
	Rhyming – tell your child lots of rhyming words like "*Egg* rhymes with *peg* and *Meg*."
Phonemic awareness	If we had the word *cupcake* and took away *cup*, I'd have *cake* left!
	Try other examples such as *cookbook, pancake, cupboard*, etc. Break words into sounds.

Real-life scenario 2: At the park or on a nature walk

Nouns	Name the things you can see or what your child is playing on or with; for example, bark, climbing frame, types of trees, names of different birds (*rosella, magpie, cockatoo*) and names of insects.

Pronouns	Note the people around you:
	"**She** is running fast."
	"Look at **his** cute dog."
	"It's **her** turn on the swing, then it's **yours**."
	"Wow, he climbed up there by **himself**."
Adjectives	Choose something to have a discussion about; for example, leaves or trees.
	What they look like – colours, different shapes and compare sizes (*tiny, little, small, big, huge, enormous, gigantic*). Which one is bigger? Which one is the biggest?
	What they feel like (texture) – soft, brittle, slimy, rough, smooth, prickly, crumbly
	What their weight is – light, "Do they float?"
	What they are for – shade, cleaning the air.
Verbs	Swing, roll, fly, slide, catch, climb, blow, push.
Prepositions	**on** the slide
	on the swing
	under the tree
	over the bridge
	next to the rock
Morphology	"Great swing**ing**."
	"There are so many leave**s**."
	"Would you like to go high**er**?"
	"The girl looks **un**happy."
	"That tree is the tall**est**."
	"Wow, you climb**ed** the tree."
	"Your hat **dis**appeared!"
Conjunctions	"We had better go home **as** it looks like it is going to rain."
	"She is very tired, **yet** she is still running."
Following instructions	Ask your child to find things for you (like a scavenger hunt).
	"Can you find me **three green** leaves?"

Phonological awareness	**Syllables** – break different words into syllables.
	Alliteration – say sentences that have the same sound at the start like "**T**allest **t**ree-top." "Go **sl**ow on the **sl**ippery **sl**ide."
Phonemic awareness	If I have the word *football*, and take away *foot*, I'm left with *ball*.
	Try other words such as *parkbench, sunshine, playground*.
	The word *park* has three sounds in it: *p-ar-k*. Do this with a variety of words.

Real-life scenario 3: At the beach

Nouns	Name the colours you can see; for example, different shades of the water like azure, light blue, dark blue, sparkly.
	Name objects: kayak, beach ball. If the children have beach equipment: strainer, funnel, shovel, bucket, rake, frisbee.
Pronouns	"**They** have dug a big hole."
	"That's **his** ball, it belongs to **him**."
	"**We** are going to set up **our** shade here."
	"Can **you** hold the towel please?"
Adjectives	Choose something to have a discussion about; for example, shells and the sand.
	What they look like – colour, patterns, shape, size, how they look similar and different. Put them in order from smallest to biggest.
	What they feel like – fine, grainy, rough, smooth, shiny.
	What their weight is – heavy, light, "Which one is the heavi**est**, which is the light**est**?"
	How many there are – "How many shells do you have?"
	If the children made a moat around a sandcastle, then talk about it using words such as *empty, full, float, sink, deep, shallow*.
Verbs	Fly, see, run, swim, surf, apply (as in apply your sunblock).

Prepositions	**in** the bucket
	on the sand
	under the towel
	above the trees
	next to the big rock
Morphology	"She is swimm**ing** out too deep."
	"These sandcastle**s** are big, but this one is the bigg**est**."
Conjunctions	"We have to put on sunblock **so** we don't get sunburnt."
	"I have my bathers on **but** I don't want to swim."
Following instructions	"Can you find three small white shells?"
	"After you pick up your towel, please pick up the shovel."
Phonological awareness	**Syllables** – break words into syllables like *sur-fing, o-cean, beach, um-bre-lla, oc-to-pus*.
	Alliteration – *sand, sun, sea, salt, sail, swim* all start with the sound /s/.
Phonemic awareness	If I had the word *beachball* and took away *ball*, I'd be left with *beach*.
	Try other words such as *sunblock, sunset, jellyfish, seaweed*.
	The word *beach* has three sounds in it: *b-ea-ch*. Do this with a variety of words.

Real-life scenario 4: Simon Says or an obstacle course

Nouns	Name body parts and parts of the obstacle course or props being used.
Pronouns	"It's **her** turn to go first."
	"Can you help **him** put the chair over there?"
Adjectives	"Simon says run **fast**, now **slower**."
Verbs	Run, walk, throw, crawl, weave, jump.
	Try to add some more complex words like *gallop* instead of *run* or *spring* instead of *jump*.

Prepositions	"Simon says go **under** the couch." "Simon says put the book **on** the chair." "Sit **beside** the table." When the children are completing the course, or if you are doing it with them, describe what they are doing using prepositions such as *over*, *between*, *through*, *under*, etc. Give instructions such as, "Throw the bean bag **over** the hoop."
Morphology	"They are listen**ing** very well." "You look **un**happy." "She **ran** fast."
Conjunctions	"Touch your ear **and** then your head. "Don't touch your eyes **after** you touch your toes."
Following instructions	Use two step instructions – "Simon says touch your nose and then your ear," "Simon says touch your head then clap three times." This is a great activity for your child to practise giving instructions to you as well. Obstacle course – Take turns giving instructions to each other; for example, "First run to the sandpit, then crawl over to the bike."
Phonological awareness	**Alliteration** – "Simon **s**ays **s**it down", "Simon **s**ays **s**tand **s**till." **Rhyming** – use words that rhyme with your child's name; for example, if your child's name is Kate, then you could say, "Simon says if your name rhymes with *late*, sit down."
Phonemic awareness	"Simon says *s-i-t*." See if your child can blend the sounds together to form a word (only use words that have two to four sounds like *r-u-n, j-u-m-p, s-k-i-p*).

Remember to choose words and phonological/phonemic activities that are suitable to your child's level. In all of the above situations, interaction and conversation is key. Don't just list off all the words to your child! Oral language develops best when it is "serve and return" – the back-and-forth interactions between a parent and a child. Listen to what their comments and questions are and then add your own.

In today's busy world, we often do not set aside time for talking. Quality discussion time is important to build your child's language skills, as well as letting them know that their ideas and opinions are valued. It is a wonderful time to do this at the dinner table, as there are opportunities for the whole family to share and to respond. Long car trips also offer a great chance for conversation; forego the screen time and have talking time instead. Games such as "I Spy" and "20 questions" provide excellent opportunities for language development.

Be mindful that language modelling and conversation isn't always sunshine and roses! – for example, when you hear your children yelling at each other in the loungeroom.

Mum: What's happening in there?

Boy: It's my turn.

Girl: Campbell took it from me. I had it.

Mum: Who had the remote first? You or him?

Girl: He had it first, but it's my turn.

Mum: Why is it your turn?

Girl: He chose last time.

Mum: So, it's **your** turn to choose the **first** show, **because** he chose the first show **yesterday.** [To Boy] Can you give the remote to **her** please?

Boy: Dunno where it is.

Mum: I think I saw it go **between** the cushions, or maybe **behind** them. Nope, not **between** them. Here it is, **behind** the cushion. (This is often said through gritted teeth as Boy clearly hid the remote out of spite!)

You can see that in this back-and-forth exchange, pronouns, prepositions, questions, conjunctions have all been used. It wasn't just a case of going in all guns blazing and fix the problem. Interactions, even if they are annoying, are important.

The impact of book reading

This is top of the list when it comes to developing oral language. An amazing fact for you: reading to your child for one minute a day exposes them to around 8,000 words per year; 5 minutes per day, 282,000 words per year; and 20 minutes per day, 1.8 million words per year. The compounding effect is enormous!

When children are not independent readers, those 20 minutes should be you or another adult reading to them. Once they are competent readers, they can read on their own for 20 minutes per day, which continues to expand their vocabulary and reading ability.

I rest my case! No, not really, please keep reading for the benefits and some tips for book reading.

Book reading is a wonderful way to:

- Introduce new vocabulary, grammar, and narratives – the works! They also learn about the world around them as well as concepts and ideas that in day-to-day life may never be exposed to, such as space, pirates, magic and dragons.

- Learn about the structure of stories and print knowledge – that "squiggly lines" make up words, and that print is read from left to right and from the top to the bottom of the page.

- Nurture the development of your child's imagination.

Book reading tips

In an ideal world, each child would get a book that is suitable for their language level read to them for 20 minutes each day. However, as a mum of three children with a husband who gets home late, I know that this is simply impossible every night!

One way around that challenge is to read the same book to children of different ages if you cannot get the one-on-one time. For example, read the whole sentence to your 5-year-old, rephrase it in simpler vocabulary for your 3-year-old, then point at pictures and use single words for the baby/ toddler.

I know that sometimes you just want the children in bed but bookreading really is non-negotiable. If necessary, start the bedtime process earlier so that you have 20 minutes to read before lights out. If it doesn't work for your family at night, then try reading in the morning.

You could also ask your older child who is a fluent reader to read to your younger children. If the grandparents are visiting, then ask them to read your children a book. Going out for the night? Tell the babysitter to read to your child for 20 minutes. If you're really strapped for time a couple of nights per week, then your child can listen to an audio book. If one child is waiting with you to pick up another child from an activity, you could read a book together rather than play with your phone. In the car a lot? Listen to an audiobook together.

I can go on and on …

When reading with your child:

- Ensure reading time is interactive and fun. Don't just read *at* your child, read *with* them. You do not even have to read all the words; you can simplify the book or make up a story about a character in the book or one of the pictures.

- Make connections between the book you are reading and your child's life. For example, if you are reading about a family at a beach, remind them of a time when you were at the beach together and what you did.

- Predict what might happen next in the story. Connect storylines with your child's own experiences and how they think the character can fix the problem.

- Discuss why characters feel the way they do. Compare these feelings to a time when your child felt that way. These types of conversations whilst reading the book will help your child to understand the world, use their imagination and encourage them to think, predict and solve problems.

- Read with expression and pause at dramatic moments. This will not only engage your child with the story but will also teach them about reading with fluency. Stop at full stops, pause at commas, read questions with rising intonation, emphasise words that are in capitals or are with an exclamation mark.

- Encourage your child to take the lead. Ask them to tell you the story in a book using the pictures. Your child may use simple sentences, which will enable you to use modelling. The more your child practises telling the same story, the more they will pick up on your models and improve their language in their storytelling.

- It is absolutely fine if your child wants to read the same book over and over (and over and over and over!) again. Repetition will help your child reinforce new vocabulary and the sentence structures in the book.

- Stop and tell your child what any new words mean. Use the picture to support their understanding of the new word and give an example from their everyday life that they can relate to.

Some children, even with the most amazing interactive language experiences, still struggle to pick up oral language. If this is the case for your child, then please get them assessed by a speech pathologist.

Further information

The Hanen Centre – hanen.org

> The Hanen Centre is a wonderful not-for-profit organisation that has a great website with ideas and activities for parents to develop their child's language skills. These include "The Land of Make Believe: How and Why to Encourage Pretend Play", "The Hanen Book Nook" (where they take a popular children's book and discuss ways to promote language skills) and "How to Have Fun with Playdough and Toddlers".

"Activities to Encourage Speech and Language Development", *Reading Rocket* – readingrockets. org/article/activities-encourage-speech-and-language-development/

> This has parent tips for reading with your child as well as activities to encourage speech and language development.

"Child Development Charts", *Kid Sense* – childdevelopment.com.au/resources/child-development-charts/

> This website has checklists for milestones from 0–8 years, including fine and gross motor skills, language and play.

Your local library is a great place to get your fill of new and interesting books and often provides book activities, including weekly story time, for younger children.

3

Phonemic Awareness

I bet you have never heard of this component of reading before? Don't worry, many haven't! Phonemic awareness comes under the umbrella of phonological awareness that was discussed in chapter 1: Foundational Skills. It is the process of being able to focus on and manipulate individual speech sounds (phonemes) in spoken words. Phonemic awareness includes the knowledge that:

- words are made up of individual sounds and the child can identify where in the word the sound is.
- words can be formed by blending separate sounds together (*f-i-sh* makes *fish*).
- words can be segmented into separate sounds (*s-l-i-p*).
- words can be changed or manipulated by deleting, adding or re-ordering sounds within the word to make a different word (*trip* without the *r* says *tip*).

Remember, we are talking specifically about spoken language here, not written. Some children understand that they are making different sounds when they say a word, but many are not aware that spoken words are different sounds put together. It is this awareness of phonemes children need to develop as they learn to read and spell. For many children, this ability needs to be directly taught.

The most frequent cause of word-level reading difficulties is poor phonemic awareness, so please do not skip this chapter! And as they say, "prevention is better than cure" – early training of phonemic awareness in the first and second year of schooling can help avoid many reading difficulties.

Reading instruction is often based on presenting the written letter and saying what sound it makes. For example: this is the letter b, it makes the b sound. Instead, we should be focusing on the sound we say: /b/ can be spelled with the b or bb. Another example is the speech sound /ai/ (as in say) which can be spelled by writing the letters ai, ay, a, ey or eigh (such as rain, day, apron, grey, eight). These letter combinations that spell speech sounds will be taught in the next chapter on Phonics.

Why good phonemic awareness is important

Phonemic awareness is one of the best predictors of how well children will learn to read during the first two years of school instruction. It is not usually included in the teaching of reading at school. However, it is crucial. Children can have wonderful sound-letter links but if they can't blend sounds together to decode the word, or segment the sounds to spell a word, or manipulate sounds to learn how to read and spell new words, then they will not become a good reader.

I was asked to assess a lovely and very bright girl in Grade 1 who was struggling to learn to read and spell. Her parents and teachers had tested her sound-letter knowledge, which she had aced. They had no concerns around her behaviour, language or cognitive skills as she was a hardworking, bright girl. No one had looked into her phonemic awareness skills and when I assessed them, she really struggled. On a reading task, she was able to say each sound-letter correspondence; for example, when she saw the word *pig*, she said the sounds *p – i – g*. But when asked what the word was, she answered, "Pot." She could not blend the sounds back together. Her parents then completed 2–5 minutes of blending and segmenting activities every day and within no time Grace had caught up and surpassed her peers.

Tolman's hourglass below shows how we start our reading journey at the Phonological Awareness level, moving through to advanced phonemic skills, *then* we learn to connect sounds and letters. Speech sound awareness comes first. Children then learn to read by remembering what letters are connected to what speech sound and blending them together. Children learn to write down speech sounds with letters as they spell.

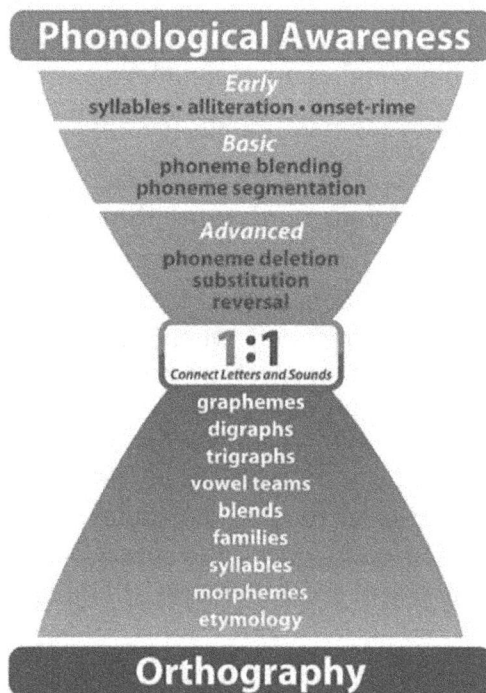

(Tolman's Hourglass, drcaroltolman.com, printed with permission.)

What should my child be able to do?

Many children are able to develop their phonemic awareness as they learn to listen and to speak without the need to be specifically taught; however, many others do not.

As it is an essential component of becoming an accomplished reader it is best to not leave the development of this skill to chance. The name phonemic "awareness" is also a bit misleading – they need to have more than just an awareness of phonemes in words. They need to be able to manipulate them with a high degree of skill and automaticity. *All* children, starting from their first year of school, should have phonemic awareness instruction and practice right through until the end of their third or fourth year of schooling (Grade 2 and 3). Once your child is proficient in phonemic awareness – hopefully by the end of their third year of schooling – there is no need to continue phonemic training.

Basic phonemic awareness skills develop during a child's first and second year of schooling, then advanced phonemic awareness skills develop in the following years. You can test your child throughout the year to monitor progress. Add dates to the table so you remember when you completed it. Don't complete the same activity without a few months in between and do not give the answers to the test materials.

Note that the phonemes, or speech sounds, in a word do not always correspond with the number of letters in the word. For example, the word *goose* has five letters, but only three phonemes (*g-oo-se*). *Match* has five letters and three phonemes (*m-a-tch*), *shoe* has four letters and two phonemes (*sh-oe*), and *burn* has four letters and three phonemes (*b-ur-n*).

We will start with practising blending onset and rime, segmenting the first sound in the word and syllable deletion before moving into basic phonemic awareness and then advanced phonemic awareness.

Blending onset and rime

Tell your child that they have to work out what word you are saying by "pushing" the sounds back together as you are going to break the word apart.

Say the first part of the word (onset), pause for one second and then say the rest of the word (rime). Model the following two examples and then once they have the idea, try the rest.

> "Listen carefully and I'll show you how to do it: *f – ish* is *fish*. Did you hear that? Here's another one, *ch – air* is *chair*. Now it's your turn."

Try these:

Examples	Correct?
sh – oe	
b – ook	
h – at	
s – un	
j – am	

Segmenting the first sound

In this activity, your child is to identify and say the first sound in a word. Tell your child to listen to the word and tell you what sound it starts with. Model the following two first so they get the idea.

> "Listen carefully, the word *meat* starts with an /m/ sound. Can you hear that? *Meat, m – eat*. Here's another one. *Sock* starts with /s/. Now it's your turn. What sound is at the start of … ?"

Try these and say the sound, not the letter name:

Examples	Correct?
chip (ch)	
pull (p)	
road (r)	
van (v)	
hen (h)	

Syllable deletion

Tell your child that you are going to say a word, then ask them to repeat it and say it again without a part of the word. For example:

Parent: Say *cupcake*.

Child: Cupcake.

Parent: Now say it again but don't say *cup*.

Child: Cake.

Another example:

Parent: Say *classroom*.

Child: Classroom.

Parent: Now say it again but don't say *class*.

Child: Room.

After your child has got the idea of what to do, try the words below:

Examples	Correct?
doorway – door = way	
skateboard – skate = board	
paper – pa = per	
object – ob = ject	
reason – rea = son	

Syllable deletion – final syllable

This is the same activity as above, but now you ask your child to not say the last syllable.

Examples	Correct?
person – son = per	
someone – one = some	

	Correct?
Tuesday – Tues = day	
sunburn – burn = sun	
sadness – ness = sad	

Children can then move on to deleting syllables from three-syllable words.

Examples	Correct?
butterfly – fly = butter	
forgetful – for = getful	
spaghetti – spa = ghetti	
cockatoo – too = cocka	
animal – mal = ani	

Basic phonemic awareness

Phoneme blending

Children start off being able to blend the onset and rime of words, before moving on to blending together separate phonemes. Remember, when saying the sounds, do not add an extra little vowel sound.

Tell your child that you are going to say a word slowly and they have to "push" the sounds back together to make the word. Model the following two examples and then once they have the idea, try the rest.

"Listen carefully and I'll show you how to do it: *w – e – t* is *wet*. Did you hear that? Here's another one: *sh – oe* is *shoe*. Now it's your turn."

Two-phoneme words:

Examples	Correct?
u – p (up)	
ou – t (out)	
o – ff (off)	
t – oo (too)	
b – e (be)	

Three-phoneme words:

Examples	Correct?
m – a – p (map)	
p – i – g (pig)	
t – ea – m (team)	

m – oo – n (moon)	
b – u – s (bus)	

Phoneme segmentation

In the early years of school, children should be able to segment (break apart) simple words with two or three phonemes. This is an important part of learning how to spell.

Tell your child that you are going to say a word and they are to break the word into its sounds (not letter names). Model the following and then ask them to try the rest.

> "Listen carefully and I'll show you how to do it: *cob* is *c – o – b*. Can you hear how the word *cob* has three sounds, *c – o – b*? Here's another one: *am* is *a – m*. It has two sounds, *a-m*. Now you try."

Two-phoneme words:

Examples	Correct?
boy (b-oy)	
on (o-n)	
us (u-s)	
toe (t-oe)	
see (s-ee)	

Three-phoneme words:

Examples	Correct?
pick (p-i-ck)	
man (m-a-n)	
chop (ch-o-p)	
late (l-a-te)	
shoot (sh-oo-t)	

Phoneme segmentation with blends

The following basic phonemic awareness skills typically develop in the second year of schooling (around 6.5 years old).

Once children have a handle on segmenting words with two or three phonemes, you can then use words with three or four phonemes and also add words with blends (two or three consonants together).

Tell your child that you are going to say a word and you want them to break the word into its sounds (not letter names). This is a similar activity to what they have done in the past but with *more* sounds.

Model the following and then ask them to try the rest.

"Listen carefully and I'll show you how to do it: *stay* is *s-t-ay*. Can you hear how the word stay has three sounds, *s-t-ay*? Here's another one: *clap* is *c-l-a-p*. It has four sounds, *c-l-a-p*. Now you try."

Examples	Correct?
star (s-t-ar)	
black (b-l-a-ck)	
snake (s-n-a-ke)	
hand (h-a-n-d)	
blue (b-l-ue)	

If your child struggled with any of the above tasks, please practise the particular areas that they found difficult with the examples below. Your child has to be quick and automatic with their responses. If your child gives you the wrong answer, then model that example several times to teach them. This should be followed by another three examples (again do each one several times) before asking your child to do the next one on their own.

The activities only take 2–5 minutes per day. Nonetheless, they can make a big difference to your child's reading. There are 15 words in each column – complete one column each practice session. Aim for five practice sessions per week. It is fine to repeat the list the following week, or simply make up your own. Remember to say the phonemes accurately without adding a little vowel.

Blending onset and rime

n – et	h – and	b – op	h – ate	l – et
c – ake	k – id	k – ick	w – all	j – am
h – ug	pl – ate	f – our	st – and	b – oom
c – up	p – ack	z – ip	b – ook	b – eep
p – op	m – et	b – all	tr – ack	t – ack
r – oom	b – an	t – eam	ch – eep	sp – ot
b – un	p – oor	l – ike	n – ame	s – un
c – all	h – op	sk – id	p – an	p – ot
st – ay	f – un	n – ot	l – id	g – ate
b – and	l – ick	g – ood	f – ork	f – ound
l – ate	p – ork	m – ore	k – ick	qu – een
m – an	sh – eep	b – oy	z – oom	h – all
b – ack	r – ake	sl – eep	j – oy	p – ick
j – et	ch – air	g – ame	b – un	f – izz
d – oor	h – am	l – ook	m – ike	l – eap

Segmenting the first sound

If your child gives you the letter name, remind them that we are listening for the sound.

finished (f)	cheese (ch)	pick (p)	zoo (z)	egg (e)
ship (sh)	wash (w)	may (m)	boat (b)	van (v)
bed (b)	hit (h)	ran (r)	shop (sh)	yacht (y)
tick (t)	leaf (l)	apple (a)	ice (i)	orange (o)
cut (c)	thin (th)	goat (g)	jump (j)	cherry (ch)
pen (p)	up (u)	need (n)	soup (s)	deep (d)
jog (j)	phone (f)	open (o)	arm (ar)	ran (r)
sigh (s)	zip (z)	poor (p)	bed (b)	win (w)
door (d)	mate (m)	circle (s)	torch (t)	oil (oi)
ace (ay)	book (b)	funny (f)	goose (g)	sum (s)
very (v)	hot (h)	this (th)	found (f)	ten (t)
chip (ch)	giraffe (j)	bed (b)	cap (c)	four (f)
like (l)	eight (ay)	heat (h)	nap (n)	many (m)
rock (r)	sand (s)	shower (sh)	pout (p)	goggle (g)
eagle (ee)	ant (a)	cupcake (c)	upon (u)	joke (j)

Syllable deletion (initial position)

Ask your child to delete the sound in the brackets. For example:

Parent: Say *sunrise*.

Child: Sunrise.

Parent: Now say it again without *sun*.

Child: Rise.

(sun)rise = rise	(jum)ping = ping	(han)dle = dle	(dark)ness=ness	(go)blin = blin
(pot)plant = plant	(ho)ney = ney	(foot)step = step	(ti)cket = cket	(air)pump = pump
(pap)er = per	(pi)cture = ture	(sti)cky = cky	(pi)llow = low	(ton)sil = sil
(com)plete = plete	(post)man= man	(fa)ther = ther	(gar)den = den	(co)lour - lour
(a)gree = gree	(la)bel = bel	(pub)lic = lic	(pro)ject = ject	(mag)net = net
(lap)top = top	(sli)ppers = ppers	(milk)shake = shake	(stu)dent = dent	(pu)ppet = ppet
(bo)ttle = tle	(l)pad = pad	(sen)tence = tence	(co)lumn = lumn	(skate)board = board

(cam)ping = ping	(pen)cil = cil	(re)peat = peat	(ath)lete = lete	(ra)zor = zor
(yu)cky = cky	(va)cuum = cuum	(neigh)bour = bour	(un)lock = lock	(bun)dle = dle
(co)ffee = ffee	(co)llect - llect	(pla)stic = stic	(sto)ry = ry	(ro)sy = sy
(grate)ful = ful	(wea)ther = ther	(mis)take = take	(cup)cake = cake	(rea)ding = ding
(e)nough = nough	(po)cket = cket	(in)side = side	(tea)cher = cher	(mu)sic = sic
(re)ceive = ceive	(ma)ttress = ttress	(ri)pple = pple	(for)mal = mal	(ze)bra = bra
(ice)cream = cream	(con)test = test	(pro)ject = ject	(be)tween = tween	(cer)tain = tain
(den)tist = tist	(li)ly = ly	(de)vote = vote	(space)ship = ship	(cen)tre = tre

Syllable deletion (final position)

sun(set) = sun	water(fall) = water	can(dle) = can	bro(ther) = bro	no(tice) = no
mon(key) = mon	ho(ney) = ho	mea(sure) = mea	mem(ber) = mem	ta(ble) = ta
win(dow) = win	de(cide) = de	quick(ly) = quick	thou(sand) = thou	win(dow) = win
cray(on) = cray	lap(top) = (lap)	vi(sit) = vi	wor(ker) = wor	back(ward) = back
cha(llenge) = cha	ma(nage) = ma	lau(ghing) = lau	snow(ball) = snow	im(press) = press
work(book) = work	par(ty) = par	cir(cus) = cir	slee(py) = slee	key(board) = key
sis(ter) = sis	sci(ence) = sci	pur(ple) = pur	ath(lete) = ath	ti(ger) = ti
sta(tion) = sta	af(ter) = af	flo(wer) = flo	mis(take) = mis	out(doors) = out
back(pack) =back	stan(dard) = stan	bo(ssy) = bo	coo(kie) = coo	mon(ster) = mon
foot(print) = foot	pen(cil) = pen	sto(len) = sto	nap(kin) = nap	ju(ggle) = ju
hun(dred) = hun	ice-(cream) = ice	for(ward) = for	si(lent) = si	sand(pit) = sand
mi(nute) = mi	tea(cher) = tea	re(mind) = re	per(form) = per	wrap(per) = wrap
dra(ma) = dra	po(cket) = po	ba(con) = ba	him(self) = him	bro(ken) = bro
hel(mut) = hel	li(ttle) = li	stu(dy) = stu	ba(by) = ba	te(ddy) = te
un(true) = un	ve(ry) = ve	sil(ver) = sil	pump(kin) = pump	ha(ppy) = ha

Syllable deletion (three-syllable words)

(com)puter = puter	water(fall) = water	diffi(cult)= diffi	trian(gle) = trian	(ham)burger = burger
bicy(cle) = bicy	(mi)crophone = crophone	(ca)ravan = ravan	reflec(tion) = reflec	Octo(ber) = Octo
(a)ttention = ttention	(um)pire = pire	(tel)ephone = ephone	(po)kemon = kemon	typi(cal) = typi
octo(pus) = octo	hospi(tal) = hospi	elec(tric) = elec	(wa)tering = tering	(for)gotten = gotten
fami(ly) = fami	(pho)tograph = tograph	(won)derful = derful	(vi)deo = deo	(li)oness = oness
(u)tensil = tensil	Decem(ber) = Decem	becom(ing) = become	musi(cal) = musi	(conn)ection = ection
(astro)naut = naut	(na)tional = tional	(el)astic = astic	(zoo)keeper = keeper	kanga(roo) = kanga
sticky(tape) = sticky	Emi(ly) = Emi	(li)stening = stening	tomo(rrow) = tomo	(un)derstand = derstand
(I)taly = taly	(his)tory = tory	enjoy(ment) = enjoy	certain(ly) = certain	citi(zen) = citi
(el)ephant = ephant	(a)pparent = parent	(con)dition = dition	(ta)bletop = bletop	post(office) = post
aware(ness)= aware	centu(ry) = centu	fina(lly) = fina	maga(zine) = maga	(mos)quito = quito
charac(ter) = charac	(ba)sketball = sketball	(gov)ernment = ernment	(per)formance = formance	newspa(per) = newspa
(ki)tchenette = tchenette	(ba)nana = nana	(qual)ity = ity	(re)lation = lation	(sci)entist = entist
(rec)tangle = tangle	inter(view) = inter	proper(ty) = proper	simi(lar) = simi	success(ful) = success
(some)body = body	(su)ddenly = denly	(to)gether = gether	(co)pycat = pycat	(me)dium = dium

Phoneme blending (two- and three-sound words)

m-a-n (man)	sh-a-ke (shake)	n-or-th (north)	th-ey (they)	p-e-n (pen)
u-p (up)	m-oo-n (moon)	c-u-p (cup)	b-oo (boo)	w-i-sh (wish)
p-e-n (pen)	r-oa-d (road)	d-ay (day)	l-igh-t (light)	o-n (on)
s-u-n (sun)	d-o-ck (dock)	w-i-n (win)	s-ig-n (sign)	p-air (pair)
t-a-ll (tall)	h-igh (high)	n-o-se (nose)	r-o-pe (rope)	b-ea-d (bead)
r-a-ce (race)	b-ir-d (bird)	sh-ou-t (shout)	j-o-g (jog)	f-i-n (fin)
ch-i-n (chin)	s-a-fe (safe)	h-a-t (hat)	b-a-th (bath)	ch-a-p (chap)

n-o-te (note)	e-gg (egg)	a-m (am)	p-i-g (pig)	b-oo-t (boot)
d-oor-s (doors)	kn-ee (knee)	ch-i-ck (chick)	w-a-tch (watch)	th-u-mb (thumb)
m-u-ch (much)	j-ar (jar)	f-or-t (fort)	ph-o-ne (phone)	p-ar-t (part)
h-i-m (him)	f-ee-t (feet)	k-ey (key)	sh-e-d (shed)	s-ay (say)
i-n (in)	b-ur-n (burn)	p-i-ne (pine)	s-ee (see)	h-or-se (horse)
s-i-de (side)	w-i-th (with)	d-a-te (date)	h-o-g (hog)	n-u-t (nut)
f-oo-d (food)	p-i-t (pit)	p-a-n (pan)	p-oor (poor)	l-a-ke (lake)
h-ou-se (house)	a-ce (ace)	oi-l (oil)	b-ea-m (beam)	sh-ee-p (sheep)

Phoneme segmentation (two- and three-sound words)

boy (b-oy)	jam (j-a-m)	pit (p-i-t)	oat (oa-t)	pay (p-ay)
mad (m-a-d)	hug (h-u-g)	we (w-e)	gag (g-a-g)	shoot (sh-oo-t)
beep (b-ee-p)	eat (ea-t)	chip (ch-i-p)	hook (h-oo-k)	in (i-n)
my (m-y)	kite (k-i-te)	new (n-ew)	tea (t-ea)	might (m-igh-t)
up (u-p)	rain (r-ai-n)	feed (f-ee-d)	boo (b-oo)	rag (r-a-g)
rice (r-i-ce)	bee (b-ee)	aid (ai-d)	line (l-i-ne)	each (ea-ch)
car (c-ar)	it (i-t)	road (r-oa-d)	pea (p-ea)	page (p-a-ge)
moon (m-oo-n)	same (s-a-me)	she (sh-e)	age (a-ge)	then (th-e-m)
off (o-ff)	bed (b-e-d)	wage (w-a-ge)	can (c-a-n)	tip (t-i-p)
thin (th-i-n)	sigh (s-igh)	tie (t-ie)	yes (y-e-s)	back (b-a-ck)
oak (oa-k)	egg (e-gg)	card (c-ar-d)	bye (b-ye)	own (ow-n)
zoo (z-oo)	fog (f-o-g)	show (sh-ow)	with (w-i-th)	four (f-our)
shop (sh-o-p)	am (a-m)	gum (g-u-m)	chew (ch-ew)	reef (r-ee-f)
pot (p-o-t)	way (w-ay)	ice (i-ce)	bed (b-e-d)	toe (t-oe)
knee (kn-ee)	odd (o-dd)	on (o-n)	mow (m-ow)	chop (ch-o-p)

Phoneme blending (three- and four-sound words, including blends)

d-u-ck (duck)	g-l-a-d (glad)	j-u-m-p (jump)	b-oo-k (book)	th-a-t (that)
r-o-t (rot)	p-e-n-s (pens)	l-aw-n (lawn)	b-e-d-s (beds)	b-e-s-t (best)
s-p-i-t (spit)	sh-oo-t (shoot)	d-i-n-t (dint)	r-o-pe (rope)	c-u-p (cup)
t-u-b (tub)	d-r-u-m (drum)	f-l-oa-t (float)	d-ow-n (down)	s-t-e-p (step)
s-t-e-m (stem)	s-a-p (sap)	n-e-s-t (nest)	s-l-i-ck (slick)	w-or-m (worm)

p-l-ay (play)	h-i-de (hide)	t-i-me (time)	ch-oo-se (choose)	s-p-ea-k (speak)
sh-ee-p (sheep)	b-r-i-ck (brick)	b-ir-d (bird)	sh-u-t (shut)	p-u-m-p (pump)
k-i-te (kite)	s-p-a-de (spade)	t-a-s-k (task)	p-l-a-n (plan)	f-l-a-g (flag)
p-e-s-t (pest)	th-i-n (thin)	ch-i-ck (chick)	w-i-pe (wipe)	s-oa-p (soap)
c-l-a-p (clap)	ch-o-p (chop)	c-a-pe-s (capes)	f-e-n-d (fend)	c-r-ow-n (crown)
m-u-ch (much)	r-a-ce (race)	d-u-s-t (dust)	b-a-th (bath)	p-l-oy (ploy)
c-ar-t (cart)	l-ea-f- (leaf)	n-ew-s (news)	d-r-aw-n (drawn)	p-a-c-t (pact)
g-oa-t (goat)	h-oo-k (hook)	b-r-a-t (brat)	b-l-ee-d (bleed)	s-a-me (same)
l-e-n-d (lend)	c-oi-n (coin)	c-l-ea-n (clean)	ch-i-n (chin)	l-e-n-t (lent)
c-l-ow-n (clown)	j-e-t-s (jets)	h-ou-se (house)	p-o-t-s (pots)	s-o-f-t (soft)

Phoneme segmentation (three- and four-sound words, including blends)

slap (s-l-a-p)	scat (s-c-a-t)	end (e-n-d)	flip (f-l-i-p)	black (b-l-a-ck)
let (l-e-t)	grass (g-r-a-ss)	happy (h-a-pp-y)	kick (k-i-ck)	drawn (d-r-aw-n)
truck (t-r-u-ck)	lead (l-ea-d)	blue (b-l-ue)	boil (b-oi-l)	lobe (l-o-be)
Mummy (m-u-mm-y)	crack (c-r-a-ck)	main (m-ai-n)	great (g-r-ea-t)	lamp (l-a-m-p)
bent (b-e-n-t)	jump (j-u-m-p)	spear (s-p-ear)	brush (b-r-u-sh)	birth (b-ir-th)
glue (g-l-ue)	sun (s-u-n)	cloud (c-l-ou-d)	truck (t-r-u-ck)	keep (k-ee-p)
shoes (sh-oe-s)	star (s-t-ar)	jump (j-u-m-p)	play (p-l-ay)	from (f-r-o-m)
smoke (s-m-o-ke)	shock (sh-o-ck)	frog (f-r-o-g)	learn (l-ear-n)	clap (c-l-a-p)
much (m-u-ch)	clean (c-l-ea-n)	thin (th-i-n)	seen (s-ee-n)	date (d-a-te)
swim (s-w-i-m)	broke (b-r-o-ke)	cheese (ch-ee-se)	winch (w-i-n-ch)	snow (s-n-ow)
snooze (s-n-oo-ze)	left (l-e-f-t)	lost (l-o-s-t)	flop (f-l-o-p)	blob (b-l-o-b)
sand (s-a-n-d)	grade (g-r-a-de)	milk (m-i-l-k)	sound (s-ou-n-d)	shark (sh-ar-k)
skip (s-k-i-p)	fly (f-l-y)	tap (t-a-p)	spoon (s-p-oo-n)	lunch (l-u-n-ch)
flew (f-l-ew)	chewy (ch-ew-y)	click (c-l-i-ck)	roast (r-oa-s-t)	nest (n-e-s-t)
block (b-l-o-ck)	from (f-r-o-m)	mend (m-e-n-d)	must (m-u-s-t)	broom (b-r-oo-m)

Advanced phonemic awareness

Advanced phonemic awareness continues to develop during a child's third and fourth year of schooling (ages 7-10).

Blending more sounds together

Now that your child can blend three- and four-sound words together, they should be able to do five- and six-sound words.

Tell your child that you are going to say some sounds slowly, and they need to "push" them back together to make a word.

Examples	Correct?
c-l-a-m-p (clamp)	
c-l-i-ck-er (clicker)	
s-t-r-o-ng (strong)	
d-r-i-pp-i-ng (dripping)	
g-r-u-m-p-y (grumpy)	

Phoneme deletion (at the start of words)

Tell your child that you are going to say a word, and you want them to then say the word again but leave out a sound. Model the following and then ask them to try the rest.

"Listen carefully and I'll show you how to do it. If I said *hip* without the *h*, it would be *ip*. Now you try. Say *sat* and then leave out the *s*."

If your child is unable to do the example, then give them the answer.

Try the following examples:

Examples	Correct?
man, without the *m* (an)	
fish, without the *f* (ish)	
seas, without the *s* (ease)	
rock, without the *r* (ock)	
bead, without the *b* (ead)	

Phoneme deletion (at the end of words)

Examples	Correct?
wheat, without the *t* (we)	
cup, without the *p* (cu)	
bone, without the *n* (bow)	
farm, without the *m* (far)	
book, without the *k* (boo)	

Once children master taking away sounds in words, try harder words that have two consonants next to each other. This skill may not develop until a child is 8 years old.

Examples	Correct?
snake, without the *s* (nake)	
truck, without the *t* (ruck)	
blue, without the *b* (lue)	
drop, without the *d* (rop)	
glow, without the *g* (low)	

Phoneme substitution (at the start of words)

Tell your child that you are going to say a word, then ask them to change a sound in the word to make another word. For example, change the *m* in *meat* to *n*. The correct answer is *neat*.

Examples	Correct?
change the *p* in *park* to *d* (dark)	
change the *l* in *let* to *m* (met)	
change the *b* in *bat* to *s* (sat)	
change the *s* in *see* to *m* (me)	
change the *k* in *kite* to *n* (night)	

Phoneme substitution (in the middle of words)

Examples	Correct?
change the *o* in *hot* to *u* (hut)	
change the *a* in *tap* to *i* (tip)	
change the *e* in *pen* to *a* (pan)	
change the *u* in *cut* to *o* (cot)	
change the *l* in *hit* to *a* (hat)	

Phoneme substitution (at the end of words)

Examples	Correct?
change the *t* in *part* to *k* (park)	
change the *m* in *home* to *p* (hope)	
change the *n* in *been* to *m* (beam)	
change the *d* in *mad* to *p* (map)	
change the *s* in *miss* to *t* (mitt)	

Blending more sounds together

s-p-r-ai-n (sprain)	t-r-a-ck-er (tracker)	g-l-oo-m-y (gloomy)	s-c-r-ea-m (scream)	j-u-m-p-er (jumper)
s-t-u-m-p (stump)	d-r-i-v-e-n (driven)	s-l-e-p-t (slept)	t-oi-l-e-t (toilet)	t-w-i-s-t-er (twister)
M-o-n-d-ay (Monday)	b-l-e-n-d (blend)	c-r-a-ck-i-ng (cracking)	ou-t-s-i-de (outside)	s-a-fe-t-y (safety)
p-l-a-n-t-s (plants)	b-ir-th-d-ay (birthday)	s-t-o-m-a-ch (stomach)	s-w-i-m-s (swims)	s-n-u-gg-le (snuggle)
b-l-o-n-d (blond)	w-a-tch-i-ng (watching)	s-n-ea-k-er (sneaker)	w-o-m-b-a-t (wombat)	s-l-u-m-p (slump)
j-u-m-p-s (jumps)	b-r-a-ck-e-t (bracket)	s-w-i-tch-e-s (switches)	ch-e-ck-u-p (checkup)	c-l-ea-n-s (cleans)
s-m-o-k-i-ng (smoking)	p-e-n-c-i-l (pencil)	g-r-i-zz-l-y (grizzly)	j-a-ck-e-t-s (jackets)	sh-a-d-ow-s (shadows)
c-o-n-c-er-n (concern)	s-c-r-ee-n (screen)	b-r-igh-t-e-n (brighten)	p-i-ll-ow-s (pillows)	s-p-r-ay-s (sprays)
p-r-i-n-t (print)	h-e-l-m-u-t (helmut)	s-t-o-n-e-s (stones)	c-r-e-a-te (create)	s-l-i-pp-i-ng (slipping)
d-r-i-n-k-s (drinks)	l-u-n-ch-e-s (lunches)	i-n-c-r-ea-se (increase)	s-n-a-ck-s (snacks)	p-o-ss-i-b-le (possible)
s-c-r-u-n-ch (scrunch)	c-r-u-s-t (crust)	r-e-p-l-a-ce (replace)	b-r-ai-n-y (brainy)	h-ea-d-a-che (headache)
ch-i-ck-e-n (chicken)	p-r-o-m-p-t (prompt)	c-oo-k-i-ng (cooking)	m-u-sh-r-oo-m (mushroom)	s-w-a-m-p (swamp)
b-e-d-b-u-g (bedbug)	c-i-t-ie-s (cities)	t-w-i-n-s (twins)	b-l-u-n-t (blunt)	m-o-n-i-t-or (monitor)
h-a-n-d-le-s (handles)	s-t-a-m-p-s (stamps)	wr-i-t-i-ng (writing)	s-t-r-ea-m-s (streams)	i-m-a-g-i-ne (imagine)
i-n-s-i-de (inside)	t-i-ss-ue-s (tissues)	c-o-m-p-e-te (compete)	s-p-ee-d-s (speeds)	b-e-d-h-ea-d (bedhead)

Phoneme deletion (at the start of words)

Ask your child to delete the sound in the brackets. For example, "Say *heart* without the *h*." The correct answer is *art*.

In some cases, the spelling of the answers have been changed to real words to make the exercise easier.

(h)eart = art	(r)an = an	(h)eat = eat	(s)and = and	(w)ent = ent
(n)ice = ice	(m)at = at	(g)et = et	(j)ar = ar	(r)ich = ich
(c)ot = ot	(sh)ore = ore	(ch)eese = ease	(l)amp = amp	(b)oat = oat
(j)og = og	(l)imp = imp	(z)ink = ink	(n)ought = ought	(s)ad = ad
(f)ight = ight	(f)ix = ix	(p)oor = oor	(m)ouse = ouse	(n)ame = ame
(y)ear = ear	(p)oke = oke	(l)ead = ead	(j)am = am	(f)ox = ox
(th)in = in	(b)all = all	(f)ish = ish	(ch)air = air	(t)oast = oast
(d)ent = ent	(j)ump = ump	(m)ind = ind	(k)ick = ick	(g)ape = ape
(kn)ock = ock	(m)oon = oon	(r)ace = ace	(sh)oot = oot	(y)es = es
(h)elp = elp	(t)ap = ap	(t)en = en	(f)ive = ive	(d)am = am
(b)ill = ill	(w)ag = ag	(wh)eel = eel	(sh)eep = eep	(qu)it = it
(p)each = each	(ch)eck = eck	(g)ift = ift	(b)and = and	(h)ive = ive
(r)ake = ache	(v)est = est	(s)at = at	(d)oor = oor	(m)int = int
(qu)een = een	(h)is = is	(c)oat = oat	(c)ame = ame	(l)edge = edge
(h)eart = art	(r)an = an	(h)eat = eat	(s)and = and	(w)ent = ent

Phoneme deletion (at the end of words)

sear(ch) = sir	far(m) = far	mea(t) = me	war(m) = war	for(t) = for
mi(ne) = my	char(t) = char	pri(me) = pry	scar(f) = scar	soa(k) = so
knee(s) = knee	shoe(s) = shoe	pla(ne) = play	roa(d) = row	Da(ve) = day
stor(m) = store	wee(k) = we	bar(b) = bar	mee(k) = me	bee(n) = bee
floa(t) = flow	shor(n)= shore	faw(n) = four	pi(ne) = pie	pea(ch) = pea
rai(n) = ray	gloo(p) = glue	bea(ch) = bee	shoo(t) = shoo	sli(de) = sly
foa(m) = foe	hur(t) = hur	ti(me) = tie	though(t) = Thor	bri(dge) = bri
brow(n) = brow	joi(n) = joy	see(p) = see	tee(th) = tee	coi(n) = coy
four(th) = four	shee(t) = she	shor(t) = shore	ca(ge) = Kay	sou(p) = Sue
fer(n) = fur	sig(n) = sigh	free(ze) = free	tea(ch) = tea	show(n) = show

pa(ge) = pay	broo(m) = brew	choo(se) = chew	ow(n) = owe	weigh(t) = weigh
car(t) = car	too(th) = too	shi(ne) = shy	loo(se) = loo	hou(se) = how
bir(th) = bur	toa(d) = toe	par(k) = par	boa(t) = bow	wor(m) = were
plea(se) = plea	tea(k) =tea	nee(d) = knee	lai(d) = lay	toa(d) = toe
no(te) = no	cu(be) = cue	shoo(t) = shoe	roo(m) = roo	see(m) = see

Phoneme deletion (with blends at the start of words)

(c)lap = lap	(s)peech = peach	(c)lay = lay	(g)lam = lamb	(s)lid = lid
(s)pot = pot	(g)loom = loom	(s)pin = pin	(b)rick = rick	(b)lend = lend
(b)limp = limp	(th)roat = wrote	(b)room = room	(c)ream = ream	(t)rash = rash
(d)rank = rank	(d)rink = rink	(t)ruck = ruck	(s)tair = tear	(c)rib = rib
(f)lag = lag	(b)rush = rush	(s)tart = tart	(c)lean = lean	(g)rim = rim
(s)wat = what	(p)lot = lot	(f)leece = lease	(s)not = not	(s)mile = mile
(b)right = right	(p)ram = ram	(s)tuck = tuck	(g)litter = litter	(d)rank = rank
(t)rain = rain	(g)rump = rump	(c)rack = rack	(p)luck = luck	(c)lung = lung
(g)lamp = lamp	(s)nack = nack	(s)nail = nail	(t)race = race	(p)ride = ride
(t)ried = ride	(s)lump = lump	(d)rink = rink	(c)rane = rain	(p)ray = ray
(p)lace = lace	(g)lance = lance	(s)wing = wing	(s)way = way	(f)ly = lie
(s)lip = lip	(s)lam = lamb	(b)lock = lock	(p)rice = rice	(s)kate = Kate
(g)rant = rant	(c)row = row	(s)top = top	(f)lock = lock	(b)reak = rake
(s)pat = pat	(f)log = log	(b)last = last	(g)rew = roo	(s)peak = peak

Phoneme substitution (at the start of words)

tap – t to k = cap	pen – p to b = Ben	same – s to n = name	chip – ch to s = sip	such – s to m = much
book – b to t = took	port – p to f = fort	path – p to b = bath	yum – y to g = gum	zip – z to l = lip
rake – r to b = bake	hand – h to s = sand	rich – r to w = witch	farm – f to h = harm	deep – d to j = jeep
sheep – sh to l = leap	hid – h to r = rid	shoot – sh to b = boot	bit – b to l = lit	hill – h to b = bill

ball – *b* to *m* = mall	dog – *d* to *l* = log	cube – *k* to *t* = tube	sort – *s* to *f* = fort	new – *n* to *p* = pew
jump – *j* to *b* = bump	need – *n* to *b* = bead	camp = *k* to *l* = lamp	ran – *r* to *t* = tan	fern – *f* to *t* = turn
tape – *t* to *k* = cape	ripe – *r* to *w* = wipe	dug – *d* to *b* = bug	bird – *b* to *h* = heard	got – *g* to *d* = dot
moon – *m* to *n* = noon	day – *d* to *s* = say	night – *n* to *l* = light	mate – *m* to *f* = fate	pack – *p* to *r* = rack
pin – *p* to *t* = tin	back – *b* to *j* = jack	zoo – *z* to *d* = do	loop – *l* to *g* = goop	shoe – *sh* to *b* = boo
chop – *ch* to *h* = hop	coat – *k* to *g* = goat	face – *f* to *p* = pace	ten – *t* to *p* = pen	miss – *m* to *k* = kiss
sound – *s* to *f* = found	that – *th* to *m* = mat	pick – *p* to *k* = kick	coin – *k* to *j* = join	van – *v* to *f* = fan
phone – *f* to *b* = bone	bell – *b* to *f* = fell	bill – *b* to *w* = will	quick – *qu* to *p* = pick	pain – *p* to *r* = rain
boy – *b* to *j* = joy	hose – *h* to *n* = nose	down – *d* to *t* = town	get – *g* to *n* = net	chap – *ch* to *s* = sap
mat – *m* to *h* = hat	tap – *t* to *m* = map	dawn – *d* to *l* = lawn	pop – *p* to *t* = top	jet – *j* to *p* = pet
run – *r* to *f* = fun	nut – *n* to *k* = cut	bolt – *b* to *v* = volt	beef – *b* to *l* = leaf	duck – *d* to *l* = luck

Phoneme substitution (in the middle of words)

hit – *i* to *o* = hot	flip – *i* to *a* = flap	town – *ow* to *a* = tan	miss – *i* to *e* = mess	leg – *e* to *a* = lag
sand – *a* to *e* = send	deep – *ee* to *i* = dip	pain – *ai* to *e* = pen	soak – *oa* to *oo* = sook	seen – *ee* to *u* = sun
pat – *a* to *i* = pit	gum – *u* to *ai* = game	not – *o* to *u* = nut	tray – *ay* to *oo* = true	dug – *u* to *i* = dig
song – *o* to *u* = sung	fan – *a* to *i* = fin	short – *or* to *ee* = sheet	vat – *a* to *e* = vet	roof – *oo* to *u* = rough
mount – *ou* to *i* = mint	bet – *e* to *a* = bat	hut – *u* to *a* = hat	keep – *ee* to *i* = kip	head – *e* to *i* = hid
get – *e* to *o* = got	loss – *o* to *e* = less	tam – *a* to *o* = tom	bend – *e* to *a* = band	jog – *o* to *i* = jig
ban – *a* to *e* = Ben	house – *ou* to *i* = hiss	ten – *e* to *i* = tin	tea – *ea* to *oo* = to	room – *oo* to *a* = ram
sheet – *ee* to *u* = shut	rope – *o* to *i* = rip	sick – *i* to *o* = sock	luck – *u* to *i* = lick	beef – *ee* to *u* = buff
cup – *u* to *a* = cap	bid – *i* to *ir* = bird	sawn – *aw* to *u* = sun	lid – *i* to *e* = lead	wig – *i* to *a* = wag

hit – *i* to *ai* = hate	mat – *a* to *u* = mutt	might – *igh* to *e* = met	right – *igh* to *a* = rat	sport – *or* to *a* = spat
fort – *or* to *i* = fit	play – *ay* to *ee* = plea	bun – *u* to *i* = bin	sheep – *ee* to *o* = shop	sick – *i* to *ee* = seek
log – *o* to *e* = leg	hip – *i* to *oo* = hoop	brown – *ow* to *a* = bran	boy – *oy* to *ee* = bee	lock – *o* to *ee* = leek
bird – *ir* to *ee* = bead	dock – *o* to *e* = deck	steal – *ea* to *i* = still	pop – *o* to *i* = pip	thorn – *or* to *i* = thin
red – *e* to *i* = rid	jet – *e* to *o* = jot	leap – *ea* to *a* = lap	boss – *o* to *u* = bus	top – *o* to *a* = tap
coat – *oa* to *u* = cut	rug – *u* to *a* = rag	mow – *ow* to *ee* = me	sort – *or* to *i* = sit	lawn – *aw* to *ee* = lean

Phoneme substitution (at the ends of words)

leaf – *f* to *ch* = leach	mug – *g* to *t* = mutt	step – *p* to *m* = stem	cat – *t* to *p* = cap	tape – *p* to *k* = take
thick – *k* to *n* = thin	lead – *d* to *p* = leap	rain – *n* to *z* = rays	word – *d* to *m* = worm	meat – *t* to *n* = mean
cart – *t* to *d* = card	cheap – *p* to *z* = cheese	pin – *n* to *t* = pit	mush – *sh* to *k* = muck	need – *d* to *z* = knees
rug – *g* to *n* = run	pet – *t* to *k* = peck	coach – *ch* to *t* = coat	mutt – *t* to *ch* = much	fish – *sh* to *n* = fin
pig – *g* to *p* = pip	seed – *d* to *s* = sees	room – *m* to *f* = roof	chip – *p* to *n* = chin	moss – *s* to *p* = mop
rope – *p* to *d* = road	rob – *b* to *t* = rot	park – *k* to *m* = palm	buzz – *z* to *m* = bum	chart – *t* to *m* = charm
lid – *d* to *k* = lick	bean – *n* to *ch* = beach	life – *f* to *k* = like	pine – *n* to *p* = pipe	lob – *b* to *p* = lop
hen – *n* to *m* = hem	men – *n* to *s* = mess	fish – *sh* to *t* = fit	teach – *ch* to *m* = team	tease – *s* to *m* = team
top – *p* to *s* = toss	tape – *p* to *m* = tame	mob – *b* to *k* = mock	with – *th* to *ch* = witch	lip – *p* to *m* = limb
taught – *t* to *n* = torn	verb – *b* to *s* = verse	beef – *f* to *m* = beam	less – *s* to *t* = let	boom – *m* to *t* = boot
heat – *t* to *p* = heap	sheet – *t* to *n* = sheen	log – *g* to *t* = lot	pen – *n* to *k* = peck	knife – *f* to *t* = knight
tight – *t* to *m* = time	card – *d* to *t* = cart	bead – *d* to *p* = beep	take – *k* to *m* = tame	cake – *k* to *m* = came
hen – *n* to *d* = head	wish – *sh* to *ch* = witch	rat – *t* to *m* = ram	curb – *b* to *v* = curve	leach – *ch* to *p* = leap
rough – *f* to *g* = rug	fizz – *z* to *t* = fit	bliss – *s* to *p* = blip	tick – *k* to *m* = Tim	bug – *g* to *k* = buck
not – *t* to *k* = knock	dead – *d* to *b* = deb	bridge – *j* to *k* = brick	cheese – *z* to *t* = cheat	map – *p* to *s* = mass

Phoneme substitution (mixed)

met – *m* to *n* = net	sand – *s* to *h* = hand	tap – *t* to *m* = map	hat – *h* to *s* = sat	cup – *p* to *t* = cut
hit – *i* to *u* = hut	rake – *r* to *m* = make	pen – *n* to *t* = pet	got – *o* to *oa* = goat	book – *b* to *l* = look
bat – *b* to *r* = rat	mud – *d* to *t* = mutt	luck – *l* to *d* = duck	face – *f* to *l* = lace	ten – *e* to *i* = tin
tag – *g* to *p* = tap	tree – *ee* to *ay* = tray	bow – *ow* to *ee* = bee	night – *igh* to *u* = nut	had – *a* to *i* = hid
card – *c* to *h* = hard	must – *m* to *j* = just	ship – *sh* to *ch* = chip	trap – *p* to *k* = track	leaf – *f* to *p* = leap
phone – *ph* to *b* = bone	jazz – *z* to *k* = jack	bag – *g* to *d* = bad	pain – *p* to *r* = rain	table – *t* to *k* = cable
pot – *o* to *a* = pat	nut – *u* to *o* = not	birth – *ir* to *oo* = booth	fat – *t* to *n* = fan	cheep – *ee* to *o* = chop
let – *l* to *s* = set	bath – *b* to *p* = path	mess – *s* to *t* = met	dead – *d* to *h* = head	shoot – *sh* to *b* = boot
thin – *n* to *k* = thick	roast – *oa* to *e* = rest	pet – *e* to *i* = pit	mug – *m* to *d* = dug	rain – *ai* to *u* = run
dog – *g* to *l* = doll	met – *e* to *i* = mitt	fox – *f* to *b* = box	mean – *n* to *t* = meat	that – *th* to *n* = nat
shop – *o* to *i* = ship	hike – *h* to *b* = bike	frog – *g* to *m* = from	fish – *sh* to *t* = fit	jump – *j* to *b* = bump
tooth – *t* to *b* = booth	cop – *p* to *g* = cog	bud – *u* to *ee* = beed	ride – *r* to *s* = side	lock – *o* to *u* = luck
bed – *b* to *h* = head	song – *o* to *i* = sing	door – *d* to *p* = poor	cut – *u* to *o* = cot	late – *t* to *m* = lame
hip – *p* to *m* = him	pox – *x* to *p* = pop	tape – *p* to *k* = take	handle – *h* to *k* = candle	much – *ch* to *d* = mud

Reminder: these skills need to be practised until your child can do it automatically. You can practise a column a day, then when your child has completed that area, start again from the last column so that your child does not remember specific words.

If your child is struggling with reading at any age, even when they are in secondary school, check their phonemic awareness and work on these skills if they are found to be poor.

You may think that your child will not be willing to complete these activities as there are no pretty pictures to go along with them. But they only take 2–5 minutes and a sticker or stamp may be an appropriate reward at the end.

Further information

If your child has completed all of the above activities and is still struggling with phonemic awareness, please look at the resources listed below.

Specific Learning Difficulties Association of South Australia (SPELD SA) – speldsa.org.au/Phonemic-Awareness-Tasks

> *SPELD SA* has a wonderful website that has free resources for many areas, including phonemic awareness.

Florida Center for Reading Research – fcrr.org/student-center-activities/kindergarten-and-first-grade

> This has some great activities that includes picture support.

"Appendix 5: Recommended Apps List", *AUSPELD* – uldforparents.com/further-reading/appendix-5-recommended-apps-list/

> This is a great list, organised into separate areas depending on what your child needs to work on.

If your child continues to find phonemic awareness difficult, then please get their hearing assessed and book an assessment with a speech pathologist.

letter cards

s	a	t	i
p	n	c	k
ck	e	h	r
m	d	g	o
u	l	f	b
ai	j	oa	ie

ee	or	z	w
ng	v	oo	oo
y	x	sh	ch
th	th	qu	ou
oi	ue	er	ar
y (ee)	a_e	e_e	i_e
o_e	u_e	ay	oy

ea	y (ie)	igh	ow
ir	ur	ew	au
aw	al	ph	wh
ff	ll	ss	zz
mb	wr	wh	kn
air	are	ear	ea

4

Structured Phonics

Phonics involves matching the sounds of spoken English with individual letters or groups of letters. I have referred to this throughout the book as sound-letter links.

Due to the complexity of English, phonics instruction should be explicitly taught in a systematic way so that children aren't left to discover the sound-letter links on their own. Instruction should follow a sequence of sound-letter links, initially teaching what is referred to as the simple code, then moving on to the complex code. (Refer to the Sounds and Letters Chart on pages 8 and 9.)

In structured phonics, morphology is introduced early and "tricky" words are taught through segmenting and blending rather than through memorisation of the shape (logograph). Unfortunately, not all children are being taught systematically. Instead, they are only taught the sound-letter link when they come across it in a word. Evidence has shown that using a systematic approach far outweighs any other (Rose, 2006 and DEST, 2005).

This book is based on the speech-to-print way of teaching reading; that is, we start with what the children know – words and individual speech sounds – and then we teach them the print, or the letters, that can be used to write down those speech sounds. Letters on a page don't "say" anything. (I have tried throughout the book to not use the phrase "What does this letter say?") We "say" words but use letters to record our words.

Over time, the pronunciation of words has changed. However, the spelling has not. The percentage of modern English words originating from each language group are roughly as follows: Latin 29%, French (Latin) 29%, Germanic 26%, Greek 6%, and proper names 4%. We have a complex orthography. This will be discussed further in chapter 5: Spelling.

I work with a gorgeous Grade-1 girl (second year of school) who has a specific reading difficulty. Her teacher was great and very supportive, but does not have the resources (or time) to put together a structured program for her. Little Sarah was often in sickbay complaining of a headache or stomach ache. When Sarah was in class, she "mucked" about when it was anything to do with reading, spelling or writing. She has an awesome sense of humour and used this to entertain the class. Clearly, she was avoiding the work as it felt hard and her self-esteem was low. Due to this, she fell further behind.

I assessed Sarah and found that she didn't know all of the sound-letter links that she should at that stage of the year and she had significant difficulties with blending spoken sounds together (phonemic awareness) as well as blending sounds together from what she herself had sounded out. Each week I saw her at school and sent home daily activities. The progress that Sarah made was amazing. Her reading and spelling levels improved dramatically in six weeks and she no longer hangs out in the sick bay. In class she is engaged and confident.

I'm not telling you this story so you can send accolades my way, but rather to illustrate a point: it wasn't really *me* that made the difference as I only saw Sarah once a week, it was her parents. They were committed to her daily practice and encouraged her progress. The power of knowledge in the hands of a parent should not be underestimated.

This is what I hope to give you in this book: power to help your children thrive.

Crucial building blocks

The English writing system is tricky. Anyone who tries to learn English as a second language will attest to that! Children need to be taught sound-letter links in a systematic way, starting with one sound to one letter correspondence and building to more complex ones. For example, digraphs are two letters used to spell one speech sound – *ch*, *sh*, *ay*, *ar*, *oi*. Trigraph are three letters used to spell one sound – *-igh* as in *night*, and *-dge* as in *judge*. Sometimes, even four letters are used (quadgraph); for example, *-eigh* in *eight* or *neighbour*.

For a child to read and to spell a word like *chop* they need to know that it has three sounds but four letters to write. The child needs to know that to read and spell the *ch* sound they need to put two letters together. For the word *stair*, your child would need to know that it has three speech sounds (*s-t-air*), but five letters to write. These sound-letter links need to be taught to automaticity, which means that your child does not struggle to recall it quickly.

Children need to be really good at blending these sounds to form words; however, they cannot "sound out" forever. So, what happens from this early, slow-sounding out stage to then being able to recognise words in a fraction of a second?

Contrary to popular thought, we do *not* store the words in our visual memory. We actually store them by a process called orthographic mapping: creating links between the spelling of words and their pronunciation. Therefore, a child has to have good phonemic awareness and sound-letter knowledge. In a nutshell, to help children map words into their long-term memory, we need to teach them how to break spoken words into individual sounds and make connections between the sounds and letters in written words.

Luckily, we do not have to teach children to map every word; they do it on their own and unitise sounds in common groups so they don't have to sound out all parts of the word. Whole words become known automatically. The best and most efficient way to get to this point is to ensure right from the start that words are mapped correctly, which is done by sounding out the sounds. If a child guesses the word from the first letter or from the picture or context, then they have missed out on the mapping process.

Some languages don't have as many speech sounds, and not as many ways to spell them, so beginner readers can pick it up relatively quickly. In English, however, there are approximately 44 speech sounds (phonemes) and over 170 graphemes to spell them, although many are infrequent. This book will cover what sound-letter links and spelling choices your child should be directly taught in their first three years of schooling.

The sequence I am following in this book is from *Jolly Phonics*. The reason I have chosen this sequence is due to the many corresponding free resources available to support you and your child, particularly the decodable readers and worksheets on the *SPELD SA* website (listed in Further Reading).

Other phonics programs include *SoundsWrite, Letters and Sounds, InitiaLit, Little Learners Love Literacy, PLD,* and *Get Reading Right*.

What should my child know at what stage?

It is important for you to know what is deemed "appropriate" knowledge for your child's stage of schooling. This way you know what sound-letter links to work on, as well as what not to worry about yet!

The first step is to ask your child's teacher what phonics program they are using so that what you practise is revising what your child has learnt at school.

Each phonics-based program teaches the sound-letter links in different orders and rates and call them different things; for example, Phase 1, Unit 1, Week 1, Stage 1, Set 1, etc.

To check what sound-letter links your child already knows, use a white board or a piece of paper and write down a letter and ask your child what we commonly say when we see that letter. You're not looking for the letter name but rather the speech sound associated with that letter. If you are unsure of what the sound should be, please refer to the Sound and Letter Chart for examples. Place a tick or cross (and date) next to the letter in the chart on page 81, or on the Sound and Letter Chart, to keep a record. Remember that your child must automatically know it. If it takes them two tries or too long to say the sound, then they will still need to work on it.

The first year

At the end of a child's first year of school, they should be able to say the sound-letter link highlighted light grey in the table on page 81 and be able to read the following words. Knowledge of these may depend somewhat on the phonics program followed, so use this as a rough guide.

hat	win	jet	top	cod
mug	can	hen	box	kid
vaf	rez	bux	yos	jiv
shop	luck	hoot	fish	then
with	thing	quack	chap	book
zuck	woth	yish	rech	quog
chimp	stop	stuck	kings	clam

You can see that I have added words that are made up. This is so we can really check your child's sound-letter knowledge, as they can't rely on words they know by sight. The last row has four sounds that your child has to blend together. If your child makes an error, it is important to know which sound-letter link they got stuck on, so please take note of that.

The second year

At the end of their second year of schooling, your child should be reading at approximately 50–60 words per minute. They should be able to complete the sound-letter links in dark grey on the table and read the words shown below. There are quite a few in this list, so if your child tires, then continue testing at another time. You may like to use a piece of paper to cover the words, only exposing one line at a time so it's not too overwhelming.

rain	coat	pie	seen	fork
out	boil	blue	fern	cart
lake	theme	time	bone	cube
stay	toy	leaf	snow	third
turn	grew	cow	sight	
aib	zoaf	kiep	theeb	dorg
coum	toid	gue	shern	parb
zame	ebe	fipe	loke	hute
raym	noy	jeat	clow	kird
surk	fewn	owp	pight	

Again, this list has real words and non-words, with an example of each sound-letter link in both. The grapheme *ow* can be said in two ways – for example, as in *cow* and *snow* – so in the non-words, either is fine.

The third year

At the end of their third year at school, children should be reading at approximately 90 words per minute, know the rest of the table (white areas) and be able to read the following words:

paw	haunt	walk	phone	cent
page	when	stiff	well	kiss
fuzz	lamb	wrist	whole	knight
chair	spare	bear	bread	swap
lawg	maunt	zalk	pheeb	cip
gelp	whib	leff	yill	zess
slazz	pimb	wret	knack	slair
zare	plear	flead	wab	

Jolly Phonics

Order of sound-letter links taught (SPELD website)								Tricky words
s	a	t	i	p	n			
c	k	ck	e	h	r	m	d	
g	o	u	l	f	b			
ai	j	oa	ie	ee	or			
z	w	ng	v	oo	oo			I, the
y	x	sh	ch	th	th			he, she
qu	ou	oi	ue	er	ar			me, we
No new sound-letter links taught for 5 weeks (revision of what's been learnt) Lots of practise blending 2-5 sound words. The above are the most common ways to spell our 42 - 44 speech sounds. Next your child will be taught alternative spellings.								be, was, to, do, are, all
Alternative spellings of vowels y /ee/ a_e (make) e_e (eve) i_e (like) o_e (home) u_e (cube)								you, your, come, some, said, here, there, they
More alternative vowel spellings ay oy ea y ow (cow) ir ur ew ow igh								go, no, so, my, one, by, only, old, like, have, live, give, little, down, what, when, why, where, who, which
Alternative consonant and vowel spellings aw au al ph (f) c (s) g (j) wh (w) ff ll ss zz mb (m) wr (r) wh (h) kn (n) air are ear ea (e) spelling 'wa' sound, 'wo'								any, many, more, before, other, were, because, want, saw, put, could, should, would, right, two, four, goes, does, made, their

Please refer to the Sound and Letter Chart for the speech sound and the different spellings so that the instructions make sense. For example, speech sound /ai/ can be spelt *ay*, *ai* or *a_e*. Speech sound /ee/ can be spelt *ee*, *ea*, *y* and *e_e*.

Some structured phonics programs teach six sound-letter relationships per week, which is fine if your child is able to grasp them quickly and if you are revising them at home. You know your child best, so if three sound-letter relationships per week suits better, then that is fine.

You can teach your child in a different order from the above and follow the sequence that your school is teaching. However, be careful when asking your child to read the words in this book, as I have used words where we have taught the sound-letter links previously. If your school does not have a structured phonics program in place, then please follow the sequence in this book.

The important thing when teaching sound-letter links is to also teach blending, segmenting and manipulation of sounds in words as you go. This is done by completing the activities in this book.

If your child knows all the sound-letter links for their stage of schooling, but you have noticed that they find it difficult to blend the sounds back into words, then please go to chapter 3: Phonemic Awareness and practise the activities.

High-frequency words

Your child needs to know some high-frequency words that they will come across in their reading before we teach the sound-letter links for those words. This is so the books they read make sense. These words may be called "sight words" or "tricky words". Many of the so-called sight words can actually be decoded once children have been taught the sound-letter links. In the table above, it lists the suggested high-frequency words to teach and when.

There are also some words that are extra difficult as there are parts of the word that are not phonetically regular; for example, *said* and *was*. These are sometimes referred to as "heart words", as there are parts of the word that you need to learn by heart.

Script to use to teach your child high-frequency words

Please refer to the chart for when to introduce and teach around three to five words per week, with regular revision.

> "I am going to teach you how to read and spell the word *said*. Let's say the sounds in the word: /s/ /e/ /d/. Now let's write the word."

You can do this on paper or on the whiteboard.

> "We know that the letters /s/ and /d/ match the sounds; however, the *ai*-part is tricky. We need to learn that bit by heart. Some other words that have the same tricky spelling are *again* and *against*."

Write the words *again* and *against* for your child and highlight the *ai* spelling of the sound /e/. You can use a highlighter, underline it, or write it with a different coloured pen.

> "Now it's your turn to write the word *said*. Make sure you say the sounds as you write the letters. Well done. The word *said* used to be pronounced as 'sayed' but over time this changed but the spelling did not."

Here is another example:

> "I am going to teach you how to read and spell the word *was*. Let's say the sounds in the word: /w/ /o/ /z/. Now let's write the word."

You can do this on paper or on the whiteboard.

> "We know that the letter /w/ matches the sound; however, the *a* and *s* parts are tricky. We need to learn that bit by heart. Some other words that have the same tricky spelling where the *a* sounds like /o/ are *want, wash, watch, swap, wand.*"

Write the above words for your child and highlight the *a* spelling of the sound /o/. You can use a highlighter, underline it, or write it with a different coloured pen.

> "All of these words start with /w/. It is 'making' the letter *a* be pronounced as /o/."

> "Now let's look at the next tricky bit. The letter *s* is being said like a /z/ sound. Other words that have this spelling are *is, as, has* and *his*.

> "Now it's your turn to write the word *was*. Make sure you say the sounds as you write the letters."

There is a wonderful website with short animations and other activities to help children learn high-frequency words: reallygreatreading.com/heart-word-magic. Please also refer to my demonstration video for teaching these high-frequency words at educatable.com.au/readable-demo.

You will come across other high-frequency words while reading that you may not have taught your child. Just tell them what the word is and continue reading. If you want to do some direct teaching of the word, then please follow the script to ensure that your child is still orthographically mapping the word and not trying to remember it by "sight" (meaning its logograph or shape). Let your child say the parts they do know, and you tell them the tricky part. For example, for the word *friend*: "In this word the *ie* is an *e* sound, so when you get to this part, say 'e'."

Always look for other words to relate the tricky word to if you can. Below are some suggested groups. (Please use the script above.)

The spelling *e* in the following words represent the sound /ee/: *the* (this is included as some accents pronounce as "thee") *he, she, me, we, be.*

The spelling *o* in these words represent the sound /oo/: *to, do, who.*

The spelling *o* in these words represent the sound /oa/: *go, no, so.*

The spelling *y* in these words represents the sound /ie/: *my, by, why.*

The spelling *ore* in these words represent the sound /or/: *more, before.*

The spelling *oul* in these words represent the short /oo/ sound: *could, should, would.*

The first six sound-letter links

What you will need: Whiteboard and marker, a pencil and this book. Feel free to photocopy each page so you can re-use them.

A set of decodable books (see Further information at the end of this chapter for a list or use the free books on *SPELD SA* website that also have worksheets.)

First, teach your child six sound-letter relationships before teaching them how to blend them together to read words.

To help your child learn and remember we will use different senses:

- **Auditory** – saying and hearing the sounds.

- **Movement** – of the lips when saying the sounds and of the hand when writing the letters.

- **Visual** – looking at your mouth when you say the sounds and looking at the written letters.

Your child may need more practice for each sound-letter link beyond the activities included. You can find additional resources at the end of this chapter.

Each sound will be taught in the same format. There is also a set of blank game boards (found at educatable.com.au/readable-demo) that you can use for each sound; start off writing the individual sound letter links you are working on, then move on to words.

The rate at which you teach the sounds is usually three to six per week. Your child should practise the sound-letter links every day, always revising the previous one taught, as it is a cumulative approach. The words that you are going to ask your child to use in "Make a word", "Switch the sound", "Read the words" and to play the games with, are made up of only the sound-letter links taught so far, therefore giving lots of opportunity for repetition. A "lesson" may look like this:

- Phonemic awareness activity (2–5 minutes).

- Sound-letter link activities (5–10 minutes), including revising and teaching, "Make a word", "Switch the sound".

- Reading practice by reading individual words ("Read the words" and "Read, sort and write") and short decodable books (5–10 minutes).

- Reading to your child, which can be done after the above or at another time; for example, before bed.

You can see that the time for each activity varies. If you are short on time, then 12 minutes is really all you need to cover everything, with extra bookreading to your child later. The key is consistency and working it into your daily schedule.

I have included writing the letter that represents the speech sound straight away. Please ask your child to say the sound as he/she is writing it. It is *very* important for you and your child to be saying the sound without adding a *schwa* or short vowel on the end. If you are unsure, then please watch the videos suggested in the Sounds and Letters Chart on how to produce all the speech sounds.

Do the activities in pencil in this book so that you can erase and repeat or photocopy the pages to use again. At first, your child's tracing of the letters and writing them on their own is going to be very slow and shaky, which is fine. They will become quicker and more accurate with practice. It is important that they are forming the letters correctly, so please ask your teacher for extra handwriting sheets if needed. If they are really struggling, then please go back to chapter 1: Foundational Skills and practise some of the pre-writing activities.

The words in quotation marks are your script. I have included a complete script for the first sound-letter link, so please continue to use this script and simply substitute the new sound-letter link you are teaching. By the time you get into the second set of sound-letter links, you may have put your own spin on the script and your child may not need such explicit instructions.

Please do not feel you have to do every activity each time. However, your child should practise the sound-letter link in words before reading the decodable reader. Once your child is able to complete the activities faster and more easily, then you can add more to each lesson. Don't forget to read to your child every day. For a beginner reader, your week can look like this:

Monday	Tuesday	Wednesday	Thursday	Friday	Saturday
Phonemic awareness	Phonemic awareness	Phonemic awareness	Phonemic awareness	Phonemic awareness	Phonemic awareness
Introduce new sound	Revise sound	Revise sound and introduce new sound	Revise two sounds	Revise two sound and introduce new sound	Revise three new sounds
Make a word (including the writing)	Switch the sound	Make a word (including the writing)	Read the words	Make a word (including the writing)	Read the words
	Read the words	Switch the sound	Read, Sort and Write	Switch the sound	Read, Sort and Write
Decodable reader	Decodable reader	Decodable reader	Decodable reader	Decodable reader	Decodable reader

Writing letters for speech sounds

Sound /s/, spelling s

Introduce the speech sound /s/: "All of our spoken words are made up of different speech sounds. I am going to say some words that all have the /s/ sound in them – *so, six, sand, biscuit, whisper, seesaw, bus, yes, Chris*. Could you hear all of those /s/ sounds? When we want to write that speech sound down, we can use this letter."

Then point to the first *s* below. **Please remember to use the sound, not the letter name!**

S

Finger trace: "Let's practise. I'm going to say the sound /s/ as I trace my finger along each letter. Now your turn. Say the sound 'ssss' as you trace your finger along each letter."

S S S S S

Find the letter: Use the table with the different shapes and the letter *s*. Cover the *s* that you just traced your finger on above.

"These are all symbols. Which one do we write down for the speech sound /s/?"

Please do not use the letter name.

S	Δ
↓	£
4	*

Pencil trace: "Let's practise writing the letter. As you are writing it, say the sound /s/. I'll do the first one, then we'll do two together and then you can have a go by yourself."

S S S S S

Write on own: "Now try writing it on your own. Remember to say the sound /s/ as you write the letter."

―――

....

....

―――

Sound /a/, spelling *a*

Revise previous sound-letter link /s/: "Let's go over what we have learnt so far. This is the way we can write the speech sound /s/."

It is a good idea to complete the page again, minus the "Introduce the speech sound".

Introduce new sound: *an, apple, ant, cat, map, dad, sofa, cola, Africa.*

a

Finger trace:

Find the letter:

s	Δ
↓	a
4	*

Pencil trace:

Write on own:

_____

_____

_____

_____

Sound /t/, spelling *t*

Revise previous sound-letter links: /s/ and /a/.

Introduce new sound: *tea, two, table, water, petal, October, hat, boat, carrot.*

†

Finger trace:

Find the letter:

s	Δ
↓	a
t	*

Pencil trace:

Write on own:

Sound /i/, spelling *i*

Revise previous sound-letter links: /s/, /a/ and /t/.

Introduce new sound: *igloo, install, ink, mix, lid, sit, salami, mini, taxi.*

i

Finger trace:

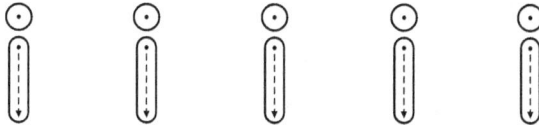

Find the letter:

*	a
s	i
Δ	t

Pencil trace:

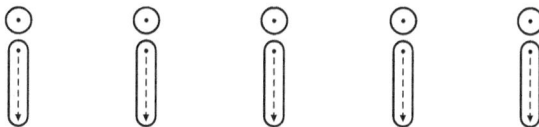

Write on own:

Sound /p/, spelling *p*

Revise previous sound-letter links: /s/, /a/, /t/ and /i/.

Introduce new sound: *pink, pet, pear, hoping, computer, super, cup, ship, flop.*

p

Finger trace:

Find the letter:

s	t
p	Δ
i	a

Pencil trace:

Write on own:

Sound /n/, spelling *n*

Revise previous sound-letter links: /s/, /a/, /t/, /i/ and /p/.

Introduce new sound: *no, nana, never, honey, dinosaur, animal, down, sun, fan.*

n

Finger trace:

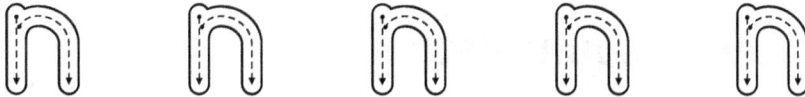

Find the letter:

a	p
t	n
s	i

Pencil trace:

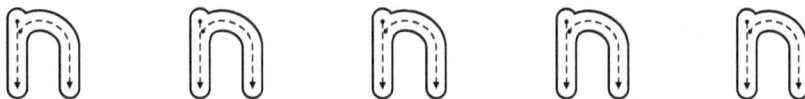

Write on own:

Revise previous sound-letter links: /s/, /a/, /t/, /i/, /p/ and /n/.

Now that your child knows the first six sound-letter links, it's time to practise how to blend them together to form a word, and then how to segment them to spell a word.

Before you start, it may be useful to watch the demonstration videos on Make a word and Switch the sound so that you know how to instruct your child. Sometimes it is easier to watch how it is done, than read it! You can find them here: educatable.com.au/readable-demo.

Below are instructions to use as a script each time you complete the activities for each new sound-letter link.

Activity 1: Revise sound-letter links

Materials needed: Letter cards. Cut out or photocopy the letters onto cardstock or laminate them. You can also add magnets onto the back to make them easy to manoeuvre on a whiteboard.

Whiteboard and marker.

Instruction script: Say a sound (not letter name) and ask your child to point to the letter we use to represent the sound.

"Can you show me the letter we can use to spell the sound /a/?"

Complete this for all of the sound-letter links taught so far, one by one. If your child has difficulty with any, then please redo the original activity page in the book.

Next, say a sound and ask your child to write the letter on the whiteboard (or a piece of paper if you prefer).

"Can you please write the letter we can use to spell /s/?"

Again, do all of the sound-letter links taught so far, one by one.

Activity 2: Make a word

Materials needed: Letter cards, whiteboard and marker (or paper if preferred). It will be easier for your child, particularly when they have learnt many sound-letter links, that you only present them with some of the letter cards. For example, if you ask them to make the word *sat*, only have those letters and one or two more. If they get confused, then only present them with the letters in the word, but have them out of order. You will see in the demonstration video that I have my letter cards with magnets up in the corner and pull down the ones needed for each word.

Instruction script: Draw lines on the whiteboard or on the paper to represent how many sounds are in the word (not how many letters, how many sounds).

> "I'd like you to make a word. Can you make me the word *sat*? First, let's say the sounds that you hear in *sat*. Great! Now what letters spell the word *sat*?"

Your child will place the letter on the first line.

You may need to help your child, particularly at the start of these activities.

> "What sound do you hear at the start? Ssssat. Yes, an /s/ sound. What can spell the /s/ sound? Great. Now what do you hear next – saaaat? Yes, an /a/ sound. And what do you hear at the end of the word s-a-t?"

Do this as you are pointing to the line where the sound is. Try not to totally break apart the word, just slow it down.

> "Great, now you have made the word! Let's sound it out and blend it together. Say the sound as my finger is underneath the letter, then say the whole word."

Put your finger under the first letter and slide your finger across so that your child says the sound as you reach each letter. They can then blend the sounds to read the word as a whole.

> "Now, can you write the word *sat* on your whiteboard? It is helpful to say the sound as you write the letter."

It is important for your child to start writing the words from the beginning. They will be messy; however, research has shown that practising writing helps children build their reading skills. Phonemic awareness grows as they read and write new words and their phonics skills are strengthened by repetition. It is fine for your child to be looking at the word they made with the letter cards as they write the word.

Follow the same instructions above. Help your child choose the letters to a word, then read the word together again, and write the word (saying the sounds as they write each letter). Use the following words from the six sound-letter links already learnt: *at, mat, pit, nap, it, pat, sit, tip, sap, nit, tap, its, pip, sip, spit, spat*. These last two have four sounds so your child may find them tricky – it is fine for you to do these ones for them as you are modelling. There is no need to do them all, particularly for beginner readers. Try to do five and then if your child tires, then stop and do the others on a different day.

When completing Make a Word activity from hereon in, use the words listed in the "Read the words" activity for each sound-letter link (Activity 4). We are not "testing" if they can do it, we are "teaching" them how to do it. There is a great saying that I think we need to remember when we are teaching anything to our children: "I do, we do, you do." This means – person teaching does it first (models), then person teaching and child do it together, and then the child does on their own.

Activity 3: Switch the sound

You can do this activity either on the whiteboard or with the letter cards. Please complete (model) the first two swaps for your child so they know what to do, before asking them to give it a try. Start with the word *at*.

> "This is the word *at*, *a-t* – *at*. What do you need to add to make it *pat*?"

If your child is unsure, then repeat it slowly while gliding your finger under the sounds as you say them.

> "Here we have *at*, what should we add to make *p-at*? Yes, that's it. A /p/ sound makes it *pat*. Which letter do we use for the /p/ sound? Great, and where does it go? Wonderful, now you have made the word *pat*. How do we change it to *sat*?"

Again, if your child has difficulty, then repeat the word emphasising the first sound.

> "This is *p-at*, what do we need to change to make it 'ssssat'? Great, we need to take away the *p* and add the *s*. Now you have made the word *sat*."

Continue with the following changes: *sat → nat → nap → tap → sap*.

Once your child has the hang of sound changes at the start and the ends of the words, then try the middle sound.

> "Now we are going to change the sound in the middle of the word. We have the word *sap*, what do we need to change to make it *sip*?"

Then continue with the following changes: *sip → sit → nit → it → at → ant*.

Again, the first time your child does this they may find it *very* difficult so give lots of help. Even if you end up doing all the sound swaps, you are still teaching through demonstration. Once your child has many letter cards, it may be difficult to find which one they need so try to have only the ones needed.

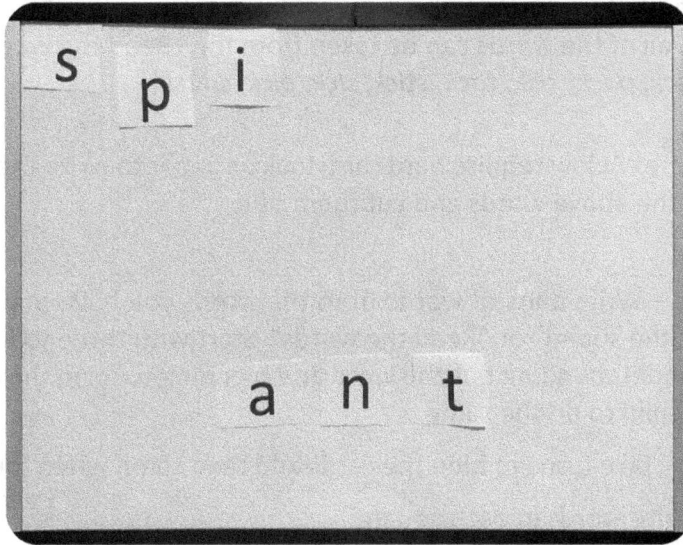

Activity 4: Read the words

Demonstrate sounding out and blending together with the first two or three words below. Help your child to read the words.

"Say the sound as my finger is underneath the letter, then say the whole word."

If your child is finding this difficult, then demonstrate sounding out and blending together another five words before asking them to try again.

at	it	an	tip
sat	its	sit	sip
tin	snip	pant	pan
tan	pit	snap	pin
tap	ant	nap	

Extra activities

Games: I have added 10x black and white masters for games. You can find them here: educatable. com.au/readable-demo. Print out as many as you like so you can use over again. You can write individual letters on them to practise sound-letter links at the start, before moving on to words that contain the sound-letter link that you are working on. For example, once you have taught your child *ck* endings, all of the words can be taken from the "Read the words" table and written on the game board (*tick, pack, kick, sack, stick, sick, pick, snack*).

Other Games: The games below require hard cardstock or paper to write the current sound-focus words. Or photocopy the above words and cut them out.

- Matching pairs – Write pairs of words from the words you have practised in "Make a word", "Switch the sound" or "Read the words". Start with three to five pairs. When it is your turn, model sounding out the word and blending to form the word. Encourage and help your child to do the same.

- Hide and seek – Take turns to hide the cards and read them when found.

- Hopscotch – Write words in each square.

- Beanbag memory toss – With the matching pairs that you wrote onto the hard cardstock, spread them face down on the ground and throw a beanbag onto one. Turn the card over and read it, then throw the beanbag onto another, trying to find the matching word.

- Torch – Using Blu-Tack, stick the words on the wall and turn off the lights. Use a torch to shine on the words for your child to read.

Now that you have demonstrated how to sound out and blend, and your child has practised making, changing, reading and writing the words, practise reading these words in connected text. This is where decodable readers come in. Decodable readers only contain the sound-letter links that your child has been taught, so they can really cement their knowledge and not be required to guess unknown words.

When reading decodable readers, your child will likely be slow and won't get through much compared to when reading predictable readers where only one word changes in each sentence. These predictable texts teach children to read from memory of the sentence structure and by guessing from the picture. They are not actually reading the words and therefore are not orthographically mapping the sound-letter links.

If you do not have access to a set of these decodable readers, please visit the *SPELD* website for free readers and worksheets (website listed in Further information). You and your child can also make up short books or sentences, using the words from the word list, and draw your own pictures to create a book.

When reading, encourage your child to sound out the word and then blend the sounds together. Tell your child to listen to the sounds and "catch" the word with their brain. Try to always attach meaning to the word, so that your child knows why they are reading – to discover meaning. You can do this by drawing a quick picture of the word. My children love this as I am a terrible drawer and they love to say how my dogs looks like cows. Or if you have the object nearby – for example, a hat or a chair – then point it out. Put the word into a sentence and relate it to what they know or have experienced. For example: "Ant. Remember when we had all of those ants after we left the honey out?"

At the beginning, reading can be very tiring as the brainpower used to work out what these funny squiggles are can be taxing. That's why the first books they read should have minimal words in them. Your child will build stamina as they go. It is better to keep it fun and stop when you can tell they have had enough as they won't take in what you are teaching them. But don't let them hoodwink you.

The next sound-letter links

If your child has mastered identifying what letters are used for the first six sound-letter links to automaticity (I just love that word!) and can blend them to read words, then they are ready to continue learning more sound-letter links.

Introduce no more than one new sound per day. In fact, you only have to introduce a new sound every second or third day, as long as you are revising the sounds already learnt each day. Be guided by your child's progress. After you have introduced a new sound-letter link, add the letter card to your pile to be used in "Make a word" and "Switch the sound" activities. There is a word list for each new sound-letter link taught. You can use words from any of the previous lists as well.

Sound /k/, spelling *c*

Revise previous sound-letter links: /s/, /a/, /t/, /i/, /p/ and /n/.

Introduce new sound: *cat, car, coffee, across, because, vacuum, panic, traffic, magic.*

Finger trace:

Find the letter:

a	p
t	n
c	i

Pencil trace:

Write on own:

_____

Make a word: (use the words from 'Read the words' below)

Switch the sound: *at → act → cat → can → cap → caps.*

Read the words:

cat	cap	can	act
cats	caps	cans	acts

Please point out and discuss with your child that when we add the *s* at the end of some words, it makes them plurals which is more than one. Your child would know this from their oral language – what child has ever asked for just one biscuit or lolly?! It's always biscuits and lollies, but it is great to be explicit and teach them about plurals in the context of reading and spelling. In the above, we have used *cans, cats* and *caps*.

Sound /k/, spelling *k*
Revise previous sound-letter links: /s/, /a/, /t/, /i/, /p/, /n/ and /c/.

Introduce the letter: "The last speech sound we talked about and wrote the letter for was /k/, with the spelling *c*. This speech sound can also be written with the letter *k*." (Point at the first *k* below.)

k

Finger trace:

Find the letter:

i	p	k
k	n	t
s	p	a

Pencil trace:

Write on own:

_____

Make a word: (use the words from 'Read the words' below)

Switch the sound: *kit → kin → kip → skip → skin → sink → ink → pink → sink → sank → tank.*

Read the words:

kip	ink	kin	kit
sink	pink	skin	sank
skip	tank		

If your child struggles blending the four-sound words together; for example, *s-k-i-n*, then stick to the three-sound words and revise the two- or three-sound words in the previous list. Remember to sound out and blend as you go. The words *ink, sink, pink, sank* and *tank*, the *n* is more like the sound /ng/, as in *sing*, but your child should be able to work out the words.

Sound /k/, spelling *ck*

Revise previous sound-letter links: /c/ and /k/ (the others will be revised when reading).

Introduce the letters: "The last speech sound we talked about and wrote the letter for was /k/. You learnt that the speech sound /k/ can be written down with the letters *c* or *k*. It can also be written with two letters together that make one sound." – whilst pointing at the first *ck* below – "This is called a digraph."

ck

Finger trace:

Find the letter:

a	p	ck
ck	n	a
s	i	t

Pencil trace:

Write on own:

Make a word: (use the words from 'Read the words' below)

Switch the sound: *ick → tick → pick → pack → sack → snack → stack → stick → sick.*

Read the words:

tick	pack	kick	sack
stick	sick	pick	snack

Sort the words:

c	k	ck

Photocopy and cut out the words below and ask your child to read each word (by sounding out and blending together as they go) and then place them under the correct spelling choice. It may be helpful for your child if you highlight or underline the /k/ sound in each word.

cat	cats	sack
tick	pick	cap
kit	kip	pack
cans	stick	can
pink	kin	ink

So, when do you use c or k to spell words? Overloading your child at the start with spelling rules can be too difficult for a beginning reader, but if they (or you!) want to know the "rule" here it is: use the c spelling of the sound /k/ before the vowels a, o and u. The k spelling of /k/ is used before e, i or y.

When your child is further along in their reading and spelling, explaining this rule and practising activities such as dictation would be useful.

Sound /e/, spelling *e*

Revise previous sound-letter links: *c, k* and *ck.*

Introduce new sound: *egg, end, extra, empty, get, nest, yes, neck.*

e

Finger trace:

Find the letter:

c	p	s
t	e	a
k	i	ck

Pencil trace:

Write on own:

_____

_____

Make a word: (use the words from 'Read the words' below)

Switch the sound: *nets → net → set → pet → pen → ten → tent → test → pest → nest.*

Read the words:

set	net	pens
nest	pet	neck
test	step	tent

Sound /h/, spelling *h*

Revise previous sound-letter links: *k, ck* and */e/.*

Introduce new sound: *hat, have, happy, house, hula hoop, beehive, behind, dollhouse.*

h

Finger trace:

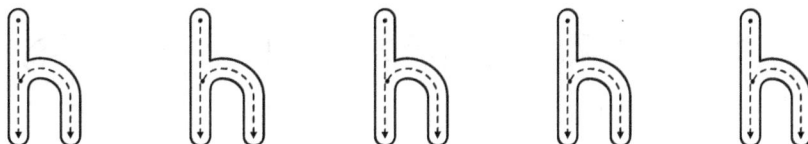

Find the letter:

h	i	k
s	e	a
t	p	ck

Pencil trace:

Write on own:

_____

Make a word: (use the words from 'Read the words' below)

Switch the sound: *at → hat → hit → it → hit → hip.*

Read the words:

hen   hit   hip   hat

hint   hens   hats

Sound /r/, spelling *r*

Revise previous sound-letter links: *ck, /e/ and /h/.*

Introduce new sound: *run, ring, rabbit, red, orange, hero, giraffe, pirate.*

r

Finger trace:

Find the letter:

k	h	s
i	e	a
p	r	ck

Pencil trace:

Write on own:

Make a word: (use the words from 'Read the words' below)

Switch the sound: *at → rat → rap → ran → rack → rick → rip → trip → trap → tap.*

Read the words:

rip	rat	ran	rent
rack	trip	trap	rest
rap	print	strap	crack

Some of these words have five sounds! For example, *p-r-i-n-t*. If these are too tricky for your child, then please do not worry – just stick to the three- and four- sound words.

Sound /m/, spelling *m*

Revise previous sound-letter links: /e/, /h/ and /r/.

Introduce the sound: *more, met, milk, lemon, farmer, number, Sam, him, drum.*

m

Finger trace:

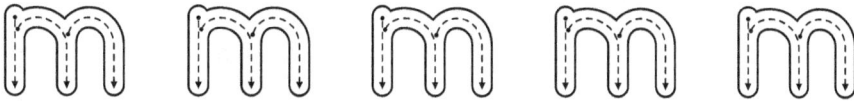

Find the letter:

h	e	s
k	n	a
m	i	ck

Pencil trace:

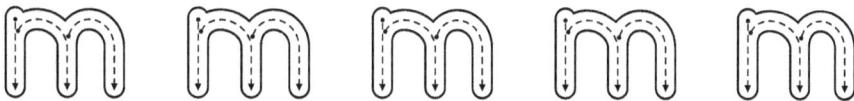

Write on own:

_____

....

....

_____

Make a word: (use the words from 'Read the words' below)

Switch the sound: *ham → him → hem → hen → men → man → mat → map → amp → stamp.*

Read the words:

ham	man	him	mat
men	map	hem	mist
camp	stem	amp	stamp

Sound /d/, spelling *d*

Revise previous sound-letter links: /h/, /r/ and /m/.

Introduce new sound: *door, down, dinosaur, bleeding, body, medal, had, made, bird.*

d

Finger trace:

Find the letter:

ck	e	m
t	p	a
k	i	d

Pencil trace:

Write on own:

_____

....

....

_____

Make a word:(use the words from 'Read the words' below)

Switch the sound: *had → dad → sad → sand → and → hand → had → hid → kid → skid.*

Read the words:

sad	end	red	dad
dip	had	den	did
and	kid	hand	skid

Now that your child has been taught the /d/ sound-letter link, we can introduce past tense *-ed* spelling. The tricky thing with *-ed* is that it can be pronounced in different ways, so you have to teach your child that if something has already happened, the correct spelling is *-ed*, not *t*. For example, jumped sounds like "jumpt"; however, if you have taught your child that the morphological ending for something that has already happened is *-ed*, then they have a better chance of spelling correctly.

Challenge words:

handed   ended   skidded   dipped

The spelling "rule" and some additional practice for *-ed* can be found in chapter 5: Spelling.

You can see that in *skidded* and *dipped* we have an additional ending consonant. However, it still only makes one sound. We add the letter if the word has one syllable, has a one single vowel and ends in one consonant; for example, *hop – hopped*, and *plan – planned*. The word *end* has two consonants, so the *d* is not repeated.

This is to "protect" the vowel so that it doesn't change its sound; for example, *hopped* versus *hoped*. This is tricky stuff and we are only introducing it here to continue working on as we go.

Sound /g/, spelling *g*

Revise previous sound-letter links: /r/, /m/ and /d/.

Introduce new sound: *get, girl, goat, begin, Lego, tiger, hug, bag, dog.*

g

Finger trace:

Find the letter:

k	d	e
h	r	ck
m	g	c

Pencil trace:

Write on own:

_____

···

···

_____

Make a word: (use the words from 'Read the words' below)

Switch the sound: *drag → rag → nag → rag → rig → dig → pig → peg → pet → get.*

Read the words:

pig	rag	get	dig
pegs	gap	gas	snag
drag	grin	gran	grip

Sound /o/, spelling *o*

Revise previous sound-letter links: /m/, /d/, and /g/.

Introduce new sound: *octopus, odd, off, op, top, rock, stop, hot.*

O

Finger trace:

Find the letter:

h	c	m
e	r	d
k	o	ck

Pencil trace:

Write on own:

_____

Make a word: (use the words from 'Read the words' below)

Switch the sound: *got → hot → hop → pop → pot → pod → pond → pod → rod → rock.*

Read the words:

got	rock	dog	top
on	hot	pot	pond
hop	pop	rod	drop

Sound /u/, spelling *u*

Revise previous sound-letter links: /d/, /g/, and /o/.

Introduce new sound: *umbrella, ugly, uncle, up, but, hug, cup, lucky.*

u

Finger trace:

Find the letter:

o	c	r
h	e	u
m	d	ck

Pencil trace:

Write on own:

_____

Make a word: (use the words from 'Read the words' below)

Switch the sound: *us → up → cup → cut → rut → cut → cud → mud → muck → duck.*

Read the words:

up	rug	sun	duck
cut	us	pump	dust
suck	hut	mud	stuck

Sound /l/, spelling /

Revise previous sound-letter links: /g/, /o/ and /u/.

Introduce new sound: *leg, lip, list, lolly, smelly, melon, doll, hill, pull.*

I

Finger trace:

Find the letter:

ck	d	r
l	m	u
e	u	o

Pencil trace:

Write on own:

_____

Make a word: (use the words from 'Read the words' below)

Switch the sound: *leg → log → lag → lap → flap → flip → lip → lick → lock → flock.*

Read the words:

lid	leg	old	glad
lap	lock	lip	cold
lick	milk	slid	flip

Sound /f/, spelling *f*

Revise previous sound-letter links: /o/, /u/ and /l/.

Introduce new sound: *fish, four, fin, toffee, left, soft, leaf, if, elf.*

f

Finger trace:

Find the letter:

o	m	r
l	f	u
e	d	ck

Pencil trace:

Write on own:

_____

....

....

_____

Make a word: (use the words from 'Read the words' below)

Switch the sound: *fat → fan → fun → fin → fit → lit → lift → flit → flip → flap.*

Read the words:

fat	if	fit	off
fog	fan	felt	fins
lift	soft	flap	frog

The /f/ sound can be spelt with one or two letters; for example, *off*. When reading that word, if your child sounds it out as *o-f-f*, please tell them that it is two letters that make one /f/ sound. We will revise double letters, so this is an introduction for your child.

A general spelling rule is that in a single-syllable word, with a single vowel which is immediately followed by the letter *f*, *l*, *s*, or *z*, the final letter is repeated. Children are normally fine reading double letters, it is the spelling that trips them up.

Sound /b/, spelling *b*

Revise previous sound-letter links: /u/, /l/ and /f/.

Introduce new sound: *bad, bump, best, bubble, rabbit, robin, grub, rub, crab.*

b

Finger trace:

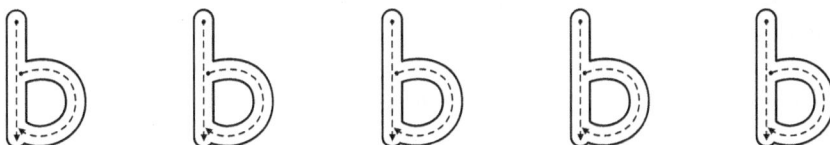

Find the letter:

ck	d	o
l	f	u
b	g	m

Pencil trace:

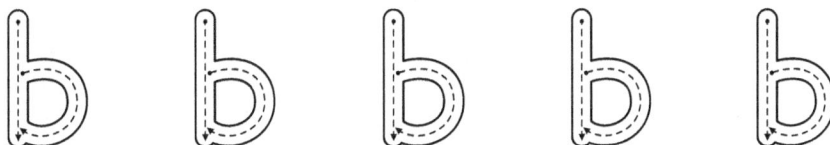

Write on own:

_____

Make a word: (use the words from 'Read the words' below)

Switch the sound: *bin → big → bag → ban → back → black → back → buck → bug → rug → rub → grub → grab.*

Read the words:

bad	beg	rub	bat
bin	cub	bed	back
big	blob	grab	grub

Teaching digraphs

You have previously introduced digraphs to your child which are two letters used to represent one speech sound. Most of the following sound-letter links are digraphs, so it is important that your child knows the concept well.

Sound /ai/, spelling *ai*

Introduce the speech sound /ai/: "All of our spoken words are made up of different speech sounds. I am going to say some words that all have the /ai/ sound in them – *aim, pail, rain, train, wait, sail*. Could you hear all of those /ai/ sounds? When we want to write that speech sound down, we can use these two letters for the one sound." – whilst pointing at the first *ai* below – "This is called a digraph."

ai

Finger trace: "Let's practise. Say the sound /ai/ as you trace your finger along the two letters."

Find the letter: "Which letters can we write down for the speech sound /ai/?"

ck	g	l
o	b	u
d	ai	m

Writing /ai/: "Let's practise writing the two letters for the sound /ai/. As you are writing it, say the sound. I'll do it first, then we'll do it together and then you can have a go by yourself."

Write on own: "Terrific writing. Now try writing it on your own. Remember to say the sound as you write the letters."

Make a word: Add the *ai* letter square and help your child make some of the words below without them seeing the words. Refer to the script in "Make a word".

Switch the sound: *aim → ail → tail → nail → snail → sail → pail → paid → pain → rain → train*.

Read the words:

aim	sail	paid	rain
tail	pain	nail	main
train	snail	mail	laid

Sound /j/, spelling *j*

Revise previous sound-letter links: /ai/ and any other the sound-letter links that your child does not know automatically.

Introduce new sound: *jam, jelly, jump, jog, jacket, jet, jolly, Jane.*

j

Finger trace:

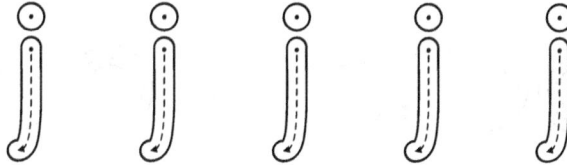

Find the letter:

d	g	oa
m	u	o
ai	j	b

Pencil trace:

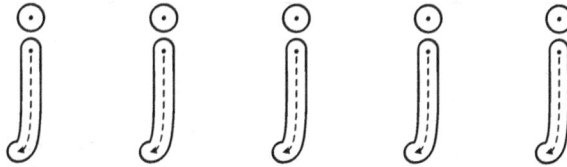

Write on own:

Make a word: (use the words from 'Read the words' below)

Switch the sound: *job → jog → jug → jut → just → jut → jug → jag → jam → jack.*

Read the words:

jog	jet	jug	jump
jam	job	just	junk
jacket	object	ninja	jackpot

I have added, for the first time, words with more than one syllable (*jack-et, ob-ject, nin-ja, jack-pot*). Your child may need extra help with these words.

There are not many other words that we can add with *j* in the middle until we have taught your child some additional sound-letter links; for example, "oy" (enjoy). Please refer to chapter 5: Spelling on why English words do not end in the letter *j*.

Sound /oa/, spelling *oa*

Revise previous sound-letter links: /ai/ and /j/.

Introduce new sound: *oat, oak, soak, boat, toast, soap, float, soak, croak, toad.*

oa

Finger trace:

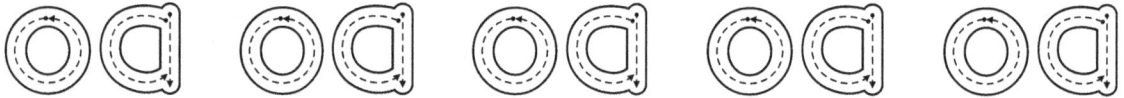

Find the letter:

j	g	oa
m	b	u
d	ai	o

Pencil trace:

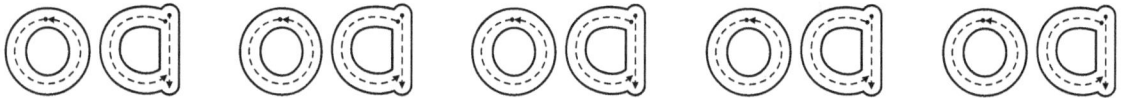

Write on own:

_____

....

....

_____

Make a word: (use the words from 'Read the words' below)

Switch the sound: *oak → oat → goat → moat → boat → coat → coast → toast → boast → roast.*

Read the words:

boat	oak	road	oat
toast	loaf	coat	soap
goat	float	groan	coast

Sound /ie/, spelling *ie*

Revise previous sound-letter links: /ai/, /j/ and /oa/.

Introduce new sound: *pie, lie, died, tried, tie, lied, cried, ties.*

ie

Finger trace:

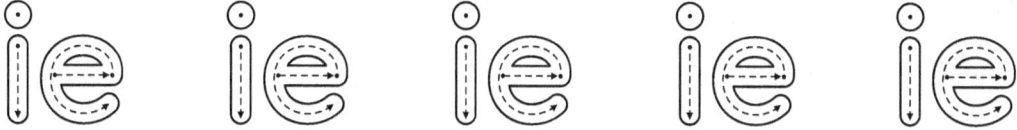

Find the letter:

ie	d	oa
j	ai	u
b	g	m

Pencil trace:

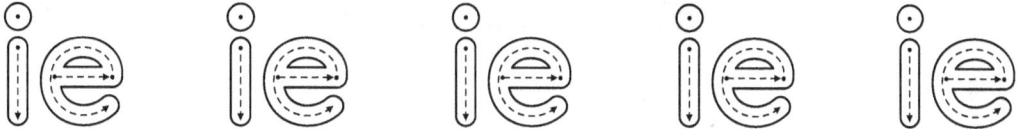

Write on own:

Make a word: (use the words from 'Read the words' below)
Switch the sound: *pie → tie → lie → die → died → lied → tied → tie → ties → pies.*

Read the words:

pie	tie	lie	lied
die	lies	ties	tied
pies	died	magpie	untie

This is another great opportunity to discuss plurals – add the *s* to *pie* to make it more than one pie, and add the *s* to *tie* to makes it more than one tie.

As we discussed previously, adding -*ed* to the end of a base word makes it past tense. Since there is already an *e* at the end, we just need to add the *d*. It is a good idea to put the words into a sentence for your child which helps them relate to what they already know.

When reading a word with -*ed* ending, for example, *jumped*, your child may sound out as "jum-ped". However, they will realise that it doesn't match to a word in their vocabulary and then change it to "jumpt".

Sound /ee/, spelling *ee*

Revise previous sound-letter links: /j/, /oa/, and /ie/.

Introduce new sound: *bee, see, sheep, meet, feet, green, sleep, peep, need.*

ee

Finger trace:

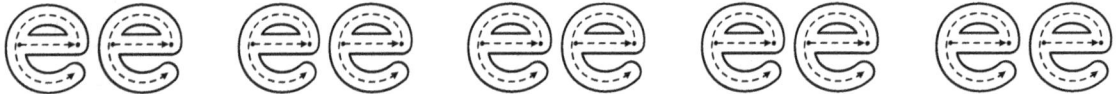

Find the letter:

ie	d	g
b	ee	u
oa	ai	j

Pencil trace:

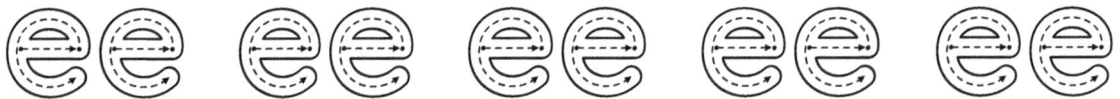

Write on own:

_____

....

....

_____

Make a word: (use the words from 'Read the words' below)

Switch the sound: *bee → been → beep → deep → keep → keen → seen → see → seed → speed.*

Read the words:

bee	see	feet	jeep
seen	need	beef	keep
deep	been	sleep	speed

Sound /or/, spelling *or*

Revise previous sound-letter links: /oa/, /ie/ and /ee/.

Introduce new sound: *or, for, sort, torn, fort, corn, fork, storm, sport.*

or

Finger trace:

Find the letter:

or	d	oo
j	ee	u
g	ai	ie

Pencil trace:

Write on own:

_____

....

....

_____

Make a word: (use the words from 'Read the words' below)

Switch the sound: *or → for → form → fort → sort → sport → port → pork → fork → cork.*

Read the words:

or	torn	for	born
fort	pork	sort	sport
horn	fork	forgot	forget

When *or* is at the end of a word – for example, *doctor* or *tractor* – in Australia we tend to pronounce this as a *schwa* which is a shortened vowel sound similar to "uh". This sound is also found in two-syllable words such as *alone* and *pencil*.

If your child is finding it difficult to read two-syllable words, then draw a line after the first syllable (for example, for/got) and ask them to sound out the first part and blend together, then sound out the second part and blend together, and finally blend the two parts to make the whole word. As words get longer, it becomes too difficult to sound out all the sounds then blend them together at the end. It is best therefore to teach them to blend as they go.

Sound /z/, spelling z

Revise previous sound-letter links: Revise the sound-letter links that your child does not know automatically.

Introduce new sound: *zoo, zebra, zip, frozen, dizzy, dozen, buzz, fizz, fuzz.*

z

Finger trace:

Find the letter:

ie	u	oo
oo	z	d
or	ai	g

Pencil trace:

Write on own:

_____

....

....

_____

Make a word: (use the words from 'Read the words' below)

Switch the sound: 1. *zap → zip → zig → zag → zigzag.*

2. *buzz → fuzz → fizz → tizz → tazz → jazz.*

Read the words:

zip	zap	zigzag	jazz
zebra	buzz	fizz	fuzz

Here are some more double letters. Again, if your child sounds out both /z/ sounds, tell them that the *zz* spelling is said as one sound.

Sound /w/, spelling *w*

Revise previous sound-letter links: /z/.

Introduce new sound: *went, win, wet, wag, cobweb, sweet, twin, unwell.*

Finger trace:

Find the letter:

ee	u	z
w	oa	d
or	ie	ai

Pencil trace:

Write on own:

_____

....

....

_____

Make a word: (use the words from 'Read the words' below)

Switch the sound: *weed → week → weep → sweep → wet → went → wet → web → well → swell.*

Read the words:

wet	win	web	went
well	wait	weed	wag
week	sweep	swan	worn
twig	will	cobweb	unwell

We have now introduced a prefix to your child: *un*. Adding *un* before a base word makes it the opposite. For example: *unwell, unhappy, undid*. We have also introduced another double letter, *ll*, which will be revised later in the chapter.

The /w/ changes the sound of *a* into the sound /o/ in some words. For example, *was, swan, wash, watch* and *swallow*. This is revised later in the chapter.

Again, if your child is having difficulty with two-syllable words, then draw a line between each syllable (cob/web, un/well) and ask them to sound out one syllable at a time before joining both together to form the word.

Sound /ng/, spelling *ng*

Revise previous sound-letter links: /z/ and /w/.
Introduce new sound: *sing, bang, song, strong, singing, hang, clang, longer, stronger.*

ng

Finger trace:

Find the letter:

ee	or	z
w	ai	oa
j	ie	ng

Pencil trace:

Write on own:

_____

....

....

_____

Make a word: (use the words from 'Read the words' below)
Switch the sound: *ring → rang → rung → sung → sing → swing → sting → sing → sang → song → long.*

Read the words:

ring	sang	song	long
hung	bang	wing	king
rang	sing	swing	sting
sleeping	sailing	seeing	jumping

Now we have introduced the spelling of the suffix *-ing*. Please discuss with your child that adding *-ing* after a base word means that the action is happening at that time. For example, *running, singing, nagging, climbing, jumping, sailing.*

When we add *-ing* to a word that has one syllable, a single vowel and ends in one consonant, the consonant is doubled. This is the same rule for when we add the suffix *-ed*. For example, *run – running, sit – sitting, step – stepping. Sleep* has a long vowel, then a consonant, so it is **not** doubled. *Sailing* has a long consonant, so it **not** doubled. *Jump* has two consonants at the end, so it is **not** doubled.

Your child may need more help to read these words and there is some more practice in chapter 5: Spelling.

Sound /v/, spelling *v*

Revise previous sound-letter links: /z/, /w/ and /ng/.

Introduce new sound: *van, very, vet, caravan, seven, travel, love, have, give.*

V

Finger trace:

Find the letter:

ng	v	z
w	or	ie
j	oa	ng

Pencil trace:

Write on own:

_____

....

....

_____

Make a word: (use the words from 'Read the words' below)

Switch the sound: *vet → vest → vent → vend → vand → van.* (Please let your child know that *vand* is not a real word, it is just for the purposes of switching the sound.)

Read the words:

vet	vest	van	vent
seven	travel	level	visit
have	give	live	sleeve

Please refer to chapter 5: Spelling on why English words do not end in the letter *v*.

Sound /oo/, spelling *oo*

Revise previous sound-letter links: /w/, /ng/ and /v/.

Introduce new sound: *book, good, cook, wood, foot and look.*

OO

Finger trace:

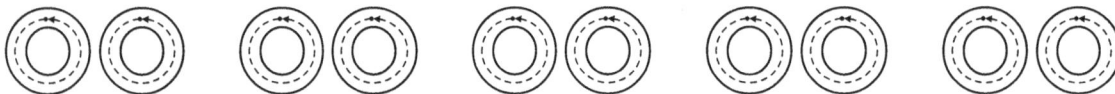

Find the letter:

ie	j	z
or	v	w
v	oo	ng

Pencil:

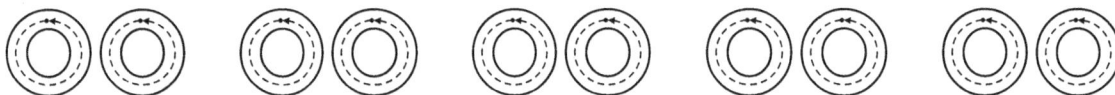

Write on own:

_____

Make a word: (use the words from 'Read the words' below)

Switch the sound: *cook → look → hook → book → took → tool → wool → woof → wood → good.*

Read the words:

good	foot	wood	woof
look	cook	hood	took
wool	book	hook	stood

The spelling *oo* can be read as two different sounds. The *oo* we have just learnt is the shorter of the two sounds, as in the words *book, good, cook, wood, foot* and *look*. There is another way to read *oo*. It can make a longer sound such as in the words *zoo, moon, soon, food, loop* and *roof*.

> "I am going to say some words that all have the /oo/ sound in them – *zoo, moon, soon, food, loop* and *roof*. Could you hear all of those /oo/ sounds? When we want to write that speech sound down, we can use these two letters to make the one sound." (Point at the first *oo* below.)

oo

Finger trace:

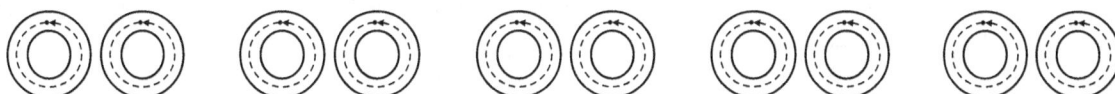

Pencil trace:

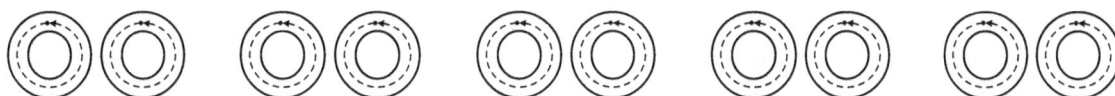

Write on own:

_____

_____

_____

_____

Make a word: (use the words from 'Read the words' below)

Switch the sound: *spoon → soon → moon → moo → zoo → zoom → boom → broom → room → roof*.

Read the words:

zoo	room	moo	broom
food	mood	hoop	roof
moon	soon	spoon	stool

Read, sort and write: Cut out the words (on page 126) and ask your child to read each word by sounding out and blending together as they go and then place (not glue) under the correct spelling (column). You may like to ask your child to highlight or underline the /oo/ spelling in each word first to make it easier for them to read. After that, take off the words, and ask your child to write the words under each spelling choice. At this stage, they are able to look at the word as they write it.

oo (as in *book*)	oo (as in *zoo*)		
		wood	moon
		took	roof
		foot	soon
		book	zoo
		good	food

When writing words during all of the "Read, sort and write" activities, your child may like lines drawn within the box to help with their letter formation. Please try to stick to the format your child has been learning at school (as some do two lines, and others do three). You could ask your child's teacher for handwriting sheets or use exercise books with pre-drawn lines. Alternatively, draw up the table for your child to write in.

When reading, your child may use the wrong /oo/ sound for that word, but mistakes are teachable moments. In this case, if your child uses the wrong sound in *m-oo-n*, ask them if this is a word that they know. If they answer "No", then ask them to say the sounds again, but use the other *oo*-sound. This is a great strategy to teach children early on; if the word is not known to them, then ask them to try it again with the vowel pronounced in a different way. This may also occur when teaching the *ow* spelling as there are two sounds it can make.

Your child may sound out words incorrectly or break up the syllables in the words the wrong way. Wait until they get to the end of the word and see if they can self-correct. I had a little boy recently who read *toward* as "tow-ard" since he saw the vowel digraph *ow*. He then said, "That's not a word I know, I'll try the vowels another way. *To-ward*." (Clever little man!)

A common word sounded out incorrectly is *island* – children may pronounce the /s/ before realising their mistake and quickly fixing it. You can see how having a good vocabulary helps with decoding as children match the word to the words they have stored in their brain. If they can't find a match, then they try the word another way, or it's close enough to what the word should be, so they work it out and pronounce it the right way.

If they do not know the meaning of the word, then they should be encouraged to ask. Children map words and recognise them automatically when the visual letters, sounds and meaning all map together after they recognise the word.

So far, we have focused on the speech sounds and corresponding letters (graphemes), rather than the letter names. This is because in order to read words, one must blend sounds together. If we focus on letter names, your child may say those instead of the sound; for example, "es" instead of /s/. Your child probably knows many of the letter names anyway through incidental learning which is fine.

It is a good idea to introduce them now that your child knows many of the sound-letter links. Many of the letter names contain the speech sounds they stand for:

- *a, e, i, o* – same as their long sound (*ai, ee*, etc).
- *b, d, j, k, p, q, t, v, z* – the letter names begin with the speech sound.
- *f, l, m, n, r, s, x* – the letter names end with the speech sound.
- *c* (*s*), *g* (*j*) – letter names start with their "soft" sound.
- *h, w, y* – letter names have no link to sounds at all.
- *u* (*y*), *y* (*w*), *w* – letter names are confused with a sound.

Digraphs and vowels do not have any letter names attached to them, so when spelling we name each letter by their letter names. For example, *play* has the *ay* spelling of /ai/.

Teaching letter names

First, determine what your child already knows. Use the letter cards and ask your child if they know what the letter's name is. You can have two piles: one pile that your child knows and one that you need to work on. With the ones you need to teach, tell your child that you are going to teach them what the letters are named or called because now that they are beginning to spell words, it is easier to say the name of the letter.

Introduce one new letter name per day or every second day, with lots of repetition and revision. You can also introduce capital letters through writing both capital and lower-case letters and play matching games of capital and lowercase letters – use wooden puzzle pieces, or magnets that have a mixture of cases or write the letters on post-it notes.

Sound /y/, spelling *y*

Revise previous sound-letter links: Revise the sound-letter links that your child does not know automatically.

Introduce new sound: *yes, yellow, yacht, yuck, yell, yap.*

y

Finger trace:

Find the letter:

ng	oo	y
z	V	w
j	or	ie

Pencil trace:

Write on own:

_____

Make a word: (use the words from 'Read the words' below)

Switch the sound: *yes → yet → yell → yep → yap → yak.*

Read the words:

yes	yet	yell	yap
yuck	yum	yelp	yep

The letter *y* has four sounds it can represent:

- Sound /y/ as in *yes, yellow* and *yet* (typically at the beginning of a word).
- Sound /i/ as in *gym*.
- Sound /ee/ at the end of a two-syllable word as in *bunny, mummy* and *baby*.
- Sound /ie/ at the end of one-syllable words as in *my, cry* and *by*.

These will be taught individually later, so please do not try to teach now.

Sound /x/, spelling *x*

Revise previous sound-letter links: /y/.

Introduce new sound: *fox, box, six, next, explain, extra.* (The letter *x* represents two speech sounds – *ks*.)

X

Finger trace:

Find the letter:

oa	w	ie
z	v	oo
x	ng	y

Pencil trace:

Write on own:

Make a word: (use the words from 'Read the words' below)

Switch the sound: *mix → six → fix → fox → box.*

Read the words:

fix	fox	box	six
next	mix	wax	text
sixteen	toolbox	exit	boxing

Sound /sh/, spelling *sh*

Revise previous sound-letter links: /y/ and /x/.

Introduce new sound: *shop, shoe, shut, washing, pushing, crashing, swish, fish, brush.*

sh

Finger trace:

Find the letter:

ch	ng	sh
w	z	v
x	or	oo

Pencil trace:

Write on own:

_____

....

....

_____

Make a word: (use the words from 'Read the words' below)

Switch the sound: 1. *shock → shot → shop → ship → sheep → sheet → short.*

2. *wish → fish → dish → dash → cash → crash → rash → lash → splash → splosh.*

Read the words:

shop	fish	shed	dish
shut	shock	wish	ship
cash	shoot	crash	splash

Sound /ch/, spelling *ch*

Revise previous sound-letter links: /y/, /x/ and /sh/.

Introduce new sound: *chair, chop, chicken marching, butcher, teacher, much, such, torch.*

ch

Finger trace:

Find the letter:

oo	ng	x
z	ch	or
w	v	y

Pencil trace:

Write on own:

_____

....

....

_____

Make a word: (use the words from 'Read the words' below)

Switch the sound: 1. *chain → chin → chick → chip → chop → chap → champ.*

2. *such → much → munch → lunch → punch → pinch.*

Read the words:

chop	chin	rich	much
chat	such	chick	lunch
chain	bench	torch	pinch

Sound /th/, spelling *th*

Revise previous sound-letter links: /x/, /sh/ and /ch/.

Introduce new sound: "This is the quiet *th* sound which is made with no voice activated – *thing, thumb, thick, birthday, toothy, healthy, path, teeth, cloth*."

th

Finger trace:

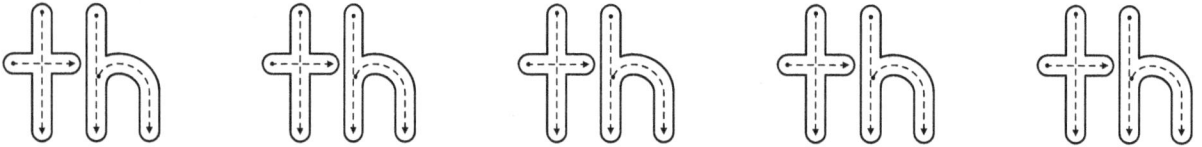

Find the letter:

v	oo	sh
ng	z	y
x	or	th

Pencil trace:

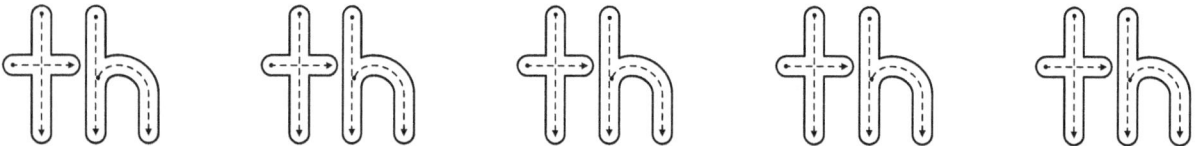

Write on own:

_____

....

....

_____

Make a word: (use the words from 'Read the words' below)

Switch the sound: 1. *thing → thin → think → thick → this → thus → thud → thug → thut → that* (*thut* is a non-word).

2. *teeth → tooth → booth → mooth → mouth → moth → loth → cloth* (*mooth* is a non-word).

Read the words:

think	cloth	thin	three
moth	thick	thing	thud
teeth	thorn	tooth	tenth

Sound /th/, spelling *th*

Revise previous sound-letter links: /ch/, /sh/ and the quiet *th*.

Introduce new sound: "This is the noisy *th* sound which is made with the voice activated – ***this, that, the, these, brother, mother, breathe, with.***"

th

Finger trace:

Find the letter:

ch	sh	z
y	th	v
x	or	oo

Pencil trace:

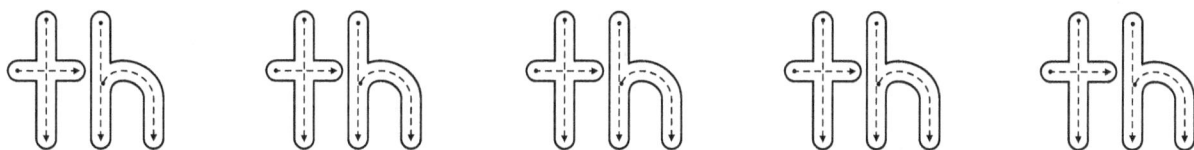

Write on own:

Make a word: (use the words from 'Read the words' below)

Read the words:

that	this	then
them	with	within

Sound /kw/, spelling *qu*

Revise previous sound-letter links: Revise the sound-letter links that your child does not know automatically.

Introduce new sound: *qu* represents two sounds, one is /kw/ – **qu**een, **qu**ick, **qu**iz, **qu**ack, li**qu**id, s**qu**irrel, s**qu**are.

qu

Finger trace:

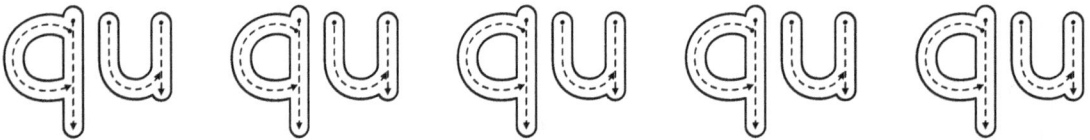

Find the letter:

x	qu	ch
y	oo	v
w	sh	th

Pencil trace:

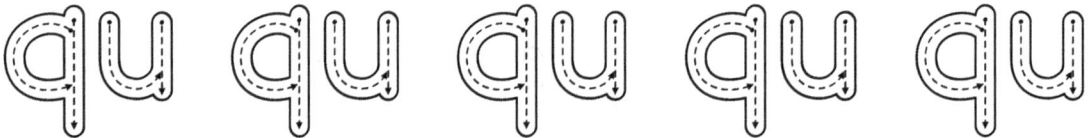

Write on own:

_____

Make a word: (use the words from 'Read the words' below)

Switch the sound: *quit → quiz → quid → squid → quid → quick → quack.*

Read the words:

quack	quiz	quick	queen
quit	quail	squid	quilt

Sound /ou/, spelling *ou*

Revise previous sound-letter links: /qu/.

Introduce new sound: *out, shout, loud, house, mouth, round, count, sound, couch.*

ou

Finger trace:

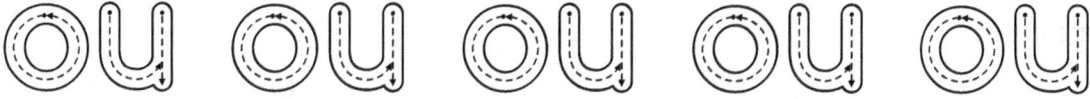

Find the letter:

oo	th	y
ch	sh	w
v	ou	qu

Pencil trace:

Write on own:

_____

....

....

_____

Make a word: (use the words from 'Read the words' below)

Switch the sound: *spout → snout → out → shout → pout → lout → loud → cloud → clout → count.*

Read the words:

out	couch	loud	sound
round	count	found	shout
cloud	spout	ground	without

You may be wondering why I have not included *house* and *mouse* in the above reading list. The reason is that we have not taught the *se* ending yet, which is another way of spelling the /s/ sound.

If you feel this will not confuse your child, then please add these words to the list. Most children will be able to read the word because by the time they sound it out, they will recognise the word. If your child pronounces the *e* at the end, then please tell them that *se* is another spelling of the sound /s/.

Sound /oi/, spelling *oi*

Revise previous sound-letter links: /qu/ and /ou/.

Introduce new sound: *oil, oink, boil, soil, join, coin, poison, toilet, spoil.*

oi

Finger trace:

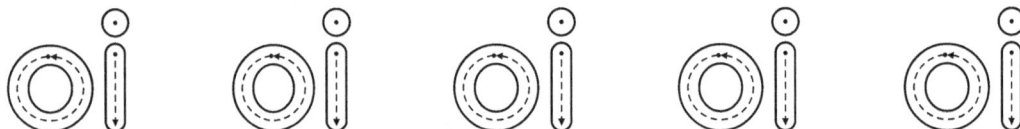

Find the letter:

oi	th	qu
ch	oo	w
sh	v	ou

Pencil trace:

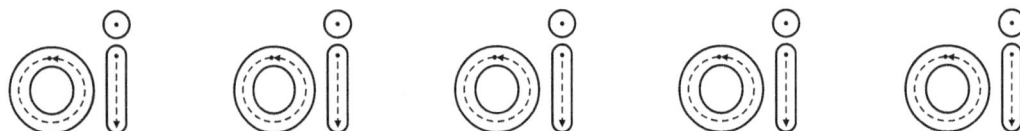

Write on own:

_____

Make a word: (use the words from 'Read the words' below)

Switch the sound: *oil → boil → soil → coil → coin → join → joins → joint → point → points.*

Read the words:

oil	coil	join	joint
boil	coin	soil	spoil
point	boiling	joining	toilet

Sound /oo/, spelling *ue*

Revise previous sound-letter links: /qu/, /ou/ and /oi/.

Introduce new sound: Sound /oo/, spelling *ue* – *blue, glue, true, Sue, untrue, gluing.*

ue

Finger trace:

Find the letter:

ou	th	ue
ch	v	w
qu	oo	oi

Pencil trace:

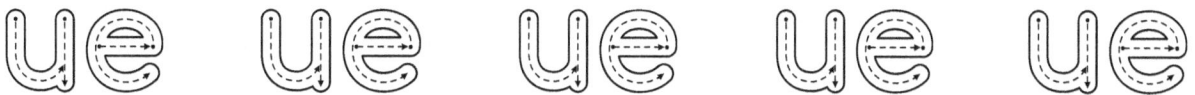

Write on own:

_____

Make a word: (use the words from 'Read the words' below)

Switch the sound: *true → rue → sue → cue → clue → blue → glue → glued.*

Read the words:

Please revise the meaning of the prefix *un-* with your child. It turns the base words – for example, *true* and *glue* – into the opposite meaning.

You can also point out that adding *d* to glue to make it *glued* means that it has already happened. "I glued the paper together at school today." Please also point out that Sue is a name, so it has a capital letter.

You may think that the words *cue* and *rescue* should be also in this list, but they have a different sound, like "yoo".

Sound /yoo/, spelling *ue*

Introduce new sound: sound /yoo/, spelling *ue* – *due, cue, venue, value, argue, statue, rescue.*

ue

Finger trace:

Find the letter:

ou	th	er
ch	ue	ar
sh	oo	oi

Pencil trace:

Write on own:

_____

Make a word: (use the words from 'Read the words' below)

Read the words:

due	cue	rescue	Tuesday
continue	venue	argue	value

Take the time to define new words that your child does not know.

The word *continue* may look very long and scary to your child, but you can help them read it by breaking it into its syllables. Sound out the first three sounds then blend together: *c-o-n – con*, then the next three sounds and blend together *t-i-n – tin*, then the last sound *ue*. Now put the three parts together: *con-tin-ue – continue*.

Sound /er/, spelling *er*

Revise previous sound-letter links: sound /oo/, spelling *ue* and sound /yoo/, spelling *ue*.

Introduce new sound: *her, herb, mermaid, person, fern, germ, tiger, sister.*

er

Finger trace:

Find the letter:

ng	oi	er
sh	e	a
k	th	ck

Pencil trace:

Write on own:

_____

Make a word: (use the words from 'Read the words' below)

Switch the sound: *her → herd → herb → verb → ver → ever → never → clever* (*ver* is a non-word).

Read the words:

As with the sound /or/ at the end of words, Australians tend not to produce the sound /er/ fully but rather shorten it into a schwa; for example, *sister* as "sista" and *silver* as "silva".

Here are some more double letters. When adding the suffix *-er* to a base word, it becomes a comparative. For example, *hot* becomes *hotter*. Again, it has one syllable, a single vowel and one consonant at the end, and the doubling is to protect the vowel from changing sound.

Sound /ar/, spelling *ar*

Revise previous sound-letter links: sound /oo/, spelling ue, and sound /yoo/, spelling ue, and /er/.

Introduce new sound: *art, arm, apart, march, party, farm, shark, car, star.*

ar

Finger trace:

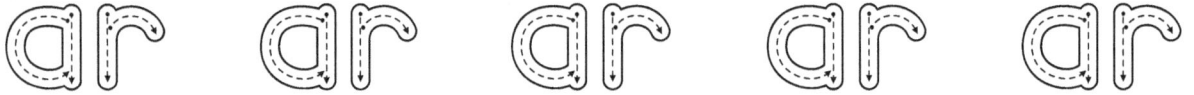

Find the letter:

ar	oi	p
y	th	a
ue	i	sh

Pencil trace:

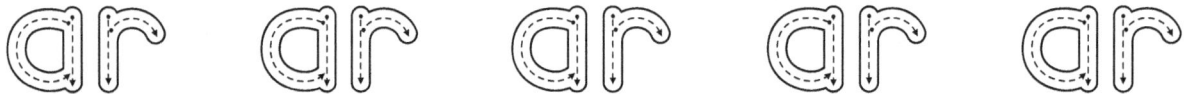

Write on own:

_____

....

....

_____

Make a word: (use the words from 'Read the words' below)

Switch the sound: *park → shark → ark → art → arm → far → car → cart → card → hard.*

Read the words:

art	far	arm	hard
star	shark	part	car
park	march	smart	sharper

Adding the comparative suffix -er to words like *smart* and *sharp* does not require the last letter to be doubled as they have a long vowel.

We have now taught your child the simple code for 42 out of the 44 phonemes (speech sounds) that we use in English. In the *Jolly Phonics* program, after that last sound-letter link is taught, they do not introduce any new ones for five weeks. During this time, there is lots of practice blending two- to five-sound words and revising all the sound-letter links. This is a great time to consolidate all that your child has learnt and ensure it is learnt to automaticity.

Over the next 5 weeks, revise each sound-letter link by completing "Make a word", "Switch the sound", reading individual words from the "Read the word" tables as well as through games and by reading lots of decodable books. Your child may start to group common letter patterns together and won't need to sound out the whole word. For example, -ack (*back, pack, sack*), -ap (*cap, map, rap, tap*), -ain (*rain, brain, chain*).

As you now know the English language does not have a one-to-one correspondence where there is one sound for each letter. It also has many different spellings of the same sounds, which is what we will now delve further into. In the first year of schooling, these alternative spellings of sounds are only introduced. In the second year of schooling, they are revised and practised until automaticity. Please do not expect that your child has to master them after the first "teaching". They will need lots of repetition and practice.

Teaching alternate vowels

Sound /ee/, spelling *y*

Introduce new sound: "There are often other spellings of the speech sounds in words. I have taught you that the spelling *ee* can be used for the speech sound /ee/. I am now going to show you another way to spell the speech sound /ee/. This spelling is at the end of two-syllable words like *bunny, very, funny, baby, happy* and *party*."

Trace with a pencil and say the sound /ee/: "Trace over the letter. As you are writing, say the sound. I'll do one first, then we'll do one together and then you can have a go by yourself."

y y y y y

Write on own and say the sound /ee/: "Great writing. Now try writing it on your own. Remember to say the sound as you write the letter."

_____

....

....

_____

Make a word: (use the words from 'Read the words' below)

You will see that there are many words below with double letters: *dolly, puppy, mummy*. There is no hard-and-fast rule here, but the middle consonant is usually doubled when the word has two syllables, the first vowel is short, and there is one consonant between the vowels (*y* works as a vowel at the end of a word). Examples include *rabbit, sudden, muffin, button*. The reason why they are doubled is to "protect" the vowel for words ending in *y* (as below) and *le*. If *happy* was spelt *hapy*, then you may pronounce the *a* as the long /ai/ sound.

The reading of these words is often easier than the spelling! When introducing the "Make a Word", tell your child that some of these words have two letters spelling the sound in the middle.

Switch the sound: *funny → bunny → runny → dunny → dummy → tummy → mummy → muddy → Maddy → daddy*.

Read the words:

dolly	puppy	bunny	silly
lumpy	bumpy	body	lucky
funny	tummy	happy	teddy

Read, sort and write: Cut out the words and ask your child to read each word by sounding out and blending together as they go and then place (not glue) under the correct spelling. You may like to ask your child to highlight or underline the /ee/ spelling (*ee* or *y*) in each word first to make it easier for them to read. After that, take off the words, and ask your child to write the words under each spelling choice, saying the sounds as they go. At this stage, they are able to look at the word if needed whilst writing.

ee	y (/ee/ sound at end of words)		
		sheep	green
		funny	body
		lucky	feet
		meet	keep
		mummy	copy

This next group of sound-letter links are tricky and are called different names, most commonly "bossy e", "magic e" or "split digraph". In this book, we are going to refer to them as one of the many jobs of final e.

Final e: In some words, the final E at the end of the word reaches back around the consonant letter and changes the sound of the vowel before it to its long sound. Here are some examples:

- *home* – the final e tells us to use the long sound /oe/.
- *made* – the final e tells us to use the long sound /ai/.
- *Steve* – the final e tells us to use the long sound /ee/.

Here are some examples of how adding the final E to words changes the vowel sound from short to long:

cut	cute
mad	made
pet	Pete
cop	cope
hid	hide

Sound /ai/, spelling *a_e*

Revise previous sound-letter links: Sound /ee/ spelt with *y* as well as any other previous sound-letter links that your child does not know automatically.

Pencil trace: Say /ai/ as writing the letters.

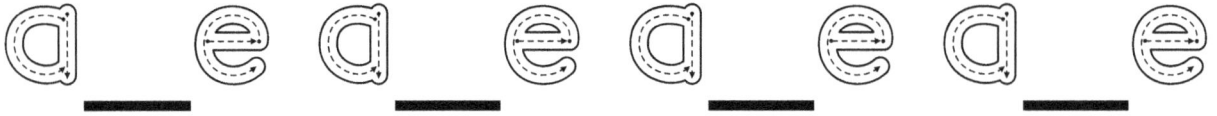

a_e a_e a_e a_e

Write on own:

Make a word: (use the words from 'Read the words' below)

Switch the sound: *ate → ape → tape → cape → cake → cave → gave → game → name → came → cake → lake*.

Read the words:

ate	game	ape	cake
bake	hate	came	snake
cave	lake	plane	made

Read, sort and write: Your child has learnt two spellings of the /ai/ speech sound.

ai	a_e		
		made	cage
		wait	pain
		paid	rain
		late	chase
		aim	bake

You can extend this activity by adding the suffix *-ing* to words such as *aiming, waiting, raining*. For now, do not try words that you have to drop the *e* to add *-ing*; for example, *bake – baking*. This will be covered in chapter 5: Spelling. You can also add the past tense suffix *-ed*, such as *waited, rained, aimed*.

Sound /ee/, spelling *e_e*

Revise previous sound-letter links: Sound /ee/ spelt with *y* and sound /ai/ spelt *a_e*.

Pencil trace:

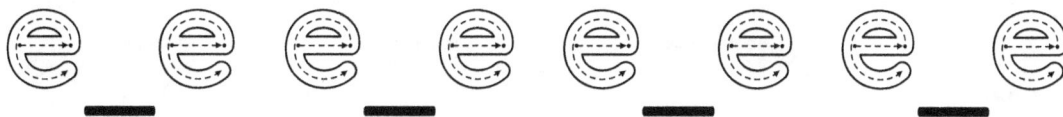

Write on own:

Make a word: (use the words from 'Read the words' below)

Read the words:

Eve	even	these	Steve
Pete	theme	uneven	compete

Please explain to your child that *Eve*, *Steve* and *Pete* are all names, therefore they need a capital letter. You may want to write your name and your child's name to show that they also have capital letters.

Read, sort and write:

ee	e_e		
		sheep	Pete
		meet	sleep
		eve	these
		tree	queen
		theme	even

Sound /ie/, spelling *i_e*

Pencil trace:

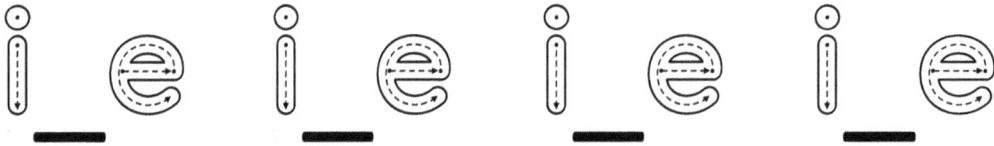

Write on own:

Make a word: (use the words from 'Read the words' below)

Switch the sound: *ride → side → tide → time → lime → life → live → hive → hike → bike.*

Read the words:

ride	nine	five	bikes
life	side	time	mine
bite	hive	kite	timed

Read, sort and write:

ie	i_e		
		pie	bike
		ride	tie
		like	died
		lies	bite
		mine	lie

Sound /oa/, spelling *o_e*

Pencil trace:

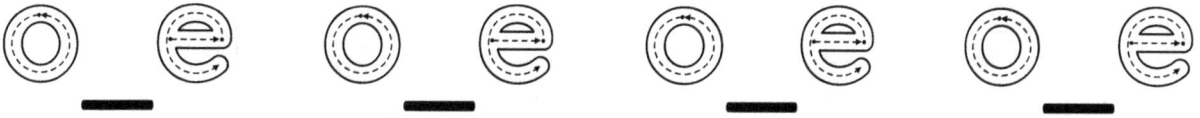

Write on own:

Make a word: (use the words from 'Read the words' below)

Switch the sound: *robe → rope → hope → home → hole → pole → poke → choke → woke → joke.*

Read the words:

home	joke	pole	stone
note	bone	hope	spoke
ropes	hole	choked	smoke

Read, sort and write: Your child has now been introduced to two spellings of the /oa/ sound.

oa	o_e		
		soap	loaf
		boat	note
		hope	joke
		bone	home
		road	float

Sound /yoo/, spelling *u_e*

Pencil trace:

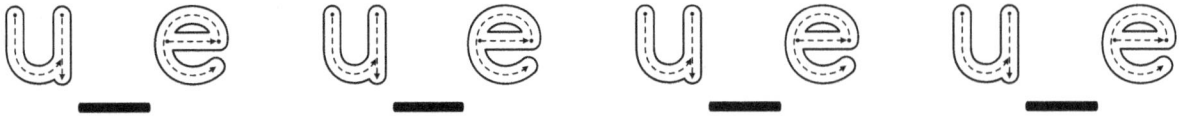

Write on own:

Make a word: (use the words from 'Read the words' below)

Switch the sound: *fuse → use → ute → cute → cube → tube → lube → Luke → fluke → flute.*

Read the words:

cute	rude	ute	used
fume	use	flute	tube
nude	cube	utes	costume

Read, sort and write: Your child has now been introduced to two spellings of the /yoo/ sound.

ue	u_e		
		argue	ute
		cute	cube
		rescue	due
		use	venue
		cue	tube

Sound /ai/, spelling *ay*

Pencil trace:

Write on own:

Make a word: (use the words from 'Read the words' below)

Switch the sound: *clay → play → lay → may → hay → way → day → say → stay → stays.*

Read the words:

say	play	stay	way
clay	hay	trays	day
staying	may	spray	played

Read, sort and write: Your child has now been introduced to three spellings for the /ai/ sound.

ai	a_e	ay			
			day	paint	make
			ate	name	chain
			wait	play	stay
			way	say	came
			train	snail	made

Your child may have noticed the pattern when doing the word sorts. The digraph *ay* is used when it is the last sound in a word or syllable (such as *playing*). The *ai* spelling is used before a consonant.

Sound /oi/, spelling *oy*

Pencil trace:

Write on own:

_____

....

....

_____

Make a word: (use the words from 'Read the words' below)

Switch the sound: *toy → boy → boys → joys → joy → toy → toys.*

Read the words:

toy	boy	joy	enjoy
enjoying	enjoyed	toys	boys
annoy	annoying	annoyed	ploy

When adding a plurals *s* to the end of the word, it often sounds more like a /z/sound. This is also the case in words such as *was, has, is.*

Read, sort and write:

oi	oy		
		boy	oil
		point	toy
		joy	joint
		enjoy	spoil
		ploy	coin

Sound /ie/, spelling *y*

As mentioned previously, the letter *y* can also be used to spell the /ie/ sound in words such as *dry*, *my*, *cry*, *fly*, *by* and *spy*.

Pencil trace:

Write on own:

Make a word: (use the words from 'Read the words' below)

Switch the sound: *shy → by → my → spy → sty → sky → try → cry → dry.*

Read the words:

fly	by	my	dry
try	sky	shy	cry
spy	fly	pigsty	myself

Read, sort and write: Your child has now been introduced to three spellings of the /ie/ sound.

ie	i_e	y			
			ride	fly	by
			die	pie	nine
			like	my	five
			sky	tie	lie
			lied	bite	spy

Sound /ee/, spelling *ea*

Pencil trace:

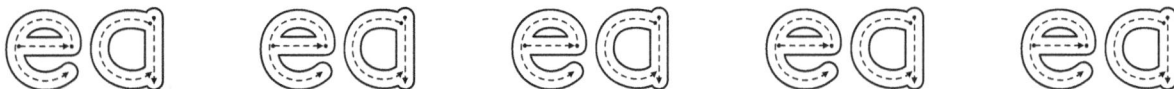

Write on own:

_____

_____

_____

_____

Make a word: (use the words from 'Read the words' below)

Switch the sound: *beach → each → eat → meat → seat → neat → heat → heap → cheap → leap.*

Read the words:

eat	meat	teach	heap
leaf	pea	seat	beak
beach	neat	dream	each

Read, sort and write: Your child has been introduced to four spellings of the /ee/ sound.

ee	y	e_e	ea				
				funny	meat	see	footy
				sheep	even	eat	bean
				mummy	leaf	tree	eve
				body	these	jeep	uneven
				theme	dusty	tea	sheet

Sound /ie/, spelling *igh*

This is a trigraph; that is, one sound, three letters.

Pencil trace:

Write on own:

Make a word: (use the words from 'Read the words' below)

Switch the sound: *high → sigh → sight → light → fight → fright → right → night → light → lights.*

Read the words:

high	fight	light	sigh
thigh	night	tight	fights
right	lights	flight	sunlight

Read, sort and write: Your child has been introduced to three spellings of the /ie/ sound.

ie	i_e	igh			
			light	pie	shine
			time	fight	die
			high	like	flies
			size	tied	right
			untie	sigh	wide

Sound /oa/, spelling *ow*

Pencil trace:

Write on own:

_____

. . . .

. . . .

_____

Make a word: (use the words from 'Read the words' below)

Switch the sound: *bow → low → blow → slow → slows → slower → lower → rower → grower → grow.*

Read the words:

low	snow	snows	bow
blow	own	slow	showed
show	slower	grow	growing

When adding the comparative suffix *-er* to words that end in *w* and *x*, do not double the consonant.

Read, sort and write: Your child has been introduced to three spellings of the /oa/ sound.

oa	o_e	ow			
			boat	throw	moat
			spoke	coat	home
			snow	shown	note
			hope	low	grow
			croak	foam	rope

Sound /ou/, spelling *ow*

Pencil trace:

Write on own:

_____

....

....

_____

Make a word: (use the words from 'Read the words' below)

Switch the sound: *now → cow → ow → owl → howl → how.*

Read the words:

how	now	owl	cow
town	clown	down	howl
frown	brown	crowd	shower

Read, sort and write: Your child has been introduced to the two main spellings of the /ou/ sound.

ou	ow		
		out	brown
		loud	shout
		down	how
		cow	count
		mouth	now

Sound /er/, spelling *ir*

Pencil trace:

Write on own:

_____

....

....

_____

Make a word: (use the words from 'Read the words' below)

Switch the sound: *birth → bird → third → thirst → thirsty → thirst → first → fir → sir → stir.*

Read the words:

bird	girl	stir	shirt
dirt	dirty	skirt	first
birth	birthday	third	thirteen

Read, sort and write: Your child has been introduced to two spellings of the /er/ sound.

er	ir		
		girl	dirt
		fern	under
		herd	skirt
		shirt	verb
		stir	finger

At the ends of words, Australians shorten the *er* sound to a schwa. So, *finger* sounds like "finga".

Sound /er/, spelling *ur*

Pencil trace:

Write on own:

Make a word: (use the words from 'Read the words' below)

Switch the sound: *hurt → blurt → blur → bur → urn → turn → burn → burnt → burst.*

Read the words:

fur	burn	turn	hurt
curl	burning	church	burst
surf	sunburn	turning	turned

Read, sort and write: Your child has been introduced to three spellings of the /er/ sound.

er	ir	ur			
			girl	dirt	burn
			fern	under	curl
			herd	skirt	turn
			shirt	verb	burger
			stir	finger	fur

Sound /yoo/, spelling *ew*

Pencil trace:

Write on own:

Make a word: (use the words from 'Read the words' below)

Switch the sound: *dew → pew → few → fewer → newer → new → stew → stews*. Please help your child with the two sounds added from *new* to *stew*.

Read the words:

new	newer	newest	dew
few	fewer	fewest	pew
curfew	stew	stews	stewing

We have now introduced another morphological ending, *-est*. This ending is the superlative, which means the "best". This can be explained by listing the adjective, comparative and superlative in that order; for example, *big, bigger, biggest*.

If you had physical objects to use in a demonstration, then that can be helpful. For example, find pencils of different lengths then say, "This one is long, but this one is longer and this one is the longest."

Read, sort and write: Your child has been introduced to three spellings of the /yoo/ sound.

u_e	ue	ew			
			few	due	cue
			nude	cube	venue
			stew	ute	new
			newer	rescue	use
			cute	Tuesday	due

Sound /or/, spelling *au*

Pencil trace:

Write on own:

_____

....

....

_____

Make a word: (use the words from 'Read the words' below)

Read the words:

Paul	laundry	August	haul
author	launch	haunt	haunted

Read, sort and write: Your child has been introduced to two spellings of the /or/ sound.

or	au		
		for	Paul
		author	or
		sort	August
		haunt	corn
		form	haunted

Sound /or/, spelling *aw*

Pencil trace:

Write on own:

_____

....

....

_____

Make a word: (use the words from 'Read the words' below)

Switch the sound: *claw → law → paw → jaw → saw → raw → draw → draws → drawn → dawn → lawn.*

Read the words:

paw	draw	saw	straw
jaw	lawn	crawl	claw
yawn	jigsaw	drawing	seesaw

Read, sort and write: Your child has been introduced to three spellings of the /or/ sound.

or	au	aw			
			straw	for	draw
			sort	Paul	sport
			paw	saw	haunt
			form	August	launch
			haul	lawn	or

Sound /or/, spelling *al*

Pencil trace:

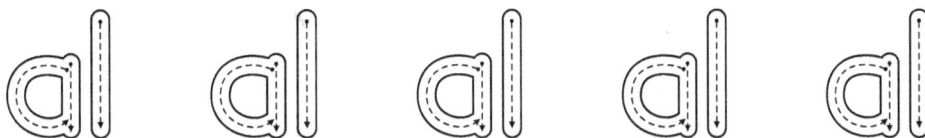

Write on own:

_____

_____

_____

_____

Make a word: (use the words from 'Read the words' below)

Switch the sound: *all → hall → fall → call → tall → talk → walk → chalk.*

Read the words:

all	hall	fall	walk
call	calling	falling	small
chalk	talk	talking	talked

Read, sort and write: Your child has been introduced to four spellings of the /or/ sound.

or	au	aw	al				
				small	paw	August	haul
				jaw	call	launch	all
				or	talk	sport	yawn
				sort	draw	saw	torn
				walk	for	Paul	haunt

Teaching alternate consonants

Sound /f/, spelling *ph*

Pencil trace:

Write on own:

Make a word: (use the words from 'Read the words' below)

Read the words:

phone	dolphin	nephew	phonic
Philip	photo	graph	phones

Photo may be a tricky word as we have not introduced *o* as a spelling of /oa/, unless you have taught the high-frequency words such as *go*, *no*, and *so*. If you have, please explain to your child that photo has the same *o* spelling that represents the /oa/ sound.

Read, sort and write: Same sound, different spelling.

f	ph		
		fish	frog
		flat	photo
		phone	nephew
		gift	if
		dolphin	photos

Sound /s/, spelling c

The way we pronounce the c spelling depends on the vowel afterwards. When followed by a, u, or o, it is a /k/ sound, often called the "hard c". When followed by an i, e or y, it is an /s/ sound, often called the "soft c".

Make a word: (use the words from 'Read the words' below)

Switch the sounds: ice → mice → dice → rice → race → face → pace → space → ace → lace.

Read the words:

city	ice	rice	dice
face	space	race	cent
circus	mice	pencil	spaceship

Read, sort and write: Same sound, different spelling.

| s | c | | |
	(sound /s/)		
		city	ice
		mice	sort
		sand	cent
		sat	star
		pencil	sit

Read, sort and write: Same spelling, different sound.

| c | c | | |
(sound /k/)	(sound /s/)		
		cat	mice
		cent	cot
		picnic	cycle
		city	circus
		cut	pencil

Sound /j/, spelling *g*

The way we pronounce the *g* spelling depends on the vowel afterwards. When followed by *a, u,* or *o,* it is a /g/ sound, often called the "hard g". When followed by an *i, e* or *y,* it is a /j/ sound, often called "soft g". *However,* there are exceptions to this rule: *get, geese, gecko, gift, give, girl* and *tiger.*

Make a word: (use the words from 'Read the words' below)

Switch the sounds: *stage → sage → age → page → cage → caged → cages → pages → ages → aged.*

Read the words:

age	page	cage	caged
huge	stage	germ	germs
gem	energy	magic	digit

I have not added words such as *fridge, bridge, hedge* as they have *dge* spelling of the sound /j/ which we have not covered yet.

Read, sort and write: Same sound, different spelling.

j	g (sound /j/)		
		jump	page
		huge	gem
		joint	jet
		jam	germ
		age	job

Read, sort and write: Same spelling, different sound.

g (*g* sound)	g (*j* sound)		
		go	tag
		gut	huge
		gem	page
		age	green
		pig	germ

Sound /w/, spelling *wh*

In some accents the *h* is pronounced, so if this is you, then please skip to the next sound.

Make a word: (use the words from 'Read the words' below)

Read the words: Some of these words have already been introduced to your child.

when	which	whip	whirl
what	why	whale	white
wheat	wheel	while	whatever

Read, sort and write:

w	wh		
		when	web
		went	what
		whale	week
		wait	whip
		which	win

Some phonics programs will cover all of the above sound-letter links in the first year of schooling (and possibly more), whereas some take two years. Many of the sound-letter links are only *introduced* and then at the beginning of the following year are *revised* with lots of practice before anything else is taught.

In your child's second year of schooling, please go back and complete the activities again. Your child may like to do the same activities as the first time or you can use different games and activities and words. The key is for them to get repeated practice in words as well as in connected text.

If you did not get through all of the sound-letter links, continue on, ensuring that you revise previous ones as you go. Over the summer school break (normally five to six weeks), your child may be reluctant to complete academic activities. It's ok not to pursue the more structured teaching during this time, but as we do often see a drop in reading skills over extended holiday periods, please ensure that your child reads to you every day.

If your child is managing well and knows all of his/her sound-letter links to automaticity and is blending and segmenting to read and to spell words, then continue on through this book.

Your child may need more repetition and practice with different activities than what I can provide in this book, so please use the resources outlined in Further information.

I cannot stress enough how important it is for children who are new to reading to practise regularly with decodable readers.

Sound /f/, spelling *ff*

A general spelling rule is that in a single-syllable word, with a single short vowel which is immediately followed by an *f, l, s,* or *z,* the final letter is doubled.

Make a word: (use the words from 'Read the words' below)

Switch the sound: *buff → puff → piff → tiff → stiff → sniff → snuff → stuff → scuff → cuff.*

Read the words:

stuff	tiff	sniff	scuff
cliff	off	puff	buff
stiff	cuff	handcuff	sheriff

Read, sort and write:

f	ph (sound /f/)	ff (sound /f/)			
			phone	stuff	frog
			off	dolphin	if
			fish	photos	stiff
			puff	lift	photo
			cliff	nephew	fun

Please take the time to explain the meaning of words that your child does not know. For example, a *tiff* is a small fight and a *scuff* is a mark left if you scrape against something. Make sure you relate it to something they have experienced with examples.

Sound /l/, spelling *ll*

Make a word: (use the words from 'Read the words' below)

Switch the sound: *ill → hill → bill → bell → sell → sill → dill → doll.*

Read the words:

bill	hill	bell	still
sell	doll	will	fell
sill	shell	drill	troll

Sound /s/, spelling *ss*

Make a word: (use the words from 'Read the words' below)

Switch the sound: *hiss → kiss → miss → mess → dress → press → stress.*

Please help your child where they have to add two sounds for "Switch the sound"; for example, *mess* to *dress* and *press* to *stress.*

Read the words:

miss	hiss	fuss	stress
press	boss	dress	mess
mass	lass	kiss	cross

In Australia, the words *class, glass, grass, pass* have an /ar/ sound, spelt with *a*. We have not taught that sound-letter link yet, so I have not included those words.

Read, sort and write:

S	C (sound /s/)	SS (sound /s/)			
			sit	kiss	boss
			city	cross	dress
			mess	cent	self
			mice	nice	yes
			bus	sock	face

Sound /z/, spelling *zz*

Make a word: (use the words from 'Read the words' below)

Switch the sound: *buzzer → buzz → fuzz → fuzzy → fizzy → fizz → frizz → frizzy → fizzy → dizzy.*

Read the words:

buzz	fuzz	fuzzy	buzzer
fizz	fizzy	jazz	frizz
buzzing	fizzing	dizzy	jazzy

Letters that we often refer to as "silent" are actually the result of a change in pronunciation over time. Centuries ago, the /b/, /w/ and /k/ sounds were pronounced in the following list of words. These sound-letter links may not be introduced until the third year of schooling.

Sound /m/, spelling *mb*

Make a word: (use the words from 'Read the words' below)

Read the words:

lamb	comb	numb	crumb
thumb	combed	dumb	limb
bomb	climb	climbing	climbed

Read, sort and write:

m	mb (sound /m/)		
		pram	aim
		climb	dream
		stem	thumb
		comb	dumb
		lamb	broom

The *b* is also not pronounced in the words *doubt* or *debt*.

Sound /r/, spelling *wr*

Make a word: (use the words from 'Read the words' below)

Read the words:

wrist	wrap	write	wrong
wring	wrung	wreck	wriggle
wry	wrote	wrench	wrapper

I haven't directly taught the *le* ending yet (usually taught in Grade 3) but your child might be able to read the word *wriggle* accurately, because by the time they decode it, they have matched the word to one they know in their vocabulary. If they do pronounce /e/, please tell them that when *le* is at the end of a word, so only say "l". You can show your child some other words with that ending too, such as *turtle, purple, little, bubble, simple*.

Read, sort and write:

r	wr (sound /r/)		
		right	write
		room	two
		wrap	rock
		red	wrist
		wrong	ran

This is a great time to discuss homophones with your child. Homophones are words that sound the same but differ in meaning and spelling. Here are some examples:

- *rap* and *wrap*
- *right* and *write*
- *rapper* and *wrapper*
- *ring* and *wring*

As there are relatively few words in English that have a silent *w* it may be difficult for your child to remember how to read and to spell them. It may be useful to look at the origin of the words. Words that has sound /r/ with the spelling *wr* usually refer to twisting. For example, *wrap* is twisting paper, your *wrist* can twist, to *wreck* means to twist something out of its usual form, to *wriggle* means to twist around, *wry* means a twisted sense of humour and *writing* is twisting the form of letters.

Sound /h/, spelling *wh*

The /w/ is also not pronounced in a small number of words starting with the *wh* spelling.

Make a word: (use the words from 'Read the words' below)

Read the words:

who	whom	whole	whose

The *w* is also kept silent in the word *two,* as well as *sword* and *answer.*

Sound /n/, spelling *kn*

Make a word: (use the words from 'Read the words' below)

Read the words:

knight	knee	knew	knock
know	knit	knife	knot
knack	kneel	knob	knuckle

Read, sort and write:

n	kn (sound /n/)		
		knight	knife
		night	nine
		knot	knew
		knee	not
		know	need

Put the word in a sentence so that your child can attach meaning to it. For example: At night time we go to bed. The word *night* is spelt with *n.* A *knight* is someone who lives in a castle and rides dragons. This is spelt *kn.*

The word *not,* as in "You are not allowed to do something" is spelt with an *n,* and the *knot* that you tie with your shoelaces is spelt *kn.*

Sound /air/, spelling *air* (trigraph)

Make a word: (use the words from 'Read the words' below)

Switch the sound: *fairy → fair → air → pair → hair → chair → stair → air → airy → hairy.*

Read the words:

air	fair	chair	fairy
pair	stair	hair	hairy
unfair	haircut	upstairs	airport

Sound /air/, spelling *are* (trigraph)

Make a word: (use the words from 'Read the words' below)

Switch the sound: *aware – ware – dare – hare – care – pare – spare – share – tare – stare – stared.*

Read the words:

care	square	stare	careful
dare	spare	rare	aware
hare	scare	scared	share

We have used a suffix here *-ful*. This ending literally means "full of". For example:

- *careful* is "full of care"
- *hopeful* is "full of hope"
- *fearful* is "full of fear"

Sound /air/, spelling *ear* (trigraph)

Make a word: (use the words from 'Read the words' below)

Switch the sound: *tear → pear → pears → bears → bear → wear → swear → swears → wears → wear.*

Read the words:

tear	tearing	wear	wearing
bear	bears	swear	swearing
pear	pears	wearable	bearable

There are only five base words with this spelling of /air/.

We have introduced another suffix *-able*. Adding this means that the base word is able to be done. For example, *breakable* is able to be broken, *readable* is able to be read, *wearable* is able to be worn, and *believable* is able to be believed.

Read, sort and write:

air	are	ear			
			hair	swear	fairy
			bear	chair	wear
			bare	stare	pair
			stair	pear	dare
			scare	spare	tear

Here are some more homophones for you to discuss with your child: *pear* and *pair*, *stair* and *stare*, *bear* and *bare*.

The spelling *ear* can also be a different sound, found in words such as *ear*, *dear*, *hear*, as well as the sound /er/ as in *learn*, *earn* and *earth*. (This is usually covered in a child's fourth year of schooling.)

Sound /e/, spelling *ea*

Make a word: (use the words from 'Read the words' below)

Switch the sound: *lead → head → dead → read → bread → spread → read → dead → deaf.*

Read the words:

head	bread	deaf	feather
heavy	spread	dead	weather
lead	read	spreads	spreading

Read, sort and write:

e	ea (sound /e/)		
		check	heavy
		head	bed
		best	dead
		get	fell
		bread	deaf

Initial /w/ changes sound /a/ to /o/

Make a word: (use the words from 'Read the words' below)

Switch the sound: *want → wand → wad → swad → swat → swab → swan → swap → swamp.* (*Swad* is a not a word.)

Read the words:

was	watch	swan	swap
want	wasp	wand	wander
swamp	swab	wallet	swat

We have not directly taught ending *-tch* as in *watch*. Please point out to your child that it is another trigraph; that is, three letters, one sound (/ch/).

I want to reiterate that the years in which the sound-letter links are taught are not rigid as each structured program teaches sound-letter links in a different order and at a different pace. What I want to emphasise, however, is that if your child has not consolidated all of the sound-letter links taught in this book by the end of their third year of schooling, then keep revising and practising until they do.

Further information

To access my demonstration videos: educatable.com.au/readable-demo.

"Decodable books", *Spelfabet* – spelfabet.com.au/phonics-resources/07-decodable-books/

   This is a comprehensive decodable readers list.

"Phonic Books", *SPELD SA* – speldsa.org.au/speld-phonic-books/

   This page offers free decodable readers and worksheets.

"Resources for Families", *Dyslexia – SPELD Foundation* (*DSF*) – dsf.net.au/resources/home-resources/

   Free phonics resources.

"Advice and Resources", *PhonicBooks* – phonicbooks.co.uk/advice-and-resources/

   The page offers free teaching resources, including advice for teachers and parents.

PhonicsPlay – phonicsplay.co.uk/resources

   Fun online reading games. Be sure to select the sound-letter link your child is currently learning.

Sue Lloyd (co-author of Jolly Phonics) has a printable word list for extra practice – tcrw.co.uk/materials-teaching-children-read-write/

"Phonics Resources", *Spelfabet* – spelfabet.com.au/phonics-resources/

   The website has word lists for extra reading practice as well as a comprehensive list of resources.

"Mr Thorne and the a-e Split Digraph" at *Mr T's Phonics* – youtu.be/W1xqLjHF53A

   This short clip talks about the final e using a_e as an example. The channel has short clips for other phonics.

5

Spelling

My son made a birthday card for his friend. On the front he drew a picture of himself and his friend and his sister. He wrote on the front that his sister is *stoopd*. This, for a 6-year-old, is great spelling! He has yet to learn that the letter *u* can be used to spell the /yoo/ sound, but he knew that in the middle of words you don't use *ue* or *ew*.

The alphabetic code is reversible. Decoding is blending sounds together to read words. Encoding is segmenting sounds to spell words. For both, you need phonemic awareness and sound-letter relationship knowledge, therefore reading and spelling should be taught at the same time, particularly in the first two years of schooling. After that, children benefit from additional explicit instruction in spelling as there are rules that are too complex for a beginner reader.

In chapter 4: Phonics, your child had to write the words as they were learning the sound-letter link. If your school is using a structured synthetic phonics approach, then spelling will be worked on simultaneously in a carefully sequenced way, which is how it should be. Unfortunately, some schools send home word lists to memorise, but the words are unrelated and do not focus on one sound pattern.

You can actually be a super reader but a terrible speller. As detailed in the "Learning to read" overview, 30% of children can learn to read without explicit synthetic phonics instructions. Unfortunately, they may not learn to spell as they have not segmented the words into their sounds and analysed patterns within words.

An example of this is my own husband: smart man, prolific reader, engineer, always wins trivia nights, but cannot spell to save his life. He was never taught at school the sound-letter relationships and the patterns in words and the English language.

Many people think that English is full of irregular spellings of words that just need to be memorised by sight. This is certainly not the case. In fact, according to P.R. Hanna, J.S. Hanna, Hodges, and Rudorf (1966):

- 50% have predictable spelling (based on sound-letter links).
- 36% are predictable except for one sound.

If you take into account where the word comes from and what it means, then only 4% of words are genuinely irregular in spelling. These words may have to be taught and learned visually.

Looking into the history of the English language and spelling is fascinating. The English language we use today is made up of many origins: Anglo-Saxon, Latin, Greek and French. In the previous chapter, your child would have been taught the *ph* spelling of the speech sound /f/; for example, *phone* and *dolphin*. These words are of Greek origin. Also of Greek origin is the *ch* spelling of the sound /k/; for example, *school, scholar, chemist* and *anchor*.

Pronunciation of words has changed significantly over time, but the spellings less so. Silent letters in words such as *climb*, *knee* and *know* hundreds of years ago would have been pronounced. *Said, friend, does* and *enough* are examples of common words that continue to use spellings from up to ten centuries ago when they were pronounced differently.

You may think it's fine if your child can't spell – after all, that's what spellcheckers are for! Unfortunately, a spellchecker only works for those that can spell relatively well. It will not be able to give correct options to words that are way off the mark, nor will it pick up correctly spelt words that are used in the wrong place.

Why spelling is important for reading

Good spelling instruction can help children become better readers as it embeds the knowledge that underpin relationships between sounds and letters as well as word meanings, including base words and suffixes. If you know how to spell a word, then it is imprinted more solidly in your memory and makes it easier for you to recall for fluent reading.

Being a good speller also makes writing that much easier since writing is a complex process. Your child can focus on formulating ideas, putting sentences together, handwriting and punctuation instead of having to stop their flow of writing to remember how to spell a word. Some children lean towards using less complicated words in their writing as they know how to spell them, thus making their written work less compelling.

Knowing the spelling patterns also helps to work out the meaning of words, which, as you know, is the goal of reading – comprehension. For example, if words that sound the same (homophones) are also spelled the same, then it is harder to work out their meaning when reading. Examples include *rain/reign/rein, by/bye, wood/would, there/their/they're, altar/alter, band/banned, allowed/aloud, road/rowed/rode*.

Spelling is also important in our society. As adults, if we come across a poorly spelt job application, or blog, we are more likely to have less confidence about the suitability of the person.

What should my child be able to do?

As we have discussed throughout the book, we have 26 letters in the English alphabet to represent around 44 speech sounds (phonemes). These phonemes can be spelt with one to four letters (graphemes) and there are 75 basic graphemes that need to be taught. There are many more graphemes, more than 170, but not all of these are necessary to teach as some are uncommon. We can spread the teaching of the graphemes over a number of years to make it more manageable for your child and for those who teach.

Some children are able to learn the right spelling choice for when there are different ways to spell a sound through reading. Most children, however, need lots of practice reading and spelling words that have the same spelling pattern in them.

It is normal for your child to make spelling mistakes, particularly in the first three years of schooling. What is important is that those errors are corrected in a positive and helpful way. A tick or a cross means nothing alone; look for patterns in the spelling errors so you know what your child needs help with.

At the beginning of Grade 2 (third year of schooling) they will need to begin to be explicitly taught some spelling rules. These are too overwhelming for a beginner reader, so please practise spelling by always writing the words and completing word sorts when learning the sound-letter relationships as shown in chapter 4: Structured Phonics. Doing this will show the spelling patterns without the cognitive overload of rules.

End of first year of schooling – Your child should be able to write down the letter or grapheme used for most of the speech sounds. Give your child a piece of paper or use a white board and ask your child, "Can you write down the letter that we use for the sound /b/?" Tick or cross next to the letter on the chart below.

s	a	t	i	p	n	c	e
h	r	m	d	g	o	u	l
f	b	j	z	w	v	y	x

The vowel digraphs may need more practice, so do not worry if your child cannot spell them just yet.

ai	oa	ie	ee	or	ng	oo	oo
sh	ch	th	th	qu	ou	oi	ue
er	ar						

They should also know all of the letter names. Your child should be able to segment, or break apart, the sounds in words to be able to write the corresponding letter. This is where a strong foundation in phonemic awareness is essential.

Please use the reading lists in chapter 4: Structured Phonics (page 75 and 76) to check your child's spelling skills (relative to what year of schooling they are up to). Use a lined piece of paper for your child to write down the word that you say. Spelling skills can develop a little later then reading for many children.

Developing spelling

Spelling is not a visual memory task, nor should it be taught as such. Spelling is a language task that, like reading, requires the teaching of speech sounds, sound-letter relationships, meaningful parts of words (bases or roots, and suffixes), origins and history of words. (Word study becomes more of a focus in the upper primary years.) Children can then apply this knowledge to the spelling of many words, not just the ones they have been taught to memorise on unrelated lists.

There are over 100 spelling rules, but there are around 30 important ones. To introduce all of these to a beginner reader will overload them. At this stage, they need lots of practice reading and spelling words that all have the same grapheme in them, not a whole heap of rules to memorise. For example, when learning to read and spell the oi grapheme, your child will note the pattern of where this grapheme is found in the word. Your child needs to be taught that spelling is breaking words into its speech sounds and writing the corresponding letter or letters down.

Once your child is ready to learn spelling rules, typically at the start of their third year of schooling, they will learn how to add suffixes to words, which sound to pronounce when and which grapheme can be used where. When we teach spelling and spelling rules, we use the name of the letters, not their sounds.

Please revise the definitions of what is a consonant and a vowel, as well as short vowels and long vowels in the glossary.

Suffix rules

A suffix is a morpheme (word part) added at the end of a base word (the word that gives it meaning). A suffix can change the base words meaning.

Regular plurals

Instruction script: "When we change a word from meaning one into more than one, we call it a *plural* and the spelling of the word often changes. With most words, we just have to add the letter *s*; for example, *dog – dogs, ball – balls, cup – cups*. The sound is pronounced as /z/ if the word ends in a 'noisy' (voiced) sound. For example, say these words out loud and hold the *s* at the end like "catsss" and "dogzzz". You can hear that in *cats*, it is a /s/ sound as the word ends in the quiet /t/, while in *dogs*, it is a /z/ sound as it ends in the noisy sound /g/. In words that end in *ch*, *sh*, *s*, *ss*, *x* or *z*, the letters *es* are added. Let's practise."

Please do not do all of this at once! It is fine to do one row at a time, then once your child has had lots of practice, complete the mixed-base examples.

Base word	Add plural (-s)	Base word (ends in ch)	Add plural (-es)
cat		torch	
dog		bench	
rat		church	
dream		peach	
tree		beach	
car		lunch	
clock		teach	
boat		branch	
river		munch	
lake		speech	

Base word (ends in *sh*)	Add plural (*-es*)	Base word (ends in *s and ss*)	Add plural (*-es*)
bush		bus	
crash		yes	
dish		plus	
lash		gas	
brush		boss	
wish		mess	
rash		cross	
splash		hiss	
gash		press	
smash		kiss	

Base word (ends in *x and z*)	Add plural (*-es*)	Base word (mixed)	Add plural (*-s* or *-es*)
box		dog	
fox		smash	
mix		kiss	
fix		fix	
six		peach	
wax		boat	
fizz		box	
frizz		cross	
whizz		torch	

Base word	Add plural	Base word	Add plural

Do not expect your child to be able to remember the rule and these spellings after their first practice. They will need many opportunities for repetition. Please use the blank table above to add more words to practise. Tip: when you add the *-es* spelling of plurals, it adds another syllable to the word.

Irregular plurals

Instruction script: "In the following words, when we change them into a plural, the whole word changes. Let's read them together and then you can write the words."

Base word	Plural	
child	children	
tooth	teeth	
foot	feet	
goose	geese	
man	men	
woman	women	
mouse	mice	
person	people	
that	those	
this	these	

The words *woman* and *women* will be difficult for your child to sound out so please help them. The word *people* is an irregular word to spell, so again, they will need lots of help and practice before they will be able to do it on their own correctly.

And some words don't change *at all* when they become plurals.

Base word		Plural	
sheep		sheep	
fish		fish	
deer		deer	
aircraft		aircraft	
moose		moose	

Keep or drop the e rule

With the following practise lists, please do not think that you have to do them all at once.

It is fine to choose one column going down. Once all three columns have been done, you can rub them all out and practise again, this time going across and completing all suffixes for the base word.

Instruction script: "If a word ends in the letter *e*, and we add a suffix that starts with a vowel, we drop the *e*.

"Adding *-ing* to words means that it is happening; for example, 'I am riding later today' and 'I am jumping'.

"Adding -ed to a word means that it has already happened; for example, 'We baked the bread yesterday.' This is called past tense. Often, we can't just add -ed to a word to make it past tense. Sometimes, the whole word changes. For example, 'I am riding later, and I also rode yesterday.' These are called irregular past tense.

"Adding -er to words changes the meaning to 'one who does something'; for example, a teacher is 'one who teaches', a singer is 'one who sings'.

"Let's look at the five examples already done, then I'll do one, then we will do two together, then you can try on your own. Where there is an *, adding that suffix can't be done."

Base word	Add -ing	Add -ed	Add -er
take	taking	* took	taker
make	making	* made	maker
ride	riding	* rode	rider
bake	baking	baked	baker
hope	hoping	hoped	hoper
brave			
bite			
smoke			
tape			
trade			
blame			
slide			
wave			
smile			
close			
joke			
argue			
rescue			
invade			

Instruction script: "If a word ends in e, when we add a suffix that starts with a consonant (-ful, -s) we **keep** the e."

Base word	Add -ful	Add -s
hope	hopeful	hopes
love	*	loves
hate	hateful	hates
force	forceful	forces
use		

plate		
shame		
peace		
grace		
care		

There are many more suffixes than the above examples, but we have not taught them in this book as they are for older children.

Instruction script: "If the base word ends with a consonant and the letter *y*, we have to change the *y* to an *i* then add the suffix."

Base word	Add plural *-es*
baby	babies
body	bodies
fairy	fairies
spy	
cry	
party	
bully	
city	
lolly	
fly	
army	
story	
candy	

Base word (some have suffix y already)	Add *-er*	Add *-est*	Add *-ly*
bossy	bossier	bossiest	bossily
brainy	brainier	brainiest	*
angry	angrier	angriest	angrily
chewy	chewier	chewiest	*
bumpy			
cheeky			
dirty			
dusty			
funny			
happy			

lucky			
messy			
shady			
silly			
easy			
dry			
fizzy			
greedy			
hungry			

Many of these words already have a suffix – *brain + y = brainy, dust + y = dusty, luck + y = lucky, mess + y = messy*. Adding the *y* changes the word from a noun (naming word) into an adjective (describing word).

Instruction script: "If the base word ends with a vowel and the letter *y*, we **keep** the *y* then add the suffix. We also **keep** the *y* if the suffix starts with *i* as you cannot have two *ii*'s together."

Base word	Add -s	Add -ing	Add -ed	Add -er
annoy	annoys	annoying	annoyed	annoyer
boy	boys	*	*	*
play	play	playing	played	player
stay	stays	staying	stayed	stayer
toy	toys	toying	toyed	*
day				
cray				
enjoy				
lay				
employ				
say				
pay				
spray				
stray				

Your child may need extra help with tricky words such as *employ*.

Many of the above cannot have suffixes added to the base words. It is useful to discuss this with your child.

"Have you ever heard of the word *dayer*? The *-er* ending changes the word into 'one who does'. I don't think you can '**do** a day'."

Also note that past tenses in the following words are irregular: *say – said, pay – paid, lay – laid.*

Instruction script: "We also **keep** the *y* if the suffix starts with *i* as you cannot have two *ii*'s together. This means some words are trickier than others."

Base word	Add *-es*	Add *-ing* (keep y)	Add *-ed*	Add *-er*
cry	cries	crying	cried	crier
dry	dries	drying	dried	drier
copy	copies	copying	copied	copier
fly	flies	flying	* flew	flyer
try				
study				
spy				
dirty				
carry				
marry				
hurry				

Suffix doubling rules

Instruction script: "When *f, l, s* or *z* are at the end of one-syllable words, and follow straight after a short vowel, they are spelt with double letters. We learnt this in the chapter on phonics. When we add suffixes to these words they do not change."

Base word	Add *-s* or *-es*	Add *-ing*	Add *-ed*	Add *-er*
sell	sells	selling	* sold	seller
buzz	buzzes	buzzing	buzzed	buzzer
sniff	sniffs	sniffing	sniffed	sniffer
stuff				
press				
chill				
toss				
spill				
stiff				
dress				
fizz				

The exceptions to this rule of spelling words with double letters at the end after a short vowel are: *yes, us, if, plus, bus, quiz.* When the final *s* has sound /z/, it is *not* doubled: *his, was, as, has, is.*

Instruction script: "When we add a suffix that starts with a vowel, we double the last consonant of the word. This is so we don't say the name of the vowel.

"This is often referred to as the 1:1:1 rule – one syllable, one short vowel, ends in one consonant.

"Let's read the first 5 together, then I'll do one, then we can do two together, then you can try on your own."

Base word	Add -*ing*	Add -*ed*	Add -*er*
hop	hopping	hopped	hopper
big	*	*	bigger
dig	digging	* dug	digger
sit	sitting	* sat	sitter
hot	*	*	hotter
clap			
cut			
skip			
pop			
step			
chop			
zip			
sun			
bag			
drum			
sad			
swim			
wet			
run			
drip			

Note: When words end in *x*, the *x* is not doubled as it has two consonant sounds *ks*. The letters *y* and *w* are also never doubled as at the ends of words they are part of a vowel digraph.

Instruction script: "If words do not follow the 1:1:1 rule, then we **do not** double the consonant. Let's look at these examples. In the word *jump*, it ends in two consonants, so we do not double the letter *p*. The word *cash* also ends in two consonants, so no doubling. The words *make* and *look* have long vowel sounds, so we do not double the letter *k*. The word *blow* ends in a long vowel and we never double after a *w*."

Base word	Add -*s* or -*es*	Add -*ing*	Add -*ed*	Add -*er*
jump	jumps	jumping	jumped	jumper
cash	cashes	cashing	cashed	*
make	makes	making	* made	maker

look	looks	looking	looked	looker
blow	blows	blowing	blowed	blower
steal				
pump				
fail				
read				
rain				
fish				
storm				
ring				
duck				
sail				
mark				
lift				
soak				
play				
post				

The following table has mixed endings so that your child can practise adding suffixes. Some require doubling the last letter, others do not. Only complete these after lots of practice.

Base word	Add -s or -es	Add -ing	Add -ed	Add -er
crack				
snow				
end				
pain				
jog				
rip				
lock				
cheat				
join				
mad				
ship				
swoop				
show				
sway				
skip				

In chapter 4: Structured Phonics, we mentioned *le* endings, but not in depth as this is not usually taught until the fourth year of schooling (Grade 3). For your own knowledge, when a short vowel is before the endings *-ble*, *-dle*, *-tle* or *-gle*, the consonant is doubled. For example: *pebble, bubble, middle, muddle, little, bottle, goggle, juggle*. In the word table, the *a* is long, therefore the *b* is not doubled like the word *bubble*.

Past tense, *-ed* endings

Children often read *jumped* as "jump-ed" as that is how it is written, before they correct to the pronunciation "jumpt" which matches the word they have in their vocabulary. When spelling, we often see children use a *t* at the end, or *id* as the sounds differ.

Instruction script: "When we are spelling regular past tense words, the *-ed* spelling can sound different, depending on what the word ends with. If a word ends in a quiet sound, it sounds like a *t*. We always use *-ed* spelling to show that it has happened. Let's read these words and listen to how *-ed* spelling sounds."

Sounds like /t/	Sounds like /d/	Sounds like /id/ or /ed/
jumped	played	dented
watched	called	needed
kissed	cleaned	wanted
looked	nailed	rounded
helped	buzzed	hunted

When the base word ends in a *t* or *d*, adding the past tense *-ed* makes another syllable.

Instruction script: "Now it's your turn to write the words."

Sounds like /t/	Sounds like /d/	Sounds like /id/ or /ed/

"Which sound to pronounce when" rules

Most the following has already been covered in the previous chapter, so please redo those pages with a focus on spelling the words. Your child needs lots of practice spelling, initially while being able to look at the words then moving on to writing independently.

- Silent final *e* has a few functions (also called silent *e*, magic *e*, bossy *e*). When a silent final e is added, it changes the short vowel into a long vowel (or its name) such as *rip/ ripe, cut/cute*. The final *e* is letting us know that we need to produce the vowel as its name in one-syllable words that have the structure vowel + consonant + e. This is also the case when it is the letter *y*; for example, *type* and *hype*.

- The silent final *e* after *th* tells us to produce a voiced sound. Say these pairs of words and listen to the different sound of the *th*: *breath – breathe, bath – bathe, cloth – clothe, teeth – teethe*.

- If we want to pronounce a /k/ sound at the start of words that are followed by an *e, i* or *y*, we need to use the letter *k*, not *c*. The letter *c* sounds like the speech sound /s/ if followed by *e, i* or *y*; for example, *cent, city, cycle*.

- The letter *o* is usually pronounced as /u/ when followed by *m, n, th*, and *v*. For example: *come, some, none, honey, money, mother, brother, love, dove*.

- The letter *c* is pronounced as /s/ when followed by *e, i* or *y*. Otherwise, *c* is pronounced as /k/.

- The letter *g* may soften to a /j/ sound when followed by *e, i* and *y*. Otherwise, *g* is produced as a /g/.

- If a one-syllable word ends in *y*, then it is pronounced /ie/; for example, *fry, cry, my, my, fly*. This is because English words can't end in *i*.

- The letters *i* and *o* may be pronounced as their long sounds, or names, when followed by two consonants; for example, *kind, find, child, climb, wild, old, host, comb, most*. You may hear this referred to as "Kind old words" or "Wild old words" as they stem from long-ago Anglo-Saxon times.

Some other silent final *e* jobs:

- Every syllable must have a written vowel (*table, pickle, bottle*) so if the *e* was not added at the end, then these words would break the rule.

- *e* is added to stop singular words that end in *s* looking like plurals. For example: *dens – dense, moos – moose, teas – tease*.

- Silent final *e* helps with sticking to the rule that no English words end in *i, u* and *v* (*have, live, love*).

- Adding an *e* informs us of the meaning of the words (*by – bye*).

Sometimes, the final *e* does two jobs in the one word. For example, in the word *nice*, it is making the *i* says its name as well as softening the *c* to /s/.

Most final *e*'s are silent, but there are 16 words where it is pronounced. Here are 12 words that are useful and appropriate for young children: *me, be, he, she, we, acne, karate, the* (not always), *recipe, catastrophe, kamikaze, simile*.

"Which grapheme can be used where" rules

Knowledge of letter-pattern rules in words is important for spelling. Here are some common ones:

- The letter *q* is always followed by a *u* and then another a vowel (*queen, quack, quick*).

- English words do not end in the letters *i, u, v* and *j*. It is important for your child to know this so that when they hear words that end in these sounds, they can make a different choice: add a final silent *e*, or choose from different spellings for the one sound, or in the case of *i*, they can use *y*.

Here are some examples:

- Words do not end in *i* – when the vowel sound *i* is heard at the end of words, it is spelt with *y*; for example, *cry, my, dry*. This rule also helps with spelling choices (*oi/oy, ai/ay* and *ei/ey*). You may think there are some exceptions to this rule, but these words are not of English origin. *Spaghetti, broccoli,* and *ravioli* are Italian; *ski* is Norwegian; *chai* is Arabic and *kiwi* is Maori (NZ); and the word *hi* is a slang word for *hello*.

- Words do not end in *u* – this helps when there are spelling choices for the same speech sound; for example, *ou/ow*. The words *cow, how, now* cannot end in *u*, therefore they can't be spelt with the *ou* digraph, so they must use *ow*. Similarly, *saw, paw* and *draw* cannot end in the letter *u* so they cannot be spelt with *au*, therefore must be *aw*. Again, you may think of some exceptions but there is always a reason! The word *flu* is an abbreviation of *influenza, menu* is French, and *tofu* is Japanese.

- Words do not end in *v* – a final silent *e* is added to the *v*; for example, *give, have, love, live*. An exception is Kiev which is a Russian word.

- Words do not end in a j - this sound at the end of words has two spelling choices, *-dge* or *-ge*. For example, *fridge, badge, large, page*. The final *e* is letting us know to produce the letter *g* as the "soft" sound /j/.

The ending *-dge* has the *d* added to protect the vowel from saying its name. The final *e* is at the end of the word to let us know to produce the soft *g*, and we do not want it "reaching around" to tell the vowel to say its name. The *d* stops that from happening, therefore this spelling is used after a single short vowel. (We did not cover this in phonics, as it is usually taught later.)

There are three exceptions to the rule that English words do not end in *i, u, v* and *j*: *you, thou* and *I*. These are very old English words.

- The letters *ck* is only used at the ends of words and after a single short vowel; for example, duck, stick, lock. When the word has a long vowel, or another consonant, it is the k spelling; for example, steak, meek, make, hook, milk, sulk.

History and meaning of words influence spelling

The meaning as well as the history (or etymology) of words influence the way they are spelt. Children are introduced to this in their first three years of schooling, and it becomes more important to teach as children become older and more proficient readers.

From their fourth year of schooling onwards, structured word enquiry is needed to continue all the great reading and spelling work they have done so far.

Some great examples of this are:

- **Two** – So why do we spell *two* with *w*? Pronunciation has changed over time, but the spelling has not. *Two* comes from the Old English *twa*, meaning two, and the *w* was pronounced back then. The spelling shows us the meaning of the word. When teaching this word, teach your child how the *w* is related to other words meaning two like *twice, twin, twelve* (ten plus two), *twenty* (two lots of ten) and *between* (in the middle of two things).

- **One** – This used to be pronounced "own". It is related to the words *only* and *alone* as they both mean one.

- **Silent letters** – If your child questions you as to why it is spelt that way, instead of just saying, "That's how they are spelt and you just have to learn it" or "English is just too hard", it is more helpful to explain the origin of the word. Clearly, we are not going to know all of the origins, which is where the free online etymology dictionary is particularly useful! Your child may also like to use their "spelling voice" and pronounce these words with the "silent" letter when spelling them so that they remember to include them.

How to teach spelling

We do not want to give children random lists of words or lists of spelling rules to memorise. We want to teach them to find and understand the patterns in the spelling of words. When we teach sound-letter relationships during phonics instructions, we also ask the children to spell the words. We are also asking them to sort the words by looking at their spelling pattern; for example, by completing a word sort of "hard c" and "soft c", your child will uncover the pattern before you even teach them the rule. Another example is when completing the word sort for *ai* and *ay* words, your child will notice the pattern that *ai* is never found at the end of a word; again, this is before you have told them the rule that no English word ends in *i*.

Spelling activities

Your child may need to practise spelling additional words to what is in the previous chapter. Use the template below (photocopy as many times as you like) and add the words you want to practise in the first column. Remember to not give random lists of words; group the words together by sound-letter relationship.

Instructions: In the two "Read the word" columns ("sounding out" and "altogether"), please write the words for your child. Ask your child to read the word by sounding out and blending together. In the second column, ask your child to spell the word, making sure that they say the sound as they write the grapheme. In the next column, ask your child to read the word without sounding it out.

Fold the paper so that your child cannot see the word and ask them to spell the word again on their own. Then unfold the paper and check the spelling. If incorrect, look at where the error was, point that out to your child and start the process again.

Sound:				
Read the word (sounding out)	**Spell the word**	**Read the word (altogether)**	**Spell the word**	**Check the word**

Board games: Use the blank board games and add words that have the spelling pattern you are practising. When it is your turn, read the word you land on out load for your playing partner to spell on a piece of paper.

When it is your partner's turn, they read out loud the word they land on for you to spell. Ensure that your counters are over the words, so that your child is retrieving the word from their memory, and not copying from the game board. Of course, this game can only be used with the graphemes that you have already taught and frequently practised.

Dictation: It sounds rather old fashioned, but it is a great way to monitor how your little one is going as well as helping them apply their spelling skills. Dictation is the step before asking your child to write their own sentences, but a step up from writing lists of words. You can also note what errors they are making, so that you know when you need to complete additional word sorts or spelling practice.

You can use the decodable books you are reading. Choose a sentence and read it out loud and ask your child to write it down. You may have to say 3-4 words at the one time, not the whole sentence. Ask your child to read it back to you and check for spelling errors. Please do not correct as they are writing. If they are all spelt correctly, great job! If not, help your child fix the error in a positive way.

General tips to help your child:

- When your child asks you how to spell a word, do not just spell it for them. Tell your child to say the word in its separate sounds (segment) and have a go at spelling it first. Remind your child to write the letter/grapheme as they say the sound (not letter names). If you know that your child can spell a word that is similar, then point out the similarities.

- If your child brings home a spelling list from school, look over the list with your child and look for any patterns. Group the words in their patterns.

- If your child needs to spell a longer word, break it into syllables, and spell each syllable; for example, *con-sid-er*.

- Some words may need what we call a "spelling" voice. For example, whenever I spell *Wednesday*, I say "Wed-nes-day", or for *finger* I make sure that I say the *-er* sound (not a schwa as in "finga").

How to "correct" spelling errors

Ask your child to look carefully at the word and see if they notice the error. If not, please correct in a positive, constructive way by letting your child know the reason behind the error. Do not just correct it.

Here are some examples:

- *play* spelt as *plai* – both are read as "play". Point out to your child that English words do not end in the letter *i*, therefore at the ends of words the spelling choice is *ay*.

- *stop* spelt as *sop* – here the /t/ sound has been missed. Ask your child to sound out all the sounds in the word and see if they have missed writing any.

- *jumped* spelt as *jumpt* – here the child has done a wonderful job of spelling all the sounds in the word. Explain to your child that when we change the word to the past tense, we always use the *-ed* spelling regardless of the sound.

After you have explained the error, ask your child to write the whole word again.

As mentioned before, only once your child reaches their third year of schooling are they able to cope with the demands of learning extra spelling rules and patterns, and more morphology and etymology. Phonics alone is not enough. Even during the first three years of learning to read, they should be explicitly taught affixes and the origins of some words and how spelling can also signify meaning.

In Grade 3 (fourth year of schooling), they will learn spellings of multi-syllable words, words with schwa's and additional prefixes and suffixes (affixes). In Grade 4, they learn Latin-based affixes and base words (also called root words). In Grade 5 and 6, they build on this with more complexity and then start on Greek affixes and bases.

Learning to spell in English is more difficult than other languages due to its many influences. On the plus side, it also gives us a larger vocabulary to choose from to express ourselves; we have around double the amount words than German, French and Spanish speakers.

Further information

"Resources for Families", *Dyslexia – SPELD Foundation (DSF)* – dsf.net.au/resources/home-resources

> They have many free resources, including printable spelling rules "Sounds of English – Grammar Booklet".

Mr Spelling – youtube.com/channel/UCAk_BNJ7wwnvCiWpbE85d9Q

> This channel has fun rap songs on spelling rules.

"Free Teaching Resources", *PhonicBooks* – phonicbooks.co.uk/advice-and-resources/free-teaching-resources/

> They have great posters that show spelling, different sounds, as well as some free decodable books.

Spellzone – spellzone.com

> This website provides words lists and spelling rules.

6

Reading Fluency

I. Love. How. Beginner. Readers. Sound. Like. Robots.

Beginner readers have to focus on working out each word, which means that their rate of reading is very slow. This is fine. As they become quicker at decoding words, as well as increase the number of words they know automatically, their rate increases and they are able to start adding expression.

Fluency in reading is being able to read accurately, at a good speed, and with expression. Expression includes intonation (rise and fall of pitch), knowing when to pause and stop, and when to add emphasis to words. My daughter has always been a very fast reader (also a fast talker!), but she reads without expression. Every year on her school report her reading ability was rated above average, but the comments were always about her reading too fast and without expression. We practised poems, speeches and reading out loud using different volumes, pitch, and emphasis, and now she is doing well.

Reading out loud makes the reader aware of the comprehension of the listener. If you read or talk too slowly it is difficult for a listener to follow as they forget the information. On the other hand, if the reader or talker is too fast, the listener doesn't have time to process the information. If the reader uses no expression, then the listener may just switch off all together, or not pick up on the really important pieces.

Fluency and comprehension

According to the National Reading Panel, which reviewed research on the teaching of fluency, children who had direct instruction in fluency are better readers.

When thinking about the "Simple View of Reading", oral reading fluency is considered the bridge between word recognition and comprehension. A fluent reader can read words automatically and effortlessly, so their attention is given to comprehending what they are reading. As the child is reading, they are problem solving and synthesising ideas, not concentrating on decoding the words.

A fluent reader can also read with expression, which helps to gain a deeper understanding of a text. It may be thought that a child has reading comprehension issues if they are not understanding what they have read. However, the difficulty often lies in word recognition and not being able to read words automatically and effortlessly and therefore the child is not able to fully concentrate on the meaning of the text.

Being able to read with expression allows children to have confidence in their public speaking and presentation skills. They are able to engage their audience through reading at a good rate and using appropriate expression and pauses.

What should my child be able to do?

As with any skill, becoming a fluent reader takes lots of practice. All of the underlying skills have to be automatic, including accuracy in word recognition. If you are not accurate, then every time you misread a word it slows you down and the meaning may be lost. It takes the average reader the first three years of schooling to get to this "sweet spot".

In the first year of schooling, oral reading fluency is about learning how speech maps onto print: how words sit on a page, how a gap between words shows a new word, and how a full stop shows the end of a sentence. In the second year of schooling, your child is still consolidating these skills whilst learning new sound-letter links and building up their bank of instantly recognisable words. This process continues until your child can read out loud at a rate similar to talking (usually halfway or the end of the fourth year of schooling).

To know if your child is able to read fluently, ask them to read an age-appropriate passage out loud to you.

Areas to note:	Comment
How smoothly are they reading?	
Do they stop and make errors or falter over words?	
Are they able to read the words but are still slow readers?	
Does your child read with expression and use different volumes and pitch? Do they use a rise of intonation for questions?	
Does your child pay attention to punctuation and pause or stop or emphasise appropriately?	
Is your child able to understand what they have read?	
Does your child often lose where they are up to on the page?	
If reading to themselves, does it take your child a long time to finish a page?	

I don't expect you to get out your stopwatch and time your child, but their teacher may assess them to calculate the "words correct per minute" (wcpm).

By the end of their second year of schooling they should be reading at 60 words per minute on an age-appropriate text. (An age-appropriate text is one that your child can read at 95% accuracy.)

By the end of their third year of schooling, your child should be reading at around 90 words per minute on an age-appropriate text and can now be thought of as an "independent reader".

Children should now be reading at a level of automaticity where whole words are recognised quickly and seemingly without effort.

By the end of their fourth year of schooling, due to their increasing automaticity of all of the areas required for fluency, an average reader will be able to read 100–120 words per minute. Most of their attention should be focused on comprehending the text.

Developing fluency

If you feel that your child's fluency is not developing, then please contact your child's teacher and tell them what you are seeing at home and ask them to discover why. It is so important that your child receives help early on if they are not developing oral reading fluency.

The key to successful intervention is to determine why your child is not reading fluently. Do they need additional systematic phonics instruction and/or phonemic awareness alongside fluency practice? Or is their word recognition good but they lack the vocabulary to comprehend what they have read? Older children may need to work on vocabulary, background knowledge and metacognitive strategies (thinking about thinking) as well as motivation. Until the cause is determined it is difficult to assign and practise the right strategies.

Remember, the goal of developing fluency is **not** for your child to "speed read". Going too fast won't allow young readers time to comprehend and add expression. When practising reading fluency, be careful not to encourage your child to read *faster*.

Fluency activities for early readers
The most important thing that you can do to develop fluency is to help your child improve their decoding skills. Do this through accurate word decoding (systematic phonics in chapter 4) using decodable books and lots of practice.

When you are reading to your child every night, make sure that you are using lots of expression – different voices and pitches – as well as pausing at punctuation. You can point out that you had to read a particular sentence in an excited voice because it ended in an exclamation mark.

You can practise expression with words that your child can decode. Ask your child to read the words below. First tell them what the punctuation mark means, then you read the word with the appropriate expression. Next, read it together, then let the child read it on their own. You can practise lots of words by writing them on your whiteboard.

"Cat." – read as a statement.

"Cat?" – read as a question.

"Cat!" – read in an excited or alarmed manner.

Example 1

"Sit."

"Sit?"

"Sit!"

Example 2

"Fun."

"Fun?"

"Fun!"

Example 3

"Dad."

"Dad?"

"Dad!"

Example 4

"Hop."

"Hop?"

"Hop!"

Example 5

"Jump."

"Jump?"

"Jump!"

Now let's add some more words.

Example 1

"Sit, Dad."

"Sit, Dad?"

"Sit, Dad!"

Example 2

"Jump, Mum."

"Jump Mum?"

"Jump, Mum!"

Example 3

"Hot dish."

"Hot dish?"

"Hot dish!"

Example 4

"Wet cat."

"Wet cat?"

"Wet cat!"

Example 5

"Ten pens."

"Ten pens?"

"Ten pens!"

You can do more of these fluency activities each day, either writing your own on your whiteboard or a piece of paper.

Fluency activities for middle-stage readers

As children become better readers and some words are known automatically, their reading rate will increase.

When your reader is able to read short sentences, ask them to read the sentence again to practise reading more smoothly.

If your child tends not to notice any punctuation, and runs all sentences into each other, then take the time to go over what each punctuation mark means. Explain to your child that using the punctuation marks when reading is important as it gives meaning to the sentence.

Here is an example of how ignoring punctuation can markedly change the meaning of a sentence. "Let's eat, Grandpa" has a different meaning to "Let's eat Grandpa". Make sure your child stops at full stops, pauses at commas, uses inflection for questions, and uses a different tone for an exclamation mark and question mark.

If your child makes a mistake or gets stuck on a word, help them with the word and then ask them to re-read the whole sentence, not just the word they found difficult.

If your child is reading too fast, then remind them to slow down so that they can understand what they are reading.

Ask your child to read the following sentences, paying attention to the punctuation marks – talking marks, full stops, exclamation marks and question marks. You can read the sentence to your child first if needed.

"The man jumped." – read as a statement.

"The man jumped!" – read in an excited manner.

"The man jumped?"– read as a question.

"The man jumped, scared." – paying attention to pausing at the comma.

Example 1

"At the shop."

"At the shop?"

"At the shop!"

"At the shop, happily."

Example 2

"The dog ran."

"The dog ran?"

"The dog ran!"

"The dog ran, excitedly."

Example 3

"You went into the city."

"You went into the city?"

"You went into the city!"

"Yesterday, you went into the city."

Another activity to help your child's fluency is to start with one word and then continue to increase the number of words in each line.

Example 1

Tom

Tom dug

Tom dug a

Tom dug a big

Tom dug a big hole

Tom dug a big hole in

Tom dug a big hole in the

Tom dug a big hole in the wet

Tom dug a big hole in the wet sand.

Example 2

Dad

Dad can

Dad can jump

Dad can jump, hop

Dad can jump, hop and

Dad can jump, hop and skip.

Example 3

Kate

Kate and

Kate and Bill

Kate and Bill went

Kate and Bill went to

Kate and Bill went to the

Kate and Bill went to the shop

Kate and Bill went to the shop to

Kate and Bill went to the shop to get

Kate and Bill went to the shop to get milk.

These next examples have more complex sound-letter links in them, so make sure your child is at this level.

Example 1

The

The huge

The huge shark

The huge shark was

The huge shark was eating

The huge shark was eating fish

The huge shark was eating fish and squid

The huge shark was eating fish and squid in

The huge shark was eating fish and squid in the deep

The huge shark was eating fish and squid in the deep sea.

Example 2

A

A duck

A duck went

A duck went back

A duck went back under

A duck went back under the

A duck went back under the water

A duck went back under the water quickly.

Example 3

The

The smart fox

The smart fox went

The smart fox went over

The smart fox went over the

The smart fox went over the gate,

The smart fox went over the gate, chasing

The smart fox went over the gate, chasing the

The smart fox went over the gate, chasing the goose.

Example 4

When

When we

When we camp

When we camp in

When we camp in summer

When we camp in summer, we

When we camp in summer, we have

When we camp in summer, we have a great

When we camp in summer, we have a great time.

Example 5

In

In the city

In the city we

In the city we explore

In the city we explore the

In the city we explore the lanes

In the city we explore the lanes and

In the city we explore the lanes and the alleys.

You can do more of these fluency activities each day. Simply write your own on your whiteboard or a piece of paper and add more words to each sentence. You can also use the book your child is reading; reveal one word at a time and cover the rest of the words using your finger or a strip of paper.

Remember, they have to go back to the start each time you add another word so they can practise reading at a pace that is similar to talking. If there is a particular sound-letter link that your child needs to practise, then use lots of words that contain that sound. It is also important when doing these exercises to explain the meaning of any word that your child doesn't know in order to build their vocabulary.

Fluency activities for competent readers

Once your child is a good reader, they can practise reading lots of different types of books out loud. Whilst it's wonderful that they can head off and read on their own, it's still really beneficial to listen to them read out loud each day, if only for five minutes.

As mentioned already, reading for 20 minutes per day is ideal, but what that looks like depends on your schedule and their competency. It could be that they read for 10 minutes on their own, 5 minutes out loud to you, and then another 5 minutes on their own. Use questions to check their understanding of the text and to show your interest in the book, which in turn, will make them more interested in reading as it is a shared experience. If they are reading a chapter book, ask them to tell you what has happened so far before they read out loud to you. Make them feel as if you are interested in the story and not just there to critique their reading skills. You can also read a page to them, modelling fluency and expression.

Other activities for competent readers to develop fluency are:

- Rehearsing poems, speeches, song lyrics or a part of a play until they are using lots of expression and great fluency. Your child can perform them to you.

- Telling jokes, so they know where and how to pause for the punchline.

- Reading lots of different styles and genres of texts.

Be mindful that reading fluency will change depending on the task and text. For example, great readers will probably not be fluent if given a very technical manual to read with specific vocabulary, as they will have to decode unfamiliar words. This is totally fine and is all part of the learning process.

Repeated reading

The text used for repeated reading should be fairly easy for your child to *read* (90- to 95%-word *accuracy*). First, make sure you go over any tricky words that your child may have difficulty reading and also define any words that your child doesn't know. Then ask your child to read the text up to four times, until they achieve a good level of fluency. Each read-through should only be one to two minutes, so choose a paragraph or a short page from a book to use for this exercise. You can do this every time your child reads out loud to you. It could be a book from school, their favourite book at home, or a poem. Choose a section of the text for them to re-read to build their fluency. Make sure you praise them for their great pausing and expression.

Another way is to model the text first. Often the saying in teaching "I do, we do, you do" is used to show that you will first model the activity (I do), then do it together (we do), before the child is asked to do it on their own (you do). In this case, it's "I read, we read, you read". Ask your child to point to the words as you read them, then read the page together, again with your child pointing at the words, and then ask your child to read the text by themselves. They could read another two to three times by themselves. This strategy allows your child to hear what fluent and expressive reading sounds like, then gets to have a practice run with you and then do it on their own.

Early stage, middle-stage and any struggling readers, should not be left to read silently on their own as they may continue to make the same word reading errors if they are not corrected. These incorrect words will then be stored in their memory.

For reluctant and new readers who wish to read alone, it is always a good idea to check if they are *actually* reading! It's often more likely they are just staring at the book or in their room quietly playing Lego!

Lastly, to help your child become a fluent reader they must read *a lot*. Many studies have found a strong correlation between the amount a child reads and their reading ability. This of course is difficult when you have a struggling reader who does not want to read. In this case, continue with daily reading in games and activities and short decodable sentences and books until they have built up their ability, confidence and willingness.

Further information

Konza D. (June 2011) "Research into practice." Edith Cowan University. ecu.edu.au/__data/ assets/pdf_file/0005/663701/SA-DECS-Fluency-doc.pdf
This paper discusses what fluency is and the strategies to help develop it.

Hasbrouck J. "Developing Fluent Readers." Reading Rockets. readingrockets.org/article/ developing-fluent-readers
This is an article about teaching fluency to beginner readers as well as maintaining fluency.

7

Vocabulary

There was one book in which I really struggled with the vocabulary. I could read the words easily (due to good decoding skills) but I had no idea what was going on. It took so much brainpower to keep re-reading sentences and paragraphs to try to understand the language that I only lasted one chapter and had to admit defeat. I won't tell you the name of it as it's rather embarrassing, but I have *never* not finished a book before.

That same struggle is going on for children as they build their vocabulary. It's not enough to simply be able to read the words; children must be able to understand what they are reading.

Vocabulary is the words and word meanings that one knows. It is not just the words one can read (decode) without knowing the meaning. Vocabulary is one part of oral language and learning new and varied vocabulary starts way before a child begins school.

Vocabulary is not merely learning the definitions of a long list of words but also about how these words relate to each other and how the meaning can alter in different contexts. We all have a receptive vocabulary (word meanings we know when listening or reading) and an expressive vocabulary (words we use when speaking or writing). Typically, our receptive vocabulary is greater than our expressive vocabulary.

Beck, McKeown and Kucan, renowned professors and researchers, classify vocabulary into three "tiers". Tier-1 words are everyday words that your child hears frequently; for example, *jump, run, talk, sing, dog, cat, happy, sad, boy, girl, red, yellow, chair, table*. Tier-1 words normally have only one meaning. These words may not need to be specifically taught and are learnt through your child's daily interactions with you and others at home, daycare, school, at the shops, on the TV, etc.

Tier-2 words are used less frequently in conversation and are found in written texts in many different topic and subject areas. Examples include *obvious, maintain, verify, description, measure*. Your child may need specific teaching of these useful words. Why are they useful? Because they are used for multiple purposes across many subjects not only at school, but also in day-to-day life. Knowledge of these words will increase your child's understanding of what they hear and read as well as allow them to express what they know in a more complex way.

Tier-3 vocabulary are subject-specific words. Each subject at school or hobby or sporting interest has its own particular vocabulary. For example, in science, your child will learn words such as *matter* and *atom*. In piano, it could be *keys* and *tone* and *treble clef*.

The impact of good vocabulary

Having a strong knowledge of words and word meanings will allow your child to understand more of what they read and hear. It also enables them to use more complex words and to have more variation in their writing and speaking. Vocabulary in pre-school is a strong predictor of a child's reading comprehension skills and therefore should be focused on by parents before they start school.

A wide vocabulary is also said to help develop phonemic awareness as the more words that a child knows that sound alike, the more attention they need to pay to individual phoneme differences. For example, *speed* and *stead* sound exactly the same except that the *p* changes to *t*.

When learning to read, a child may sound out a word incorrectly due to the variance in how a sound-letter correspondence can be said, but then they match that word to a word that they have stored in their vocabulary and change the way the sound is produced to read the word correctly. For example, when reading the word island, a child may sound it out as "is-land". Once they can't find a word that matches is-land in their vocabulary store, they realise that it is supposed to be island. Or they may sound out break as "breek", but then they adjust as they don't recognise the word breek in their vocabulary and so change to *break*. Another example is *tongue*. Try and sound that out! Vocabulary works hand-in-hand with decoding skills. The better your vocabulary is, the better reader you will become.

If a child has good decoding skills and good vocabulary, it is not often that they will struggle with reading comprehension. As your child reads, if they don't have to use all their brainpower to recall individual word meanings, they can dedicate it to comprehension and remembering what they have read. They will be able to pay attention to subtle clues that give more information, then make inferences and gain a deeper understanding of what is written.

If a child has poor vocabulary, then they may not understand what they are reading or they will use so much effort to read that they do not enjoy it. This may lead to reading avoidance, which in turn means less exposure to new vocabulary … and so a vicious cycle is created. This is exactly what happened to me with that book I mentioned earlier, and I gave up reading it as a result. We don't want this for our children.

What should my child be able to do?

The rate at which vocabulary grows is amazing! So amazing in fact that there are a range of studies on the matter, which all unfortunately differ somewhat in their estimations. At age two years, children should roughly have a vocabulary of 200–300 words. By the time they are three years old, it grows to 900–1000 words, and by the time they enter school they have around 2,200 words. By the time they are six years old, they have an expressive vocabulary of 2,600 words but a receptive vocabulary of an astounding 20,000 words! Then by age 12, they should understand around 50,000 words.

Some say that the average child in the first three years of schooling learns 1000 new words per year, and after that the rate increases to between 2000–3000 new words per year (Nagy and Scott, 2000). Others say they learn 5000 words per year (Miller and Gildea, 1987). One study showed that 8-year-olds learn 20 new words per day! Confused? Overwhelmed? Despite what the experts say, it is impossible to determine the exact size of your child's vocabulary, or for me to list all of the vocabulary that your child needs to know – nor should the real number really matter. What you simply need to be aware of is that your child's vocabulary is constantly growing, that they are replacing simpler words with harder words, that when you read or talk to them they can understand more complex vocabulary than perhaps you are using, and that they can tell you the meaning of some Tier-2 vocabulary when asked.

If you would like a vocabulary list to refer to, I have added the Blaxcell Street Public School vocabulary plan in Further information. (Note: kindergarten is the first year of schooling.) They have kindly made this free to access on *Specific Learning Difficulties Association of South Australia* (*SPELD SA*).

The challenge with word lists is that the words are out of context. To truly teach the meaning of new vocabulary it has to be meaningful – not just a definition from a list of words. There are many words that appear frequently in particular genres or subjects and should be taught while reading books or in a practical situation with you.

Developing vocabulary

As parents, we have the greatest influence on our child's language and vocabulary foundations. The more words that your child is exposed to, the better.

There are two main ways that you can help your child deepen and broaden their vocabulary. One way is through multiple exposure to words during the process of shared reading time (and when your child is an independent reader, from their own reading) and by being surrounded by a language-rich environment. The second way is explicit teaching of words that you have chosen.

Shared reading at home

We have already discussed this in chapter 2: Oral language, but I want to reiterate its importance. Bookreading should be an interactive experience, not just an adult reading out loud whilst their child remains passive. When reading you will come across more Tier-2 words than you would in everyday conversation, which gives you a great opportunity to teach new vocabulary.

Children should be reading – or being read to – books that vary in style and topic. If you just read about sport, then you will become highly knowledgeable in that area only and miss out on building an extensive vocabulary. For children who struggle to read, it is important that their parents still read out loud to them daily, regardless of age, to expand their vocabulary.

While reading to your child you can explore word meanings further by choosing a word to talk about. It's important to remember that teaching vocabulary is not just about prattling off a definition. Instead, use the steps below.

Step 1: Offer a child-friendly definition using words your child already knows, then use other words that mean the same (synonyms) and are opposites (antonyms). Discuss what category it belongs to, compare it to other words, give real life examples, refer to a picture if you have one or, my children's personal favourite, act it out. Children are more likely to remember the word if given these rich explanations.

Step 2: Connect the meanings of words to something in the child's own experience. Making it relatable is a great way to make it memorable.

Step 3: Give lots of different examples. Do not try and teach more than 10 new words in this direct way per week. Your child will be learning many other new words through listening and reading.

Here is an example of the above steps. A sentence in a book may read: "The girl **collapsed** onto the log." Ask your child if they know the meaning of the word and ask them to tell you what they know about it. "Do you know what *collapsed* means?" If your child doesn't, then talk about what *collapsed* means (to fall down) and relate a real and specific example about a time that you were "so tired you collapsed in a heap on the couch". Then ask your child if they have ever been so tired that they collapsed, and thereby relate the word to their own experiences.

Make sure your child says the word out loud. You can discuss that *collapse* is the base word but that in the story the word used is *collapsed* which is past tense. You can then refer back to the story and ask your child, "Tell me again how the girl got onto the log?" Try to use the word again later in the day.

Children need to hear new vocabulary many times and in different contexts before they can remember and use it. This is particularly true if a word has multiple meanings. For example, you could say, "I am so tired after doing all the dishes I am going to **collapse** into this chair." This will help your child commit it to memory.

This does not take a long time but it's a very valuable few minutes of the day. Do not do this with *every* new word in a book as you will lose the flow of reading and the load on your child's memory will be too great. Just two or three words will be sufficient.

Language-rich environment

In everyday conversations with your child, choose vocabulary that is not commonly heard by them. Use more complex language than normal. Here are some examples of vocabulary you can use instead of the "easier" words:

- hot – steaming, boiling

- big – enormous, immense

- sad – unhappy, despondent

- buy – purchase

- wet – soaked, drenched

- tired – weary, exhausted

- good – terrific, outstanding

- come out – emerge, appear

- bad – awful, terrible, appalling

- take off – remove

- guess – estimate

- give – distribute

The words you choose will depend on your child's language level and age, but do not underestimate them!

Below are examples of the different levels of phrasing a parent can use. The first example is at the supermarket.

Parent level-1: Stop touching that.

Parent level-2: Wow, what a big onion. Let's put that back.

Parent level-3: Wow, what a huge onion. I haven't seen one that enormous before. It's much bigger than the others. Should we put it back next to this onion or on top of the pile?

Another example that could happen at the park.

Parent level-1: Look at that big dog.

Parent level-2: Look at that huge dog running.

Parent level-3: Look at the enormous dog sprinting. Wow, it's running so fast. Why do you think it may be running so fast?

As you can see, Parent level-3 is giving better language models by using more complex vocabulary and sentence structure.

A friend of mine encourages her children to share new vocabulary that they may have learnt at school at the dinner table each night. The parents also have to contribute. This is a lovely way to be taught new vocabulary and also encourage a curiosity and love for learning new words.

Language-rich environments also include exposure to new experiences. For example, visiting zoos and museums or different playgrounds and parks. You will find new vocabulary to use and discuss in a forest versus at a beach.

Language-rich conversation during play

I am *still* playing with toy animals with my 8- and 6-year-old boys. When they were younger, I would subtly talk about different categories of animals, what they looked like and how they moved and sounded, and how they act similarly or differently from each other.

Now, I am talking about habitats and predators, using other higher-level vocabulary, but still within the environment of play. Words are not just stored in our brains like a dictionary with a list of definitions, but rather are stored with lots of related ideas around them.

Board games

There are some great board games available that build your child's vocabulary as well as offer a great way to spend time together. *Pictionary, Balderdash, Scrabble, Monopoly, Charades* and crossword puzzles are just a few. Use the same strategies of replacing easier vocabulary with more complex words in the games as well as in general chit-chat whilst playing.

Quality TV shows and apps

Meaningful conversations and interactions during bookreading and everyday life are the best ways to learn new vocabulary, but there is also a place for technology.

Before the arrival of YouTube and Netflix in 2015, my two eldest children would watch the same episodes of *Dinosaur Train, Octonauts* and *Little Einstein* over and over again. Their knowledge of dinosaurs, ocean creatures, countries and even famous composers was impressive. I remember going to a dinosaur exhibit where my oldest rattled off a million facts and figures and then me being very embarrassed when she told the guide how she had learnt it all from TV.

Unfortunately, for my youngest, with the existence of YouTube and Netflix, he watches random shows without the benefit of repetition and good quality content. In a nutshell, good quality shows, such as wildlife documentaries and educational shows that can be watched numerous times or shows that you can watch together and then discuss can be useful in building vocabulary. (Please see Further information below for recommendations of TV shows and Apps.)

Explicit teaching of vocabulary

So, what words should we teach first? Some words are far more useful than others – these are the ones we should focus on initially. For example, knowing the meaning of *pedagogy* is not as beneficial as the word *instruction*. Knowing the word *ignore* would come before teaching *discount* or *omit*. Choose words that your child is learning at school or from daily life that are immediately useful for them.

There are many words that we come across that are not part of our everyday oral language interactions, but that are still good to know. Many of these can be learnt through bookreading and conversation, but some may take additional teaching to gain a deep knowledge of the words.

A great way to help you remember how to teach these words is to use a visual tool called a semantic map. (Semantics is the study of the meaning and relationship between words.) You don't have to fill out the map to teach vocabulary, but it can be used as a guide when discussing new vocabulary so that your child gains a deep(er) understanding of the word. It is a good idea for older children to write the word so that you are tapping into meaning (semantics), how the word sounds (phonology) and how it is written (orthography).

The first semantic map is for younger children, as they may not have the language skills or the memory for all areas of the semantic map. For them, focus on a child-friendly definition, how the word sounds, other words that mean the same, and lots of example sentences related to their world or what they know. If possible, incorporate a physical example of the word. For example, if the word is *whimper*, then say something in that tone of voice.

The second template is for older children. They may want to use the map for their own self-study of vocabulary words from school. There are also many vocabulary templates online.

Blank Template (younger children)

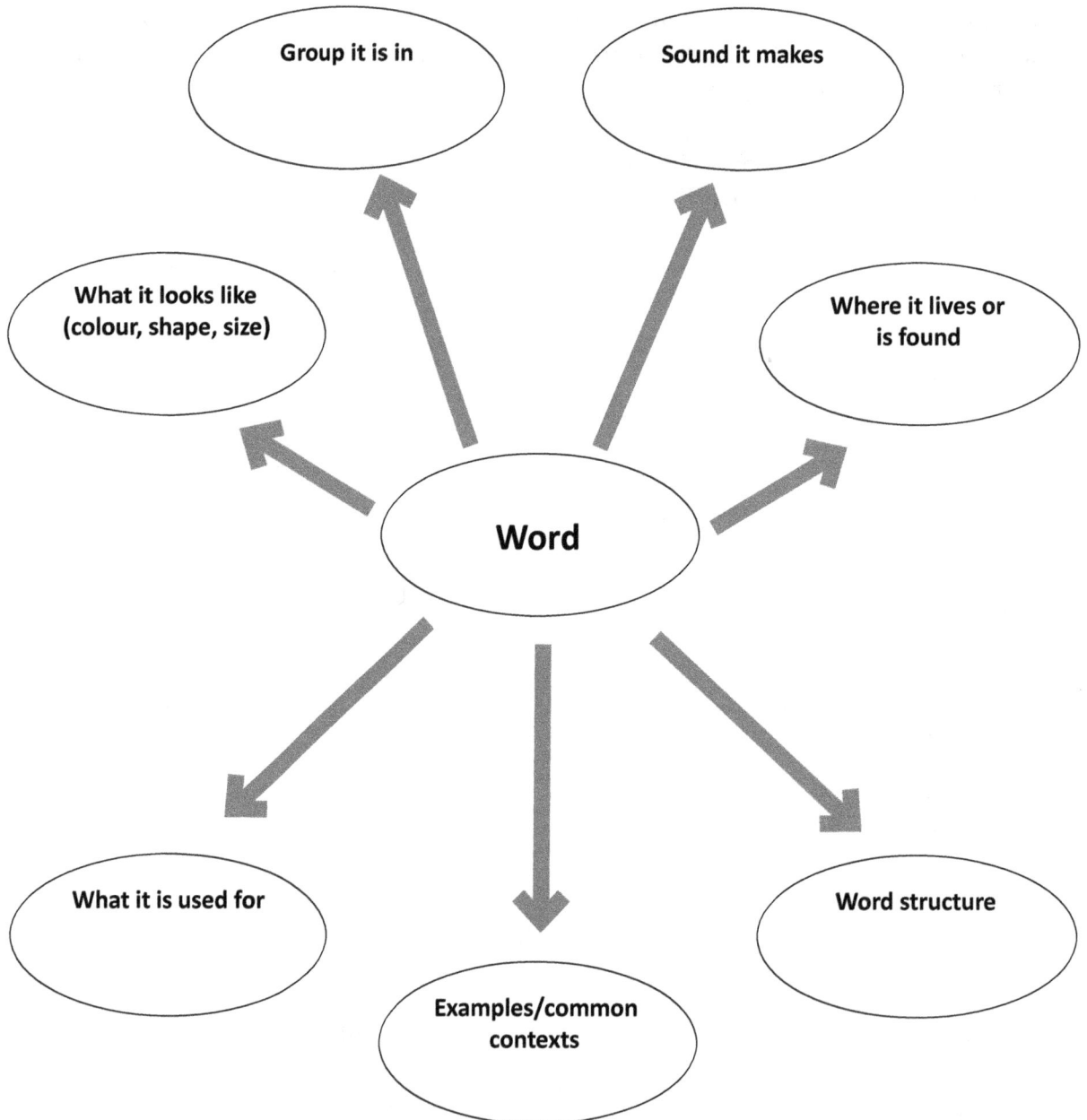

Group it is in

Sound it makes

What it looks like
(colour, shape, size)

Where it lives or
is found

Word

What it is used for

Examples/common
contexts

Word structure

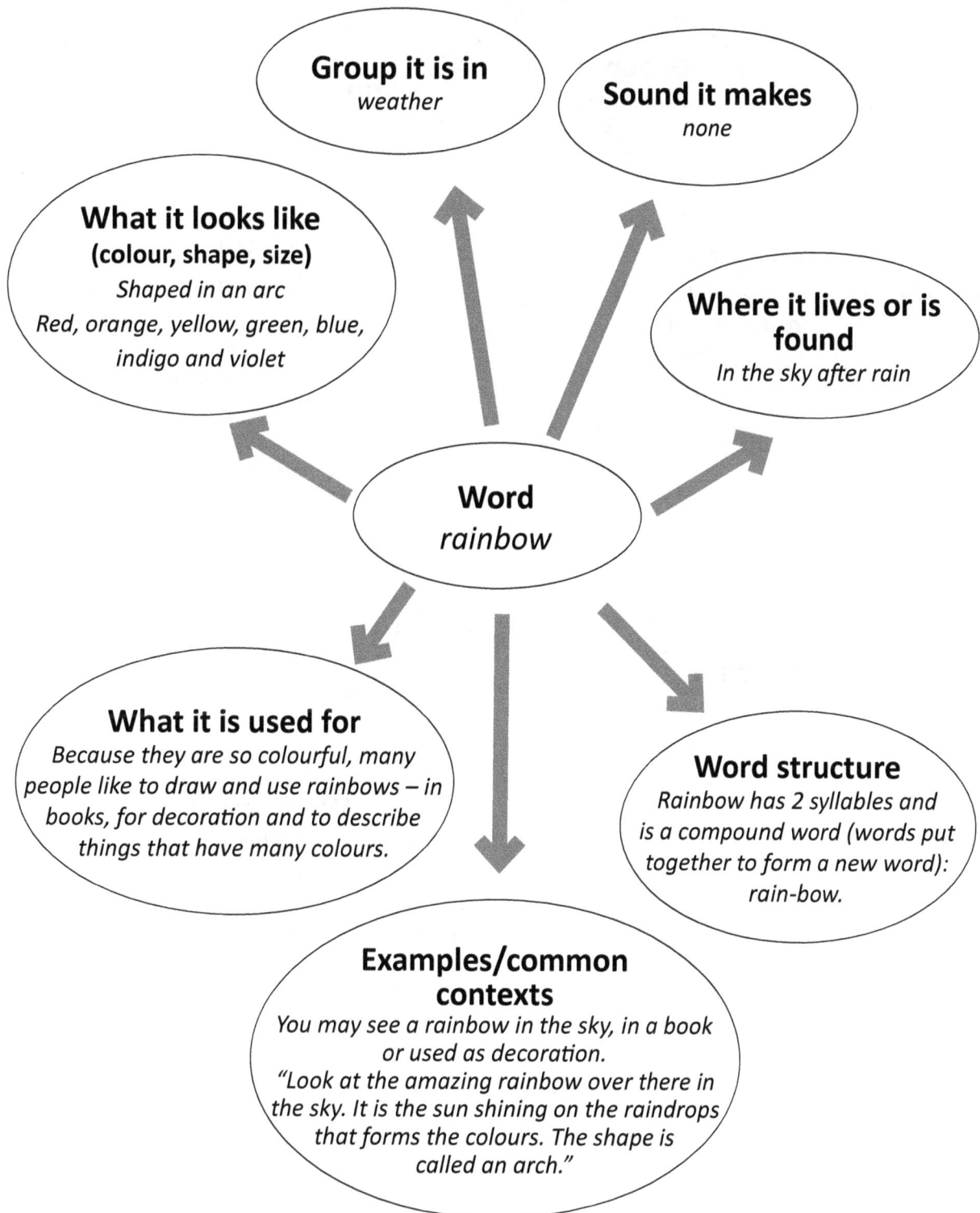

Example 1

Group it is in
weather

Sound it makes
none

What it looks like
(colour, shape, size)
Shaped in an arc
Red, orange, yellow, green, blue,
indigo and violet

Where it lives or is
found
In the sky after rain

Word
rainbow

What it is used for
Because they are so colourful, many
people like to draw and use rainbows – in
books, for decoration and to describe
things that have many colours.

Word structure
Rainbow has 2 syllables and
is a compound word (words put
together to form a new word):
rain-bow.

Examples/common
contexts
You may see a rainbow in the sky, in a book
or used as decoration.
"Look at the amazing rainbow over there in
the sky. It is the sun shining on the raindrops
that forms the colours. The shape is
called an arch."

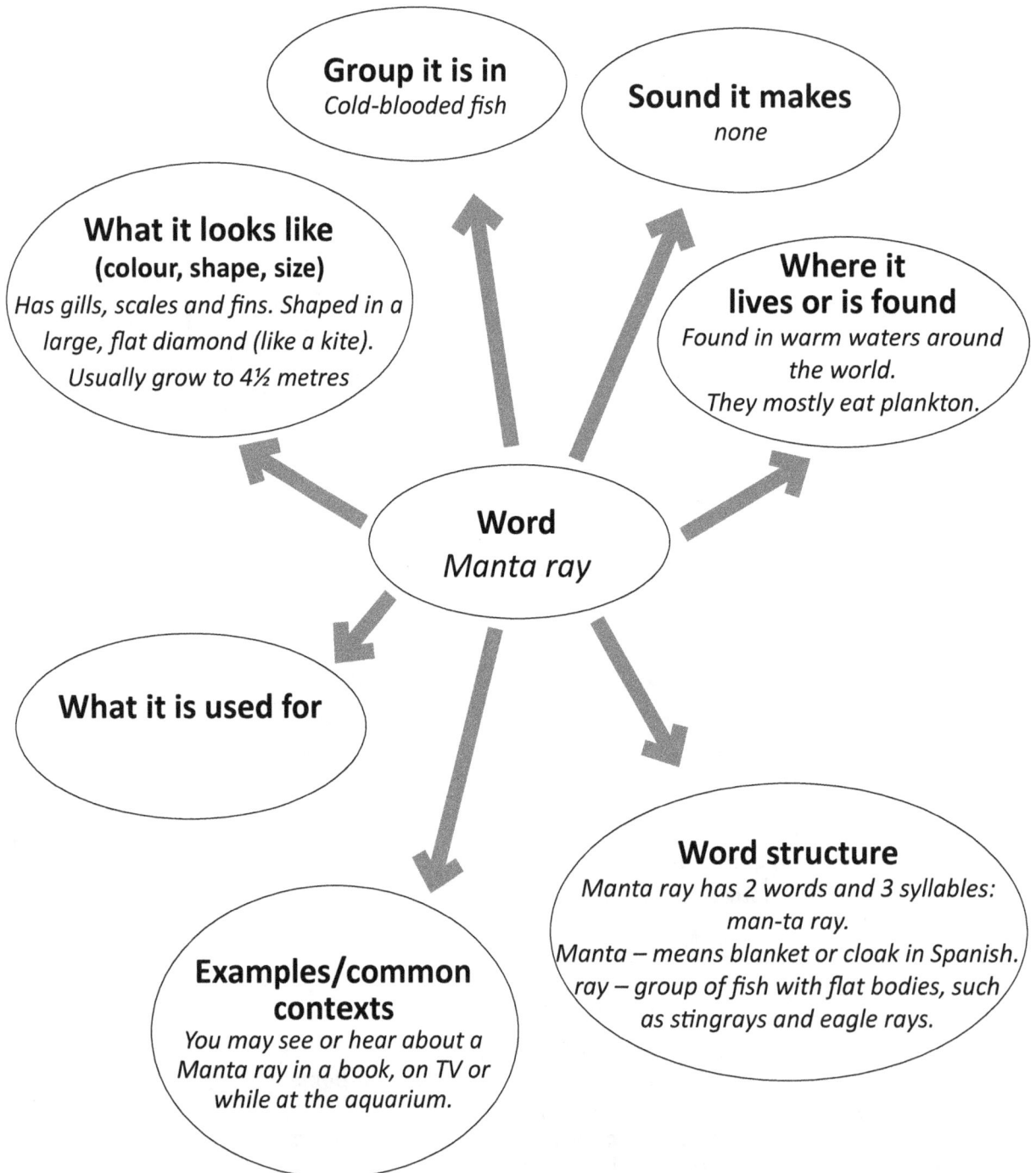

Example 2

Group it is in
Cold-blooded fish

Sound it makes
none

What it looks like
(colour, shape, size)
Has gills, scales and fins. Shaped in a large, flat diamond (like a kite). Usually grow to 4½ metres

Where it lives or is found
*Found in warm waters around the world.
They mostly eat plankton.*

Word
Manta ray

What it is used for

Examples/common contexts
You may see or hear about a Manta ray in a book, on TV or while at the aquarium.

Word structure
*Manta ray has 2 words and 3 syllables: man-ta ray.
Manta – means blanket or cloak in Spanish.
ray – group of fish with flat bodies, such as stingrays and eagle rays.*

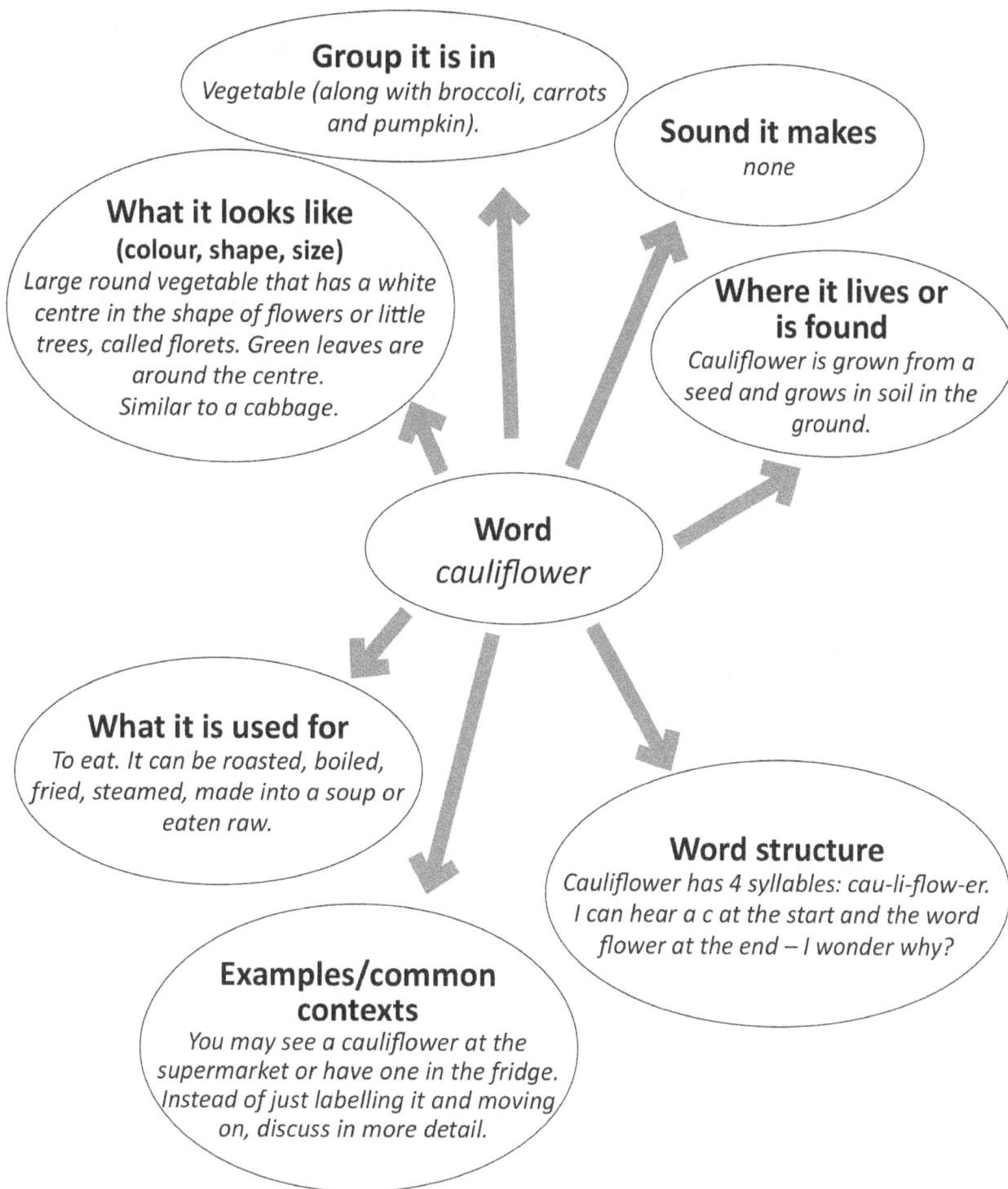

Example 3

Group it is in
Vegetable (along with broccoli, carrots and pumpkin).

Sound it makes
none

**What it looks like
(colour, shape, size)**
*Large round vegetable that has a white centre in the shape of flowers or little trees, called florets. Green leaves are around the centre.
Similar to a cabbage.*

**Where it lives or
is found**
Cauliflower is grown from a seed and grows in soil in the ground.

Word
cauliflower

What it is used for
To eat. It can be roasted, boiled, fried, steamed, made into a soup or eaten raw.

Word structure
Cauliflower has 4 syllables: cau-li-flow-er. I can hear a c at the start and the word flower at the end – I wonder why?

**Examples/common
contexts**
You may see a cauliflower at the supermarket or have one in the fridge. Instead of just labelling it and moving on, discuss in more detail.

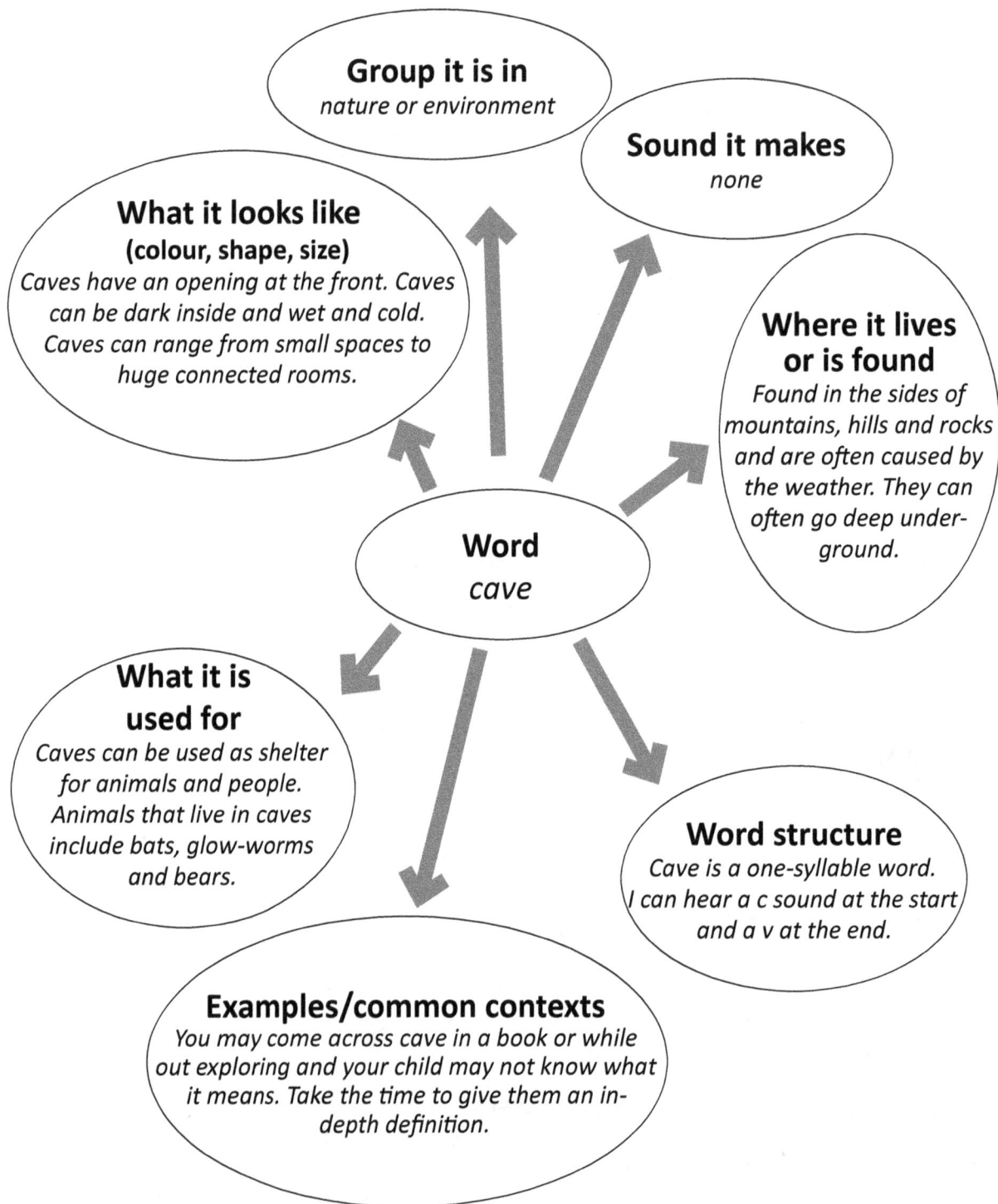

Example 4

Group it is in
nature or environment

Sound it makes
none

What it looks like
(colour, shape, size)
Caves have an opening at the front. Caves can be dark inside and wet and cold. Caves can range from small spaces to huge connected rooms.

Where it lives or is found
Found in the sides of mountains, hills and rocks and are often caused by the weather. They can often go deep under-ground.

Word
cave

What it is used for
Caves can be used as shelter for animals and people. Animals that live in caves include bats, glow-worms and bears.

Word structure
Cave is a one-syllable word. I can hear a c sound at the start and a v at the end.

Examples/common contexts
You may come across cave in a book or while out exploring and your child may not know what it means. Take the time to give them an in-depth definition.

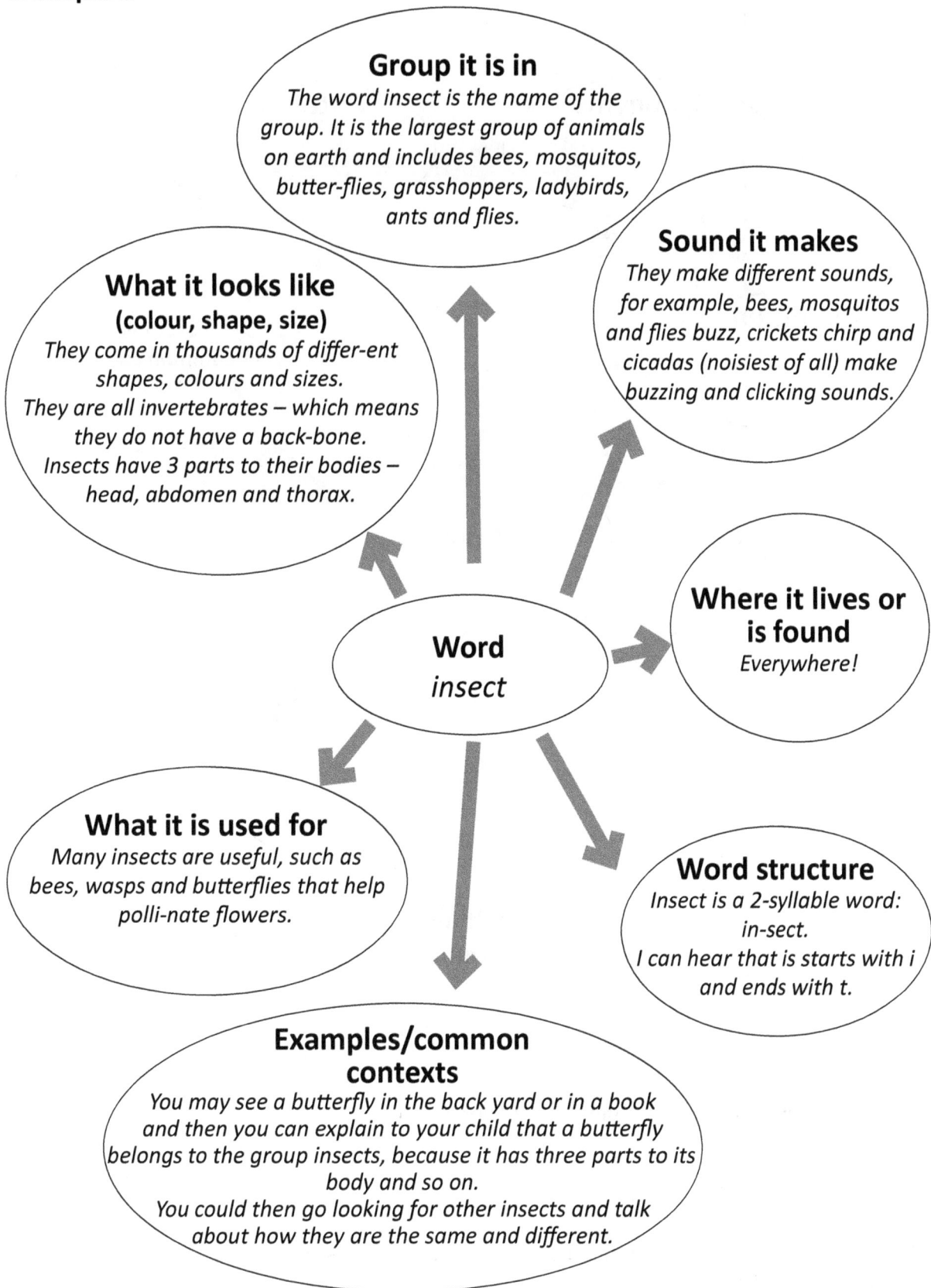

Example 5

Group it is in
The word insect is the name of the group. It is the largest group of animals on earth and includes bees, mosquitos, butter-flies, grasshoppers, ladybirds, ants and flies.

Sound it makes
They make different sounds, for example, bees, mosquitos and flies buzz, crickets chirp and cicadas (noisiest of all) make buzzing and clicking sounds.

What it looks like
(colour, shape, size)
They come in thousands of differ-ent shapes, colours and sizes.
They are all invertebrates – which means they do not have a back-bone.
Insects have 3 parts to their bodies – head, abdomen and thorax.

Word
insect

Where it lives or is found
Everywhere!

What it is used for
Many insects are useful, such as bees, wasps and butterflies that help polli-nate flowers.

Word structure
Insect is a 2-syllable word: in-sect.
I can hear that is starts with i and ends with t.

Examples/common contexts
You may see a butterfly in the back yard or in a book and then you can explain to your child that a butterfly belongs to the group insects, because it has three parts to its body and so on.
You could then go looking for other insects and talk about how they are the same and different.

Blank Template (older children)

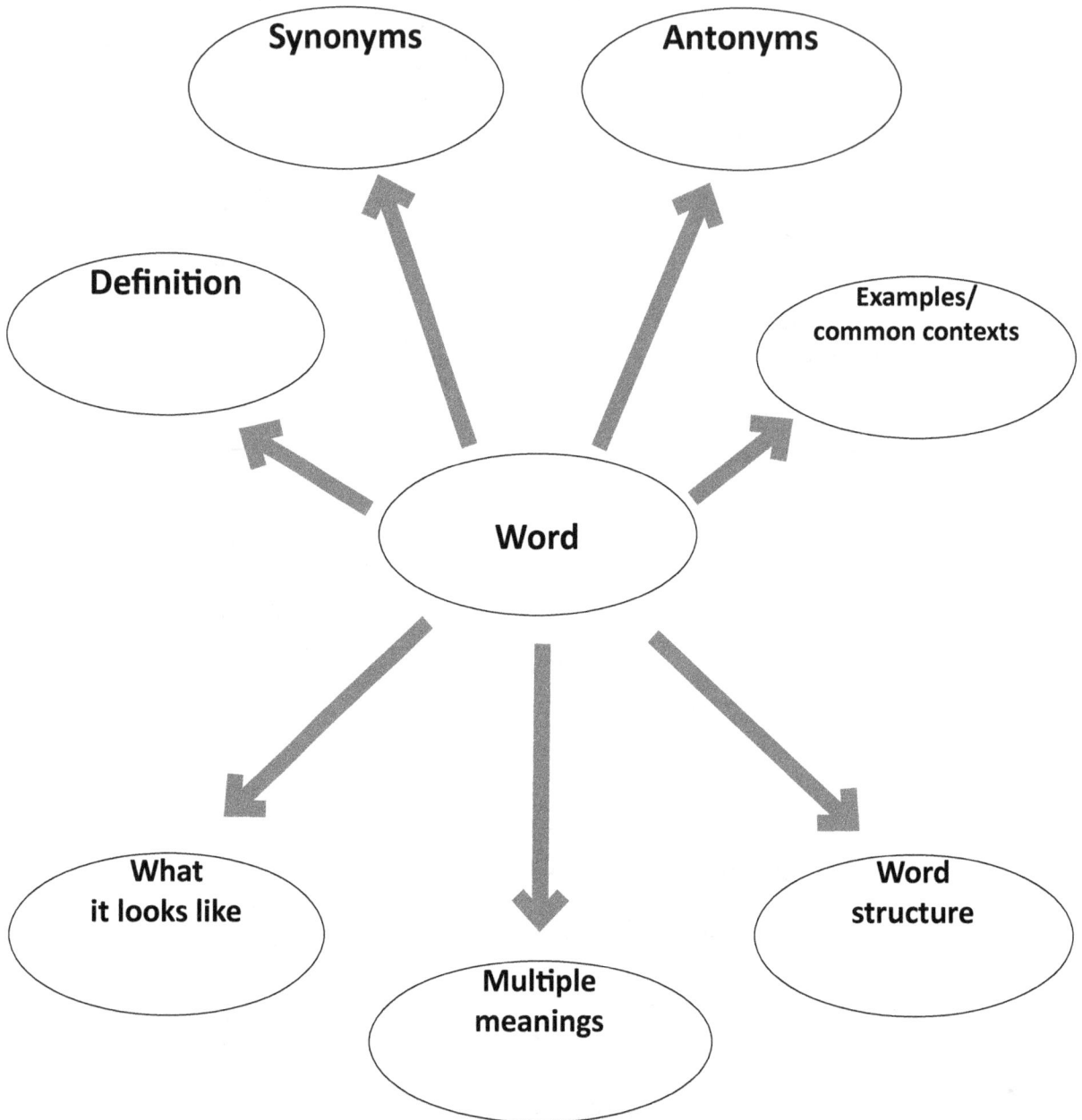

Definition – what the word means (child-friendly).

Synonyms – words that are similar in meaning.

Antonyms – words that are opposite in meaning.

What it looks like – this could include shape, size, colour, smell, visualising the word in action, acting out the word.

Word structure – phonemes in the word, how many syllables, any prefixes, suffixes.

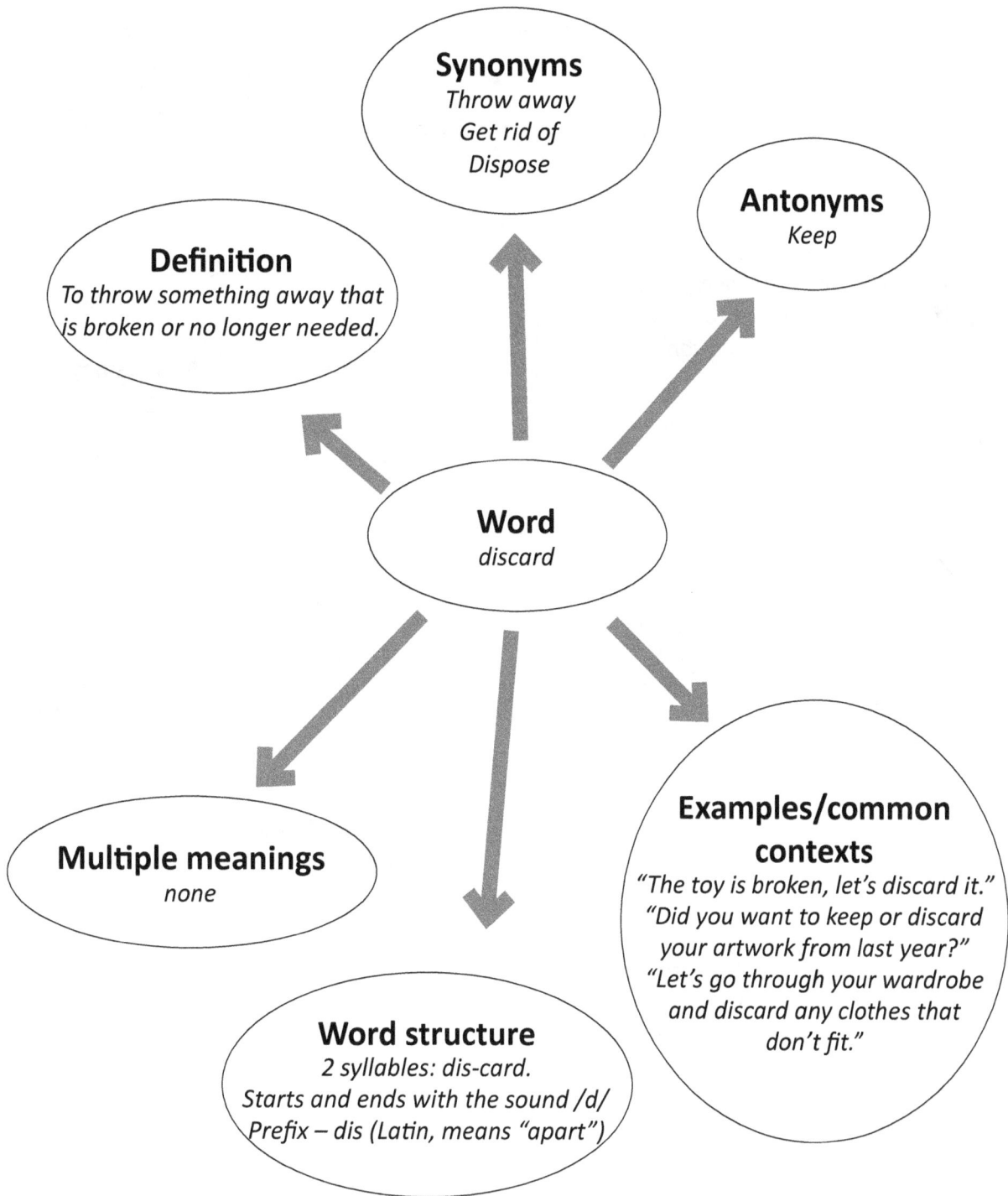

Example 1

Synonyms
Throw away
Get rid of
Dispose

Antonyms
Keep

Definition
To throw something away that is broken or no longer needed.

Word
discard

Multiple meanings
none

Examples/common contexts
"The toy is broken, let's discard it."
"Did you want to keep or discard your artwork from last year?"
"Let's go through your wardrobe and discard any clothes that don't fit."

Word structure
2 syllables: dis-card.
Starts and ends with the sound /d/
Prefix – dis (Latin, means "apart")

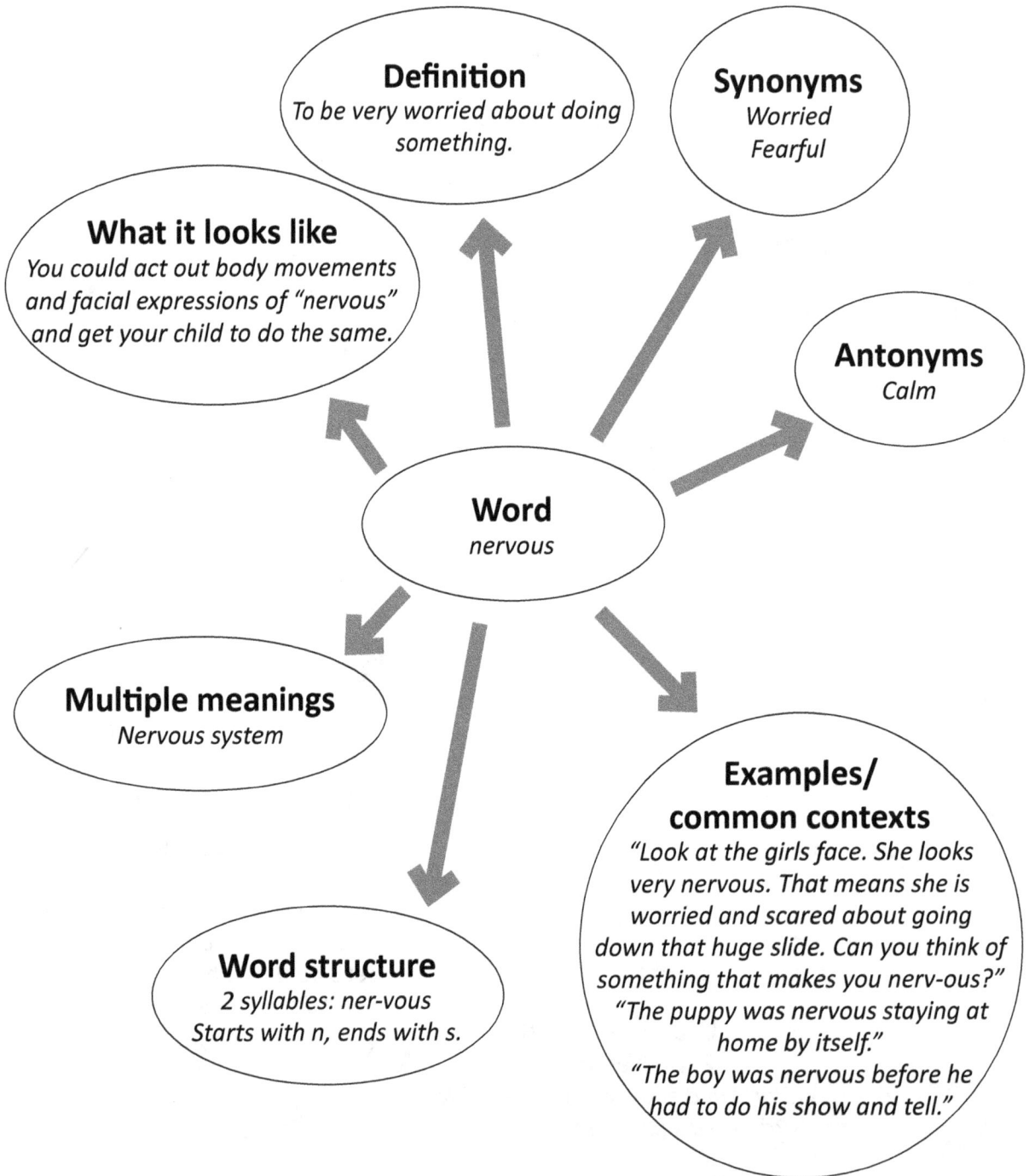

Example 2

Definition
To be very worried about doing something.

Synonyms
Worried
Fearful

What it looks like
You could act out body movements and facial expressions of "nervous" and get your child to do the same.

Antonyms
Calm

Word
nervous

Multiple meanings
Nervous system

Examples/ common contexts
"Look at the girls face. She looks very nervous. That means she is worried and scared about going down that huge slide. Can you think of something that makes you nerv-ous?"
"The puppy was nervous staying at home by itself."
"The boy was nervous before he had to do his show and tell."

Word structure
2 syllables: ner-vous
Starts with n, ends with s.

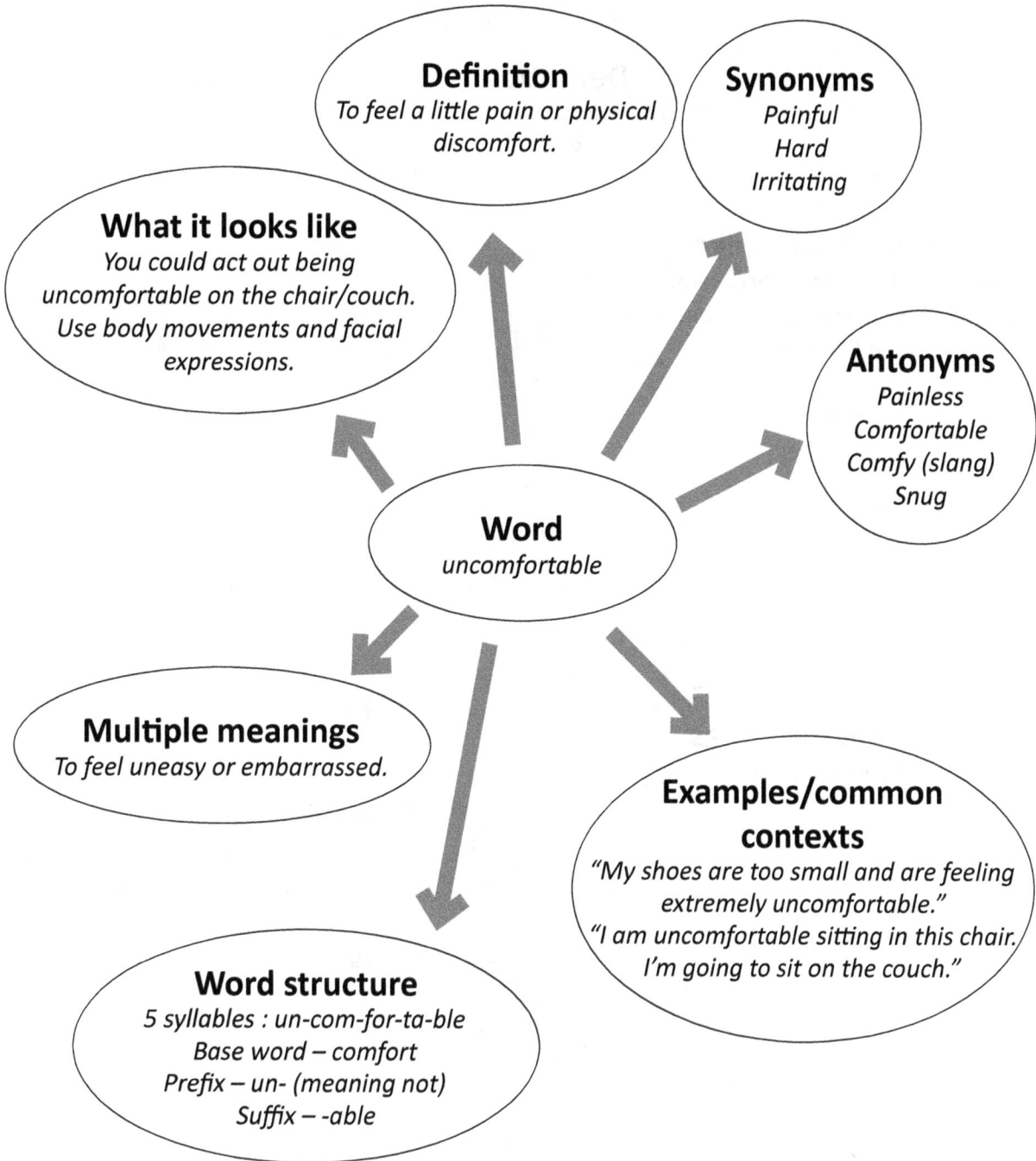

Example 3

Definition
To feel a little pain or physical discomfort.

Synonyms
Painful
Hard
Irritating

What it looks like
You could act out being uncomfortable on the chair/couch. Use body movements and facial expressions.

Antonyms
Painless
Comfortable
Comfy (slang)
Snug

Word
uncomfortable

Multiple meanings
To feel uneasy or embarrassed.

Examples/common contexts
"My shoes are too small and are feeling extremely uncomfortable."
"I am uncomfortable sitting in this chair. I'm going to sit on the couch."

Word structure
5 syllables : un-com-for-ta-ble
Base word – comfort
Prefix – un- (meaning not)
Suffix – -able

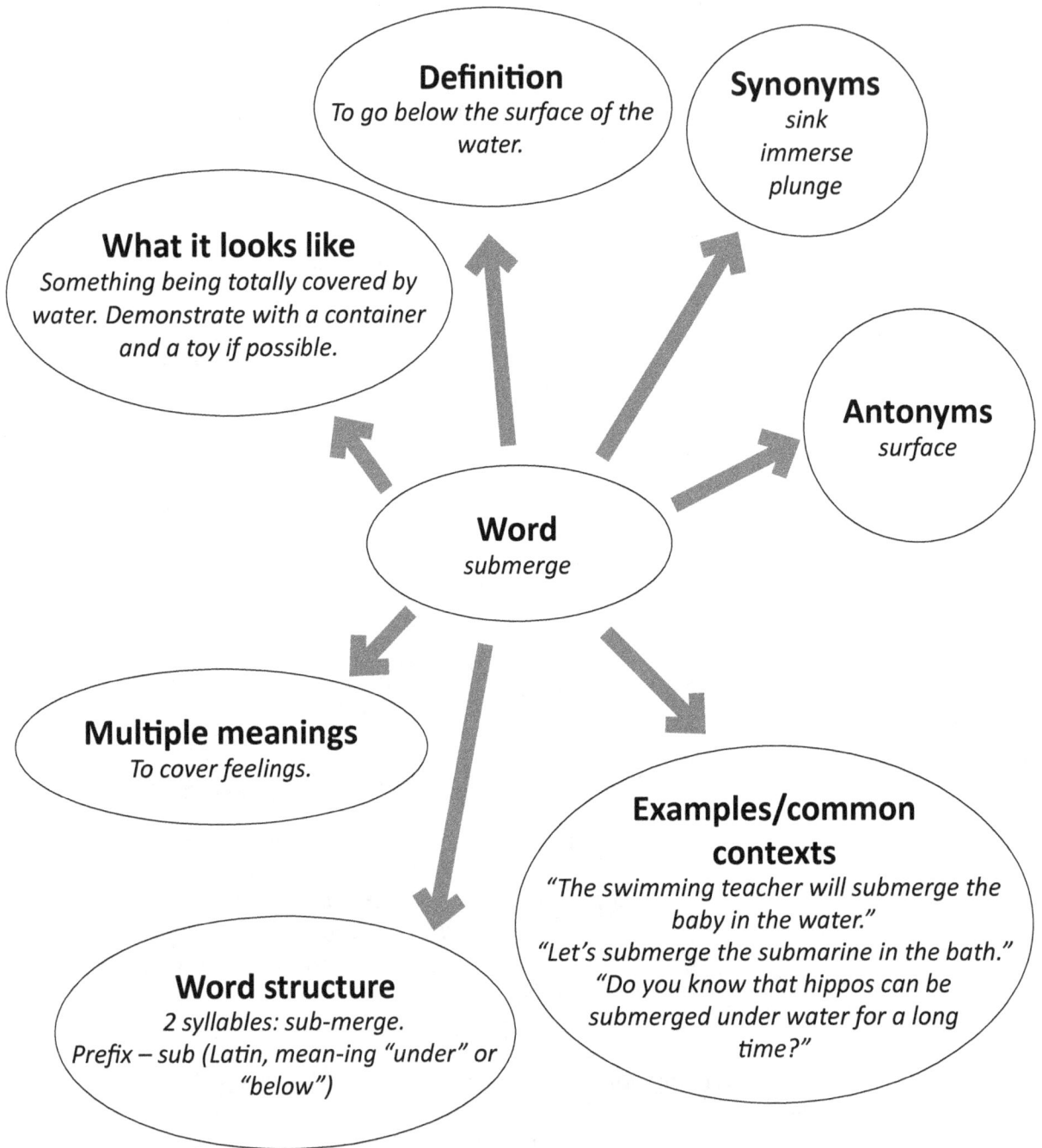

Example 4

Definition
To go below the surface of the water.

Synonyms
sink
immerse
plunge

What it looks like
Something being totally covered by water. Demonstrate with a container and a toy if possible.

Antonyms
surface

Word
submerge

Multiple meanings
To cover feelings.

Examples/common contexts
"The swimming teacher will submerge the baby in the water."
"Let's submerge the submarine in the bath."
"Do you know that hippos can be submerged under water for a long time?"

Word structure
2 syllables: sub-merge.
Prefix – sub (Latin, mean-ing "under" or "below")

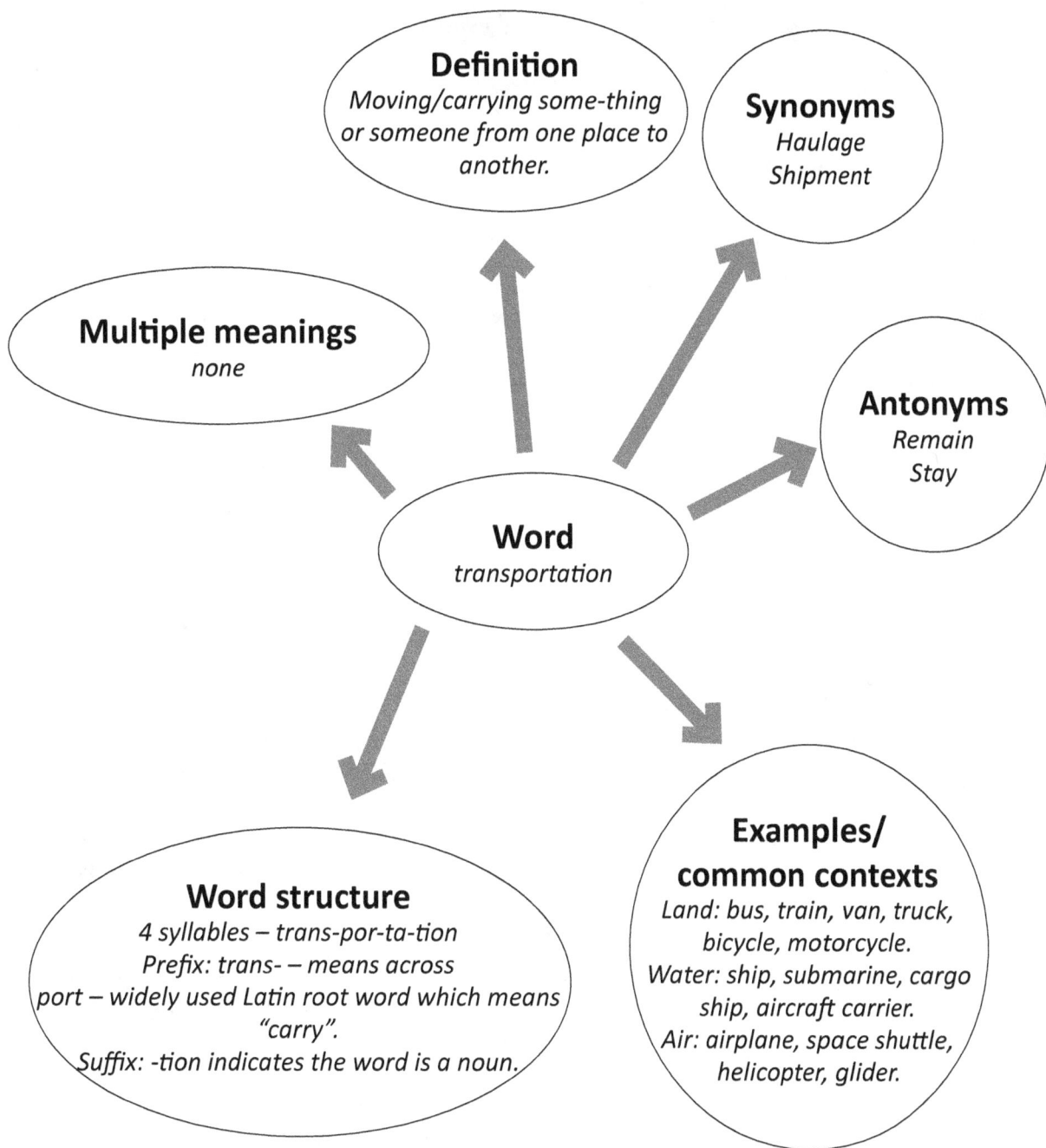

Example 5

Definition
Moving/carrying some-thing or someone from one place to another.

Synonyms
Haulage
Shipment

Multiple meanings
none

Antonyms
Remain
Stay

Word
transportation

Word structure
4 syllables – trans-por-ta-tion
Prefix: trans- – means across
port – widely used Latin root word which means "carry".
Suffix: -tion indicates the word is a noun.

Examples/ common contexts
Land: bus, train, van, truck, bicycle, motorcycle.
Water: ship, submarine, cargo ship, aircraft carrier.
Air: airplane, space shuttle, helicopter, glider.

Etymology and morphology

When it comes to word structure, keep your explanations at the level your child is at. Younger children only need to know what the word starts with, ends with, rhymes with, how many syllables, as well as simple starts and endings such as plurals and past tense. Older children can look more closely at the structure of the written word. In the example above, teaching them the Latin base or root word "port" means "to carry", will then help them understand the following words:

1. **portly** – someone who "carries" too much body weight

2. **import** – to "carry" in

3. **export** – to "carry" out

4. **portable** – easily "carried"

5. **deport** – "carry" from

6. **important** – "carried" in

7. **reporter** – one who "carries" back

8. **porter** – one who "carries"

9. **portfolio** – that which "carries" items, or those items so "carried"

This is where Google comes in very handy!

Over 60% of words in English have Latin or Greek origins, so the study of where words came from (etymology) and their morphology (structure) is important, particularly in the older years. English has evolved and has changed over time. Knowledge of this helps explain to children some of the spelling choices we have today. For example, *ch* in *chalk, cherry, chocolate* is said differently to the *ch* in *chemistry, choir, school* and *stomach*. This is because the /k/-sounding words have Greek origin.

Morphology is the study of words and the way words are put together from smaller units of meaning. The word morphology itself comes from a Greek word *morph*, meaning "shape" or "form" and *-ology* which means "the study of something". Learning about the structure of words helps children read better, comprehend text better and spell better. In chapter 4: Structured Phonics, we looked at the spelling of some morphological units and how they can be combined to form new words, therefore the following information will be partly a review.

Morphology has two main areas: base or root words and affixes (prefixes and suffixes).

A prefix is a start that you can add to a root or base word to change the meaning. A suffix is an ending that you can add to a root or a base word to also change the meaning. Many words can have both! For example, *unthankful* has the prefix *un-*, root word *thank*, and suffix *-ful*.

During the first three years of schooling, your child should learn most of the following prefixes and suffixes. They are in relative order of how tricky they are.

Prefix	Meaning	Examples
un-	not	unhappy, undone, unwell, unnoticed
re-	again	reappear, repeat, redo
dis-	opposite	disobey, disappear, disagree
pre-	before	prevent, preschool, preview

Suffix	Meaning	Examples
-s, -es	plural – more than one	dogs, apples, horses, boxes
-ing	means something is happening in the present	running, sleeping, jumping, reading, planting
-ed	past tense/already happened	walked, decided, waited, played
-ly	used to change a word to explain how an action happened or how often	quickly, calmly, loudly, cuddly, angrily weekly, hourly, monthly, annually
-ful	full of	helpful, colourful, beautiful, careful, truthful
-less	without	fearless, useless, speechless, careless, homeless
-er	person who does something; comparative	teacher, baker, driver, runner, farmer safer, bigger, weaker, nicer, faster
-est	superlative	safest, biggest, weakest, nicest, fastest
-ion, -tion, -sion	turns verbs into nouns	act – action, collide – collision, divide – division, direct – direction, describe – description
-able	able to do	washable, loveable, adorable, available, forgettable
-ness	turns an adjective into a noun meaning state or condition	redness, sleepiness, illness, darkness, happiness

In Grades 3 to 6, there are many more prefixes and suffixes that your child should be taught at school as well as important Latin root words. There is a list on the scope and sequence of Blaxcell Public School (which can be downloaded from the *SPELD SA* website with the link provided below). It is helpful for you to know so that you can reinforce them at home.

Learning vocabulary is a lifelong pursuit – even as adults we continue to add words to our "word bank". Perhaps before you started this book, the words *phonemes*, *graphemes*, *etymology* and *morphology* were not in your vocabulary – now they are!

Further information

Specific Learning Difficulties Association of South Australia (*SPELD SA*) – speldsa.org.au/image/catalog/PDFs/General%20Website/Vocabulary%20Scope%20and%20Sequence%20-%20BSPS.pdf

This is a wonderful website that has free resources for many areas, including this scope and sequence of vocabulary development.

The Florida Center for Reading Research – fcrr.org/student-center-activities

This has language and vocabulary activities, such as words that describe and word categorisation.

"8 Simple Vocabulary Games for Kids in Preschool", *Empowered Parents* – empoweredparents.co/vocabulary-games-for-kids/

A list of fun vocabulary games (no preparation needed).

ABC TV Education – abc.net.au/tveducation/programs/primary/

Free educational resources including videos, games and programs.

Banter Speech – www.banterspeech.com.au

There are several blogs on vocabulary as well as some free resources such as Visual Description Builder.

Weitzman, E. & Greenberg, J. "Shoot for the SSTaRS: A Strategy for Teaching Vocabulary to Promote Emergent Literacy." *The Hanen Centre*.

hanen.org/Helpful-Info/Articles/Shoot-for-the-SSTaRS-Strategy.aspx

This is a helpful article on how to promote vocabulary.

Talk for Writing – mailchi.mp/talk4writing/home-school-booklets

They provide wonderful booklets in grade levels to develop skills in speaking, reading and writing.

All About Learning Press have a great blog with links to free activities for teaching suffixes and prefixes as well as Latin root words, including blog.allaboutlearningpress.com/suffixes/ and blog.allaboutlearningpress.com/prefixes/.

There are many YouTube videos for teaching affixes suitable for children (and adults)!

Etymology websites

Online Etymology Dictionary – etymonline.com

Lexico: Word Origins – lexico.com/explore/word-origins

If your child has poor vocabulary knowledge or difficulty learning and remembering new words, then please get their hearing assessed and book an assessment with a speech pathologist.

8

Reading Comprehension

Reading comprehension is a complex process and combines many different skills that need to work together simultaneously. It is not just about understanding each word on the page individually, it's being able to create a mental image of what is being read and joining this information with what you already know (background knowledge). As you continue to read, you continue to add to this mental image of the characters, events, objects, places and actions described and the relationships between them.

Poor readers spend so much of their brainpower decoding words that they have little left for comprehending what they are reading. Or they make word-reading errors and therefore the meaning of the sentence changes. Or they are reading so slowly and robotically that they cannot remember what they have read. Good readers, whose word-recognition skills are automatic, can focus all of their energy on understanding what they are reading.

Some children are wonderful decoders but cannot comprehend a word of what they have read. I worked for a long time at a secondary school and completed many reading assessments. The students would be referred to me because of poor behaviour in class or poor academic progress. Often, the children would have age-appropriate decoding skills, but their reading comprehension would be that of a 7-year-old.

Simple View of Reading

Reading comprehension requires proficient skills in both **decoding** (reading written words) and **language comprehension** (understanding the words read)

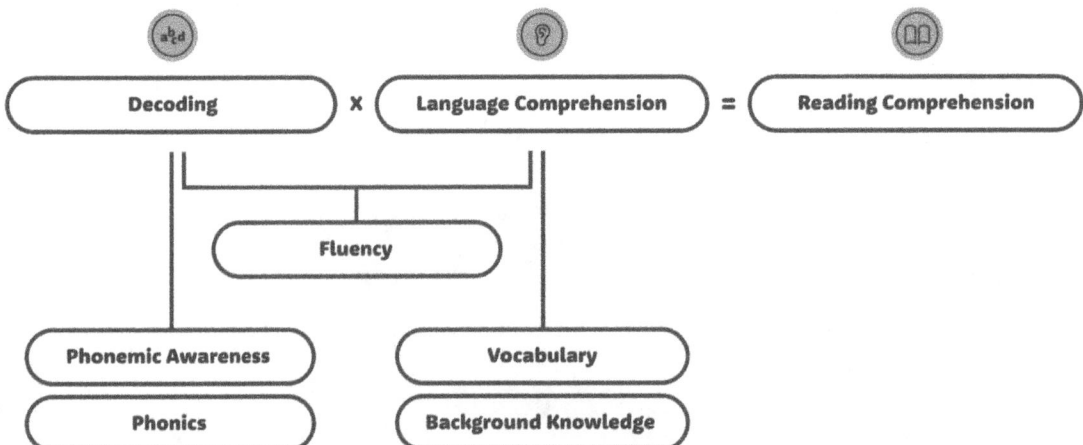

Decoding X Language Comprehension = Reading Comprehension

Fluency

Phonemic Awareness   Vocabulary

Phonics   Background Knowledge

Based on Gough and Tunmer, 1986

My job was to find out why by completing a comprehensive language assessment. One reason was that their oral language or background knowledge was poor. You can imagine how demoralising it would be for a 13-year-old to be in class all day but not understanding a word they read. Some of them act out to deflect attention away from their difficulties as their self-esteem becomes lower. Another reason was that they were never taught how to read for meaning and checking their own understanding as they went. They were simply reading because they were told to and were not engaged in the text.

According to the "Simple View of Reading", reading comprehension requires two broad skills: language comprehension and word-level reading.

If a child has good decoding skills and good language ability, then it is not often that they will struggle with reading comprehension. If a child struggles with both decoding the words as well as poor language comprehension, then mastering reading will be a real struggle for them, and they will need lots of extra help.

There is no use working on reading comprehension strategies if your child's language is poor – they need to work on vocabulary and oral language first. A child's oral language ability at the time of school entry predicts later reading comprehension. If your child's language is developing well, but they struggle to work out the words, or their reading fluency is slow, this needs to be worked on before you bother with reading comprehension strategies.

If your child has great language skills, well-developed decoding skills and good fluency but still finds reading comprehension difficult, then other factors may need to be considered. These may include attention, working memory, background knowledge, and the ability to make inferences. It needs to be determined if they are understanding the text and reading for meaning.

Why comprehension is important for reading

Quite simply, the end goal of reading is to comprehend the written message, be it a text message, an email, a worded maths question, a newspaper article, a poem, a recipe or a book. Everything discussed in this book – oral language, phonemic awareness, phonics, fluency, vocabulary knowledge – are all required for your child to able to reach the ultimate goal: comprehension of what is read.

What should my child be able to do?

When children first learn to read, their comprehension of language is far better than their ability to decode. This is because they have been exposed to and used *spoken* language up to that point in time. Once your child is a competent reader, their reading comprehension is determined by how well they understand language and their amount of background knowledge. For that reason, low language or vocabulary levels may not be picked up until later in the middle primary-school years.

In the first three years of schooling, children learn to read. After that, they should be reading to learn. Therefore, it is important that all of the areas needed for the reading comprehension process are cemented by then.

As mentioned above, there is no benefit in teaching reading comprehension strategies until all of the other areas are ruled out as factors in your child's inability to understand what they have read. If the difficulties lie in one of these areas, then working on them will in turn increase your child's ability to comprehend. Please go back to those areas of the book and support your child with the strategies and suggestions. Discuss with your child's teacher and reach out for extra assessment and support from specialists if needed.

How to know if your child has difficulties with comprehension

Your child may be very reluctant to read or may just flat out tell you that they hate reading. They may not be able to tell you exactly why, but it could be that they have no idea what is happening in the story, or why a character acted the way they did and they forget what they have read so what is the point of reading anyway!

To check if your child understands what they have read, can they:

- tell you a summary of a paragraph or page (not a word-for-word recount, but the main idea and important information)?
- re-tell the events of a book or text in a clear and correct sequence?
- answer questions about the text?
- explain why things happened in the text the way they did?
- explain how the character was feeling or what they were thinking?
- describe what the characters look like?
- describe where and when the story took place?

Developing reading comprehension

We need to get children's brains actively processing and thinking about the information that they are reading. You know the saying: "In one ear and out the other" which happens if your child is not actively listening to you. This can also occur when reading: "In one eye and out the other."

Beginner readers

When children first learn to read their ability to decode is lower than their ability to comprehend. You can still develop your child's reading comprehension through the modelling of the skills they need, as well as developing their vocabulary, oral language and background knowledge.

As you read to them, show them how you are actively processing and monitoring what you have read by:

- wondering out loud about will happen next – "I wonder if they will find the lost dog."
- questioning why a character felt or acted in a certain way or why an event happened – "I wonder why the little girl felt like that?"
- making connections between events or feelings to your own or your child's experiences – "Do you remember the time when you were really scared while camping? I think the boy is feeling scared of the noises at night time too."

- pretending that something didn't make sense to you and explain how you are going to read it again as you weren't quite sure what it meant, thereby teaching and developing the habit of re-reading to understand before proceeding.

- using questions to check their listening comprehension – "Why did they chop down the forest? Was that a good or a bad decision?"

- at the end of a page or chapter, show them how to put together a short summary of what has happened so far. Once you have modelled this a few times, ask your child to give a summary.

"The Hanen Book Nook" on the Hanen website have some wonderful examples of questions to ask paired with books. Visit *The Hanen Centre* at hanen.org/Helpful-Info/Book-Nook.aspx.

Each time your child reads, it is not necessary to do every one of the suggestions below. Try to vary them so they get a chance to practise them all whilst you are reading to them as well as when they are reading to you. A child may not become a fluent, independent reader until they are at the end of their third year of schooling.

Summarising

This involves your child telling you what is important in what they have read and putting it into their own words. My 8-year-old son can read well independently. However, he loves it when I read to him, and I like to continue to model reading fluency (rate and expression) as well as demonstrating reading comprehension by thinking out loud (as discussed above).

After he has read a few chapters on his own, I then read a few chapters to him. As a way for him to practise summarising and a way for me to check that he is understanding what he has read, I ask him to "bring me up to speed" on what has happened. If it makes no sense to me or if he doesn't include enough details, then I ask specific questions to prompt him to construct a better summary and to include more information. When I start reading, I will refer back to what he has told me to demonstrate how we continue to build on the mental image.

My daughter, on the other hand, would tell me a word-for-word recount of the chapters (*groan*). Therefore, with her, I worked explicitly on how to summarise. We discussed that she had to tell me:

- what the main idea or theme of the text was.

- what information was important.

- what the text meant in her own (and using fewer) words.

Your child initially may need a lot of help coming up with their summaries. You can help by modelling summaries, asking specific questions and then putting a summary together.

Quick summaries at the end of each chapter are a great way to help your child remember what they have read before they move on to the next chapter. If your child struggles to remember a whole chapter, then they can do a summary at the end of each paragraph. They can even write a line or two, and by the time they finish the chapter they can read over their paragraph summaries to help them continue to understand and to remember.

Questioning

As your child reads, they should interact with the text. They should pause, question or comment and think about their thinking (metacognitive skills). As discussed above, you can model this when you read out loud to them. As your child is reading out loud to you, or after they have read a page/chapter to themselves, use questions to show them what they should be thinking about as they read. With practice, your children will be able to generate their own questions as they are reading to help them stay engaged with the text.

Examples of questions include:

- Who is the main character?
- When is the story happening? (Is it set in the "olden days", or in the future? What specific year, and during daytime or night time?)
- Where is the story happening? (Is it at someone's house, at the zoo, different planet, in the city, or at school?)
- What happened? Was there a problem?
- Why did things happen that way?
- What do you think is going to happen next? What makes you think that?
- How was the character feeling? Why do you think the character was feeling that way?
- Was a solution found to the problem(s)?

You know your child best, so for some children the first four questions are all they can do initially. As they get older and have better abilities, you can push them with the other questions.

If your child is unsure of the answer, then you can model the response for them or try asking the question in a simpler way. Make sure that your child is not feeling like you are just peppering them with questions. Try and make them feel you are genuinely interested in what is happening in the book and you want to discuss it with them (even though you may hate the book and don't really care what happens to the main character!).

Comprehension monitoring

Children need to be able to recognise when they do not understand a word or a sentence, so they can stop and work out what they don't know. Was it a particular word that they don't know the meaning of? Or was it that they did not understand the inference that was made? Or the grammar used in the sentence was too complex?

Some children continue reading without checking if they understand. Comprehension is then lost, as is the enjoyment of reading. Point out to your child that if he or she was listening to someone talk and became confused with their message, they would ask the speaker to repeat what they had just said. They may even explain it in a different, easier way. The same applies to reading. Praise your child when they stop reading in order to clarify something they have not understood. It really is a wonderful skill to instil early on.

During reading, remind your child to pause if there is a word or a sentence that they do not understand and ask for some help with working out the meaning before they continue. If there is a tricky vocabulary word, then prompt them to ask you what it means (use the information in the previous chapter on Vocabulary to explain it to them) or if the text is unclear, then explain to them what clues from the text could be used to make an inference.

Remind them that they can re-read a sentence or a page to get more information to help "join the dots" or even read ahead to clarify what they don't understand. Teach them to look for clues in the text. Don't always give your child the answer; help them to re-read what they don't understand, use the context to work out the meaning, and help them draw their own conclusions using questions.

Predicting

Predicting what is going to happen next in the book is a great way of engaging your child in the text and keeping them motivated to read to the end to see if their prediction came true. You can teach prediction when you are reading out loud to your child or when they are reading to you.

To teach your child how to predict, you should model first by thinking out loud. Predict what will happen in the story and explain how you came to that conclusion (prediction), by referring to the key words or phrases in the text and also what you already know. After finishing the book, discuss with your child if it ended up happening the way you thought it would.

After you have demonstrated how to predict to your child, they can make the attempt for the next chapter or the next book. Encourage your child to tell you why they think that event is going to happen.

Here are some phrases you might like to use:

- I think this book will be about _____ because _____.
- I predict _____ will happen next because on this page I read _____.
- From what I have read so far, I think that _____ will happen.

Phrases to use when checking on your predictions:

- My prediction was right because in the story it said that _____.
- My predication was not right as what I said did not happen. _____ happened instead.
- What I thought was somewhat right as _____ happened but _____ didn't.

Inferencing

Inferencing is when we use clues from a story and add it to what we already know to make educated guesses. In other words, to "read between the lines."

We need to infer when authors do not state explicitly and exactly what is happening in a story. For example, a sentence may read "My eyes were red and puffy" and we infer that the character had been crying or has a cold. If the next sentence reads "I continued to be upset", then we can infer, with a higher degree of confidence, that she had been in fact crying.

Teach and model to your child how (and why) to infer. This can be done through looking at pictures in a book and inferring what is happening. For example, "I infer that it is the boy's birthday as there is a cake with candles and he is the one who is blowing them out." Another example, "I infer that they are watching a scary show as they are huddled together looking scared."

You can also teach inference when you are reading to your child by thinking out loud. For example, if you read a sentence that says "Jenn's palms were sweaty and her mouth was dry", then discuss how you think she may be nervous, even though the author doesn't exactly say that's how she is feeling.

If you are teaching your child whilst they are reading to you, prompt them to look for important words that will help them infer. An example could be when an author does not clearly state the location of the story, but the words *bridle*, *saddle* and *stable* are in the text. They are all words related to horses, so the story is most likely set at a horse farm.

Inferencing is a tricky skill; in the early stages of learning to read, do not expect your child to be able to do it. Lots of modelling and "thinking out loud" will be sufficient.

•

Please do not feel like you must do the above suggestions in depth every time you and your child read together. We want children to enjoy reading without being peppered with questions and compiling summaries and drawing inferences. Sometimes, a simple check and a couple of questions will do. Do not focus too much on one strategy as good readers draw on many different skills to comprehend what they are reading.

The reading comprehension process will become mostly unconscious and automatic as they progress through their schooling years and our job as parents is to continue to extend their vocabulary and background knowledge, which has more of an impact on reading comprehension in the early years of schooling than strategies.

Having rich, meaningful discussions about the book you are reading to your child or the book they are reading to you, no matter how simple, is such a worthwhile and downright lovely thing to do with your child. Instead of a movie night, have a book discussion night! Each child and adult can talk to the family about the book they are reading and what has happened, what they think will happen next, who the characters are and so on. The other members of the family can ask questions about the book.

Many complex areas come into play with your child's reading comprehension: language and background knowledge, reading ability and fluency, and general cognitive skills, attention and working memory. If you feel your child is struggling, then please talk to your child's teacher(s) or contact an educational psychologist or speech pathologist for an assessment. To be able to give your child the right support, we will need to work out exactly where their challenges are.

Further information

"The Hanen Book Nook", *The Hanen Centre* – hanen.org/Helpful-Info/Book-Nook.aspx

This has a booklist and instructions on how to use them for the practice of prediction and comprehension.

"Comprehension Ninja Series", *Vocabulary Ninja* – vocabularyninja.co.uk/product-category/reading/

This website has some free samples of reading comprehension activities for different ages.

"Student Center Activities", *Florida Center for Reading Research* – fcrr.org/student-center-activities

Choose your child's grade level and scroll down to comprehension.

9

Parent Support

We would do anything for our children to ensure that they have all the success and happiness in the world. Being able to read and write is a big part of that, not only in the areas of future employment, but their mental health and self-esteem can be impacted when they feel they cannot read well. As parents, when our children are not succeeding or progressing the way they should, we can become anxious and stressed, inadvertently making our children more anxious and stressed.

My third child has been my most reluctant reader, which is ironic, as I know more about the science of reading than ever. I am certainly not one to get easily stressed out but his lack of enthusiasm for reading was causing me heart palpitations! He was lagging behind his peers and I knew it. Unfortunately, he also knew it.

I remember a particularly bad spell where he refused to read at home, which is, as we know, critical to improvement. It doesn't matter how good the teaching is at school if your child is not practicing each day; they will not learn to read proficiently or at the same rate as their peers. Something was definitely going on and I needed to find out what.

The next time I went to help with reading at school I worked out where the problem was. The boy next to him was confidently reading *Charlie and the Chocolate Factory* each day out loud to parent helpers whilst my son was still carefully sounding out words. This is why he had shut down and didn't want to practise at home as he had lost his confidence due to comparing himself to his classmate. I had also lost all confidence and initially did the wrong thing by coming down too hard on him and "forcing" him to read; he only became more reluctant.

My worry about his reading was rubbing off on him so I changed tact. We played *a lot* of reading games, focusing on a particular sound each week, and we steered away from reading "readers" until he had found his confidence again. Now he will read every day for 20 minutes out loud and is happy to do so.

If you are feeling stressed about your child's reading ability or reluctance to read, don't give up. The first step is to work out *why* they are not progressing with their reading – it could be one of many reasons mentioned throughout the book. Then they need daily practice using whatever your child is interested in to encourage language and reading development. Play games (like the ones mentioned in this book), be a model of great reading habits, and offer lots of support and encouragement. We want our children to enjoy reading, not just to do it because you make them. It needs to be a pleasurable activity and part of your family's daily routine.

Your child's teacher

Approach your child's teacher about what they are noticing at school. Is your child refusing to read to the teacher or to other adults/peers? Are they struggling? Let them know what has been going on at home and your concerns with their reading progress. I know you may be thinking I don't want to be one of "those parents". However, you need to advocate in a proactive and calm way for your child. Storming into the school with demands is not going to get you anywhere, but neither will staying quiet.

It is important to get help as early as possible as the gap between a struggling reader and their peers can widen quickly. Don't wait until your teacher says they are not progressing as sometimes they may wait too long and there will be much more catching up to do. Trust your instincts. Request that they have additional assessment to work out what is holding them back. Is it their phonemic awareness, phonic knowledge, oral language skills, vocabulary, fluency or comprehension? Can they have additional support at school?

Ask your child's teacher what reading program or scope and sequence they are following so that you can reinforce it at home. (Scope is the content that will be covered, sequence is the order that it will be covered.) If they do not have one or are unable to explain to you how they are teaching reading, then there's a problem!

If your child's teacher thinks they are progressing well but you are still unsure, then ask them how they assess the core areas of reading and what his/her results were. Be careful to not blame your child's teachers if they have no idea of these core areas or how to assess them – they may not have been taught this during their teaching degree. If you are unhappy with the school's response to your concerns and they are not going to follow up with further assessment or extra assistance, then I suggest getting an assessment from a literacy specialist/speech pathologist.

Specialist support

Working with specialists is a partnership. Don't ever feel like you're intruding if you want to be part of the sessions. Regardless of whether your child is seeing a speech pathologist or a literacy tutor at school or outside of school, ask to attend the sessions. Ask for frequent, clear communication of ideas and activities for home practice so you can follow up at home. Ask them to provide you with evidence that the support given is evidenced-based.

Does your child need an Individual Education Plan (IEP)? These written plans are for children who require additional support at school. The IEP lays out the goals for the child and what strategies will be used to achieve them. The IEP also helps monitor their progress as they are reviewed regularly.

What happens if the support at school is not the right support? Perhaps they are just given more frequent doses of "guessing" from the context and picture? This is where it can get tricky as a parent. The teacher or reading support teacher is normally following what the school have set as extra support. You may need to rock the boat a little. Bring in evidence (this book, for example) that they need to change their reading instruction.

If you can afford to hire an experienced and knowledgeable reading specialist, such as a literacy tutor or speech pathologist with literacy experience, then I encourage you to do so.

How to support your child when the school (and you) are doing everything right

So, you have met with your child's teacher about your child's reading progress and, as far as you can tell, the teacher's reading approach is fantastic! They use a structured literacy approach with a well- thought-out and well-followed scope and sequence with no whole language/analytic phonics/guessing strategies in sight! Your child's language and cognitive skills are great and you are doing all the right things to support them at home, so why is your child still not progressing? If this is the case, then consider an assessment to look into the possibility of dyslexia. I have added resources below that include more information about the early signs of a specific reading disability (an alternate name for dyslexia) and where to turn to for assessment and support.

"Sight" words

Arrggghhh! The dreaded "sight" words. Children should not be asked to memorise words as a whole based on their shape as there are simply too many similar words and our visual memory cannot hold enough. Despite this fact, every year, children are sent home with their coloured lists of words to memorise. Everyone is getting their certificates and moving up to the next level, so, of course, you and your child want to as well. Many of these "sight" words can be decoded and do not need to be taught as a whole.

Some schools call them high-frequency words or heart words. These words *do* need to be taught so that stories read, or written, by your child make sense. They *should not*, however, be memorised as a whole nor just be practised in a random list. They should still be mapped in the same way as other words. In this book, I have called them high-frequency words as they are the most common words we come across when reading. They can be sorted into two groups: ones spelt regularly, and ones spelt irregularly. Your child can decode regular high-frequency words using their sound-letter knowledge. For example: *in, and, that, from*.

Irregularly spelt high-frequency words do not follow the normal sound-letter relationships and have at least one letter spelling a sound that we think it would not. For example, *said, give, are*.

To teach these irregularly spelt high-frequency words, continue to break the word into its sounds as you would do with any other word.

Predictable text readers

As discussed at the initial stages of learning to read, children benefit from decodable readers to practise what sound-letter knowledge they have learnt so far and use their blending skills to read (and not guess) words. Using decodable readers also helps them grow their confidence, to know that they can actually read. Too often I see children give up on reading because the readers sent home are far too hard.

Children want to please their teachers, so they often want to only read the readers sent home from school. To ensure that this is a successful and enjoyable reading experience, you can help by doing the following:

- Wait to see if they can work out a tricky word that stops their flow of reading. Do not immediately tell them the word. Prompt them to sound it out.

- Give them only the sound-letter link in the word that they have not yet learnt – not the entire word. For example, a child in their first three months of school may not have learnt *oa* so if they come across the word *boat*, you could point to the *oa* and say, "In this word, this *oa* sounds like [give them the sound]." Then it is their job to sound out and blend together, "b-oa-t". Another example: your child comes across the word *park* but they haven't learnt the *ar* diagraph yet. Point to the *ar* and tell them that this is /ar/, then ask them to sound out and blend together. If they still cannot do that, you say the sounds "p-ar-k" (whilst pointing at the letters) and ask them to blend back together.

- Ensure that your child is not guessing words by looking at the pictures instead of working out the word. Yes, I know that they may have been taught those strategies at school and your child might argue with you, but just calmly explain that when they are older and reading chapter books, they won't have as many pictures, so it will help them to remember each word by sounding it out and putting it in their memory. If your child correctly reads the word *butterfly* (a common word in early books), your child probably guessed the word as there is more than likely a picture. However, make sure they have mapped the sounds of the word onto the letters by breaking it apart with them. If your child knows the sound links for *b-u-tt* as well as the *er*, then focus on what they may not know, in this case the *y*. "Let's look at the word *butterfly*. Some parts you know how to sound out like *butt-er*, but did you know in this word the letter *y* is said as 'ie' – *butt-er-fl-y*?" Or if you are working on the *er* sound-letter link, focus on pointing that out in the word.

A great game to help your child stop the habit of guessing is through the game *snowman*. I have put a link to a video below so that you can watch Lyn Stone demonstrate.

Parent engagement

I started writing this book in 2019 and right now we are in our second lockdown in Victoria, Australia, due to COVID-19. Tomorrow, I will start the second round of remote learning with my three children. How I wish I had this book finished to help parents in this home-schooling situation! Whilst not without its challenges, one thing I really enjoyed about home-schooling was knowing what my children were learning about – something I would not have been usually privy to.

Research over the past 50 years has shown that parent and family engagement in supporting their child's learning in partnership with their school leads to much better outcomes. I think this period of remote learning, although intense, can be a time to learn from the relationships built between families and their children's teachers.

I certainly do not want to know what my children are learning about at school just so that I can drill them for another hour per day, but rather so that I can reinforce the concepts or raise the ideas in our daily conversations when appropriate.

Moving forward, I will ask for an overview of what each child will be learning over the month or term, once they are finally back at school! Some schools may not have a specific "plan" of how parents can be engaged in their child's learning at school, and as such it may be left up to the individual teacher's discretion. Nevertheless, I encourage you to request a summary of your child's learning plan for the term, not so that you can "teach" it again but so that you can discuss with them and relate it to their everyday life. This approach reinforces that you want to build a partnership with the teacher.

There are so many great opportunities to include your child's current learnings into daily home life: adding single digits at the supermarket when asking them how many oranges to get, ensuring that you have a clock with hands when they are learning about time, noticing obtuse versus right angles when wandering around the house, talking about fractions while cooking, etc. As parents, we often leave it all up to the teachers, without thinking about how we can support them to do their job to the best of their ability. It's a two-way street. We need to encourage clear communication, not just at parent–teacher interviews once a term, but as soon as a problem crops up at home that you think the teacher may benefit from knowing.

Conclusion

An acquaintance of mine was saying how her son was not a strong reader but that she had resigned herself to the fact that he was just "lazy" and would never be a good reader. Yes, some children do need more encouragement and a different approach and to work harder than others, but please, for your child's sake, never give up. Reach out for help. If it is becoming a battleground between you and your child, who else could they practise with?

On the flipside, an old client of mine, who was diagnosed with dyslexia, turned out to be a great reader and became a happy, confident young man. How? He practised for over an hour per day. Children with severe reading difficulties *can* be taught but they need good quality teaching and *a lot* of practice. Who is going to be primarily responsible for that? You are, you wonderful parent.

Further information

"The Parent Engagement Implementation Guide." *Australian Research Alliance for Children and Youth*. aracy.org.au/publications-resources/

　　An implementation guide for school communities.

"Understanding Learning Difficulties: A Guide for Parents." *AUSPELD*.

uldforparents.com

> This is a really informative guide and is well worth the read. It discusses evidenced-based programs and useful tips for parents.

Stone, L. (9 January 2019) "The Snowman Game." youtube.com/watch?v=kiiY7k4twSM

> This is a video of Lyn demonstrating a game to help children break the habit of guessing words.

"Signs of dyslexia at different ages." *Understood.* understood.org/en/learning-thinking-differences/signs-symptoms/could-your-child-have/checklist-signs-of-dyslexia-at-different-ages/

> This outlines the signs of dyslexia at different age brackets which can cause reading disability.

Australian Dyslexia Association – dyslexiaassociation.org.au

International Dyslexia Association – dyslexiaida.org

British Dyslexia Association – bdadyslexia.org.uk

The Final Word

Being able to read and to write at a skilled level, not just at a functional level, is essential for everyone … and getting started early is the best way to create a lifelong love of reading and learning. The better a child can read, the easier it is for them to learn and to cope at school; academic doors open and opportunities for careers are broadened. A lot of learning also happens while reading at home – right from when you read to your child as a baby and toddler, through to them becoming independent readers.

If your child is struggling to read, then they are rarely going to pick up a book simply for enjoyment which means they will potentially miss out on learning wonderful information about people, places and events and having their curiosity piqued about things outside their normal daily lives. Being a good reader also helps them to become a good writer through exposure to different vocabulary, sentence structures and styles of writing. Reading is also one of the most important ways to expand a child's imagination.

As children become older and more aware of their abilities, their self-esteem can be adversely impacted. Navigating through the tricky teenage years is hard enough without adding reading and writing difficulties in the mix.

As you have now learnt, there are many components to being a skilled reader that all have to come together to help your child reach the point of reading to learn. Remember, it is not a race to get to that point. It can take 3–4 years until your child is reading fluently and with expression and joy. Yes, it can feel like a battle sometimes, but I encourage you to keep going! Make the learning experience positive and fun by mixing it up and keeping it interesting for your child. Why not read outside, read in a hammock, read snuggled up in bed? And when you are teaching with the whiteboard and the letter cards, take them outside and sit on a blanket on the grass for a change of scenery. If you want to practise at the beach, write the letters that your child is learning on rocks which you can blend, segment and change. The learning doesn't have to always occur at a table.

Continue to teach and revise sound-letter links regularly, as well as listening to your child read to you every day. Continue to deepen their vocabulary and background knowledge through books, conversations, quality TV shows, visits to the museums, aquarium, etc. Continue to practise phonemic awareness and spelling. Once your child is reading independently, and for their own enjoyment, you will be so pleased that you persisted.

If your child is struggling, then please reach out for help. Discuss their progress with their teacher and seek outside assistance if you need to. The gap can widen so quickly, and once children are behind it is not easy to catch up. There may be more to your child's reading and spelling difficulties; dyslexia, dysgraphia, language delay, speech sound difficulties can all impact on your child's progress and will require specialised assessment and support.

All children need, and deserve, to be taught how to read, spell and write well in the early years. I sincerely hope that the information and activities in this book have helped or will help your child on their path to being a successful and confident reader and speller. If you need additional support for your child, then please reach out through my website, www.educatable.com.au, which lists upcoming courses and contact details.

Work with Me

If you feel that you or your child need extra support after reading this book, then please visit the *Educatable* website for upcoming online courses, workshops and other helpful information to put you and your child on the right track.

educatable.com.au

Bibliography

Beck, I. L., McKeown, M.G., & Kucan, L. (2013) *Bringing words to life: Robust vocabulary instruction* (2ⁿᵈ ed.) New York, NY: Guildford Press.

Buckingham, J., Wheldall, K., & Beaman-Wheldall, R. (2013) *Why Jaydon can't read: The triumph of ideology over evidence in teaching reading.* Policy, 29(3), 21–32.

Clarke, A. (31 July 2012) "Teaching sight words."
spelfabet.com.au/2012/07/ teaching-sight-words

Clarke, A. (7 May 2018) "What is a decodable book?"
spelfabet.com.au/2018/05/what-is-a-decodable-book/

Dehaene, S. (2009) *Reading in the brain: The new science of how we read.*
New York, NY: Academic Press.

Castles, A., Rastle, K., & Nation, K. (2018). *Ending the reading wars: Reading acquisition from novice to expert.* Psychological Science in the Public Interest, 19, 5–51.

Eide, D. (2011) *Uncovering the logic of English: A common-sense approach to reading, spelling and literacy.* Rochester, MN: Logic of English Inc.

Ehri, L.C. (2014) *Orthographic mapping in the acquisition of sight word reading, spelling memory, and vocabulary learning.* Scientific studies of reading, 18(1), 5–21.

Gillon. G.T. (2004) *Phonological awareness: From research to practice.*
New York, NY: Guilford Press.

Hasbrouck, J., & Tindal, G.A. (2006) *Oral reading fluency norms: A valuable assessment tool for reading teachers.* Reading teacher, 59(7), 636–644.

Hempenstall, K. (2016) *Read about it: Scientific evidence for effective teaching of reading.* The Centre for Independent Studies (Australia) Research report 11.

Heggerty, M. (2007) *Phonemic awareness: The skills that they need to help them succeed.* (6ᵗʰ ed.). River Forest, IL: Literacy Resources.

Hoover, W.A., & Gough, P.B. (1990) "The simple view of reading."
Reading and Writing, 2(2), 127–160.

Hoover, W.A. & Tunmer, W.E. (2018) *The simple view of reading: three assessments of its adequacy.* Remedial and Special Education, 39(5), 304–312.

Kilpatrick, D. A. (2016) *Equipped for reading success. A comprehensive, step-by-step program for developing phonemic awareness and fluent word recognition.* Syracuse, NY: Casey & Kirsch.

Kilpatrick, D. A. (2015) *Essentials of assessing, preventing, and overcoming reading difficulties.* Hoboken, NJ:Wiley.

Konza, D. (2014) *Teaching reading: Why the "Fab Five" should be the "Big Six".* Australian Journal of teacher education, 39(12), 153–169.

McGuinness, D. (1997) *Why our children can't read and what we can do it about: A scientific revolution in reading.* New York: Touchstone.

Moats, L.C. (1999) *Teaching reading is rocket science: What expert teachers of reading should know and be able to do* (Item No. 39-0372). Washington, DC: American Federation of teachers.

Moats, L.C. (2005) *How spelling supports reading: And why it is more regular and predictable than you think.* American Federation of teachers, Winter 2005/06, pp. 12–43.

Moats, L.C. (2010) *Speech to print: Language essentials for teachers* (2nd Ed.). Baltimore, MD: Brookes.

National Reading Panel. (2000). *Report of the National Reading Panel. Teaching children to read: An evidence-based assessment of scientific research literature on reading and its implications for reading instruction.* Bethesda, MD: National Institute of Child and Human Development.

Rose, J. (2006) *Independent review of the teaching of early reading: Final report.* U.K. Department for Education and Skills.

dera.ioe.ac.uk.5551/2/report.pdf

Rowe, K. (2005) *Teaching reading: National inquiry into the teaching of literacy.* Department of Education, Science and Training, Australian Council for Educational Research.

research.acer.edu.au/tll_misc/5

Scarborough, H. (2001) *Connecting early language and literacy to later reading (dis)abilities: Evidence, theory and practice.* In S.B. Neuman & D.K. Dickinson (Eds.), Handbook of early literacy research (Vol. 1, pp. 97–110). New York, NY: Guildford Press.

Seidenberg, M. (2018) *Language at the speed of sight: How we read, why so many can't, and what can be done about it*. New York, NY: Basic Books.

Share, D.L. (2011) *On the role of phonology in reading acquisition: The self-teaching hypothesis*. In S.A. Brady, D. Braze, & C.A. Fowler (Eds.), Explaining individual differences in reading: Theory and evidence (pp. 45–68). New York, NY: Psychology Press.

Snow, P. (12 May 2017) "Balanced literacy: An instructional bricolage that is neither fish nor fowl."

pamelasnow.blogspot.com.au/2017/05/balanced-literacy-instructional.html

Please enter this code

E&58#s

to access the resources for free found on
educatable.com.au/readable-demo